CHARLES BROCKDEN BROWN

Charles Brockden Brown
An American Tale

⁂

BY ALAN AXELROD

University of Texas Press, Austin

Copyright ©1983 by the University of Texas Press
All rights reserved
Printed in the United States of America
First Edition, 1983

Requests for permission to reproduce material
from this work should be sent to Permissions,
University of Texas Press, Box 7819, Austin, Texas 78712.

The publication of this work has been made possible in part
by a grant from the Andrew W. Mellon Foundation.

Library of Congress Cataloging in Publication Data

Axelrod, Alan, 1952–
  Charles Brockden Brown, an American tale.
  "Primarily a study of four novels by Charles
Brockden Brown . . . *Wieland, Ormond, Arthur Mervyn,*
and *Edgar Huntly*"—Pref.
  Includes bibliographical references and index.
  1. Brown, Charles Brockden, 1771–1810—Criticism
and interpretation. I Title.
PS1137.A9 1983   813′.2   82-13405
ISBN 0-292-71076-3

Frontispiece: oil portrait of Charles Brockden Brown (ca. 1809), attributed to
William Dunlap, N.A. Discovered in New York, 1981. Courtesy of Dr. Neil K.
Fitzgerald. Photo by Wayne Gibson.

Contents

. . . the problem of American self-recognition . . . an irreconcilable opposition between Nature and Civilization—which is to say, between forest and town, spontaneity and calculation, heart and head, the unconscious and the self-conscious, the innocent and the debauched. —Perry Miller, "The Romantic Dilemma in American Nationalism and the Concept of Nature," *Nature's Nation*, p. 199.

Preface

This is primarily a study of four novels by Charles Brockden Brown as the work of his mind and sensibility and as artifacts of the early national culture in which his mind and sensibility took shape. It is not intended as a substitute for reading the novels themselves. Those who desire a sound introductory and summary survey of the fiction should consult Donald Ringe's *Charles Brockden Brown* (New York: Twayne, 1966). Nor does this study—though it aims at a comprehensive view of Brown's career in the context of Brown's culture—attempt to be exhaustive. It does treat of many works in addition to *Wieland*, *Ormond*, *Arthur Mervyn*, and *Edgar Huntly*—works by Brown and by others, published and in manuscript, public and private; but those interested in finding and reading everything Brown wrote—what survives of all the fiction, fragments, magazine pieces, fugitive verse—should first consult Charles E. Bennett's "The Charles Brockden Brown Canon" (Ph.D. diss., University of North Carolina, 1974) and then Warner Berthoff's "The Literary Career of Charles Brockden Brown" (Ph.D. diss., Harvard, 1954), which treats Brown's non-fiction more fully than any other book-length discussion. For critical articles and other sources consult Patricia Parker's *Charles Brockden Brown: A Reference Guide* (Boston: G. K. Hall, 1980). Finally, although this study makes extensive use of biographical information, it is not a biography. Consult Harry R. Warfel's *Charles Brockden Brown: American Gothic Novelist* (Gainesville: University of Florida Press, 1949) and David Lee Clark's *Charles Brockden Brown: Pioneer Voice of America* (Durham: Duke University Press, 1952), as well as Charles Bennett's "The Letters of Charles Brockden Brown: An Annotated Census," *Resources for American Literary Study* 6 (August, 1976), pp. 164–90.

I have relied on these works and the others mentioned in the following pages as supplements to the primary sources of *Charles Brockden Brown: An American Tale*, but they represent only part of the debt I have incurred in writing the book. I am also grateful to Brown's great-great-grandniece, Mrs. Homer A. (Dorothy Burr) Thompson, for granting the release of photocopies of her "Uncle Brock's" manuscripts on deposit at the University of Texas. Many thanks to the Humanities Research Center of the

University of Texas—and especially to research librarian Ellen S. Dunlap —for furnishing the copies of those manuscripts. Ms. Grete V. Fitzell, of the Princeton University Library, kindly furnished copies of letters from the novelist to the Reverend Samuel Miller. Mr. Edwin Wolf, 2nd, at the Library Company of Philadelphia, responded fully and promptly to my inquiry about Brown's membership in the Library. Similarly helpful responses were forthcoming from Harvard University, the New York Public Library, the New-York Historical Society, and the Historical Society of Pennsylvania. Mr. Paul H. Rohmann, director of the Kent State University Press, very generously furnished me with an advance copy (in the form of corrected page proofs) of the Bicentennial Edition of Brown's *Ormond*, which had not yet been released when I was preparing my manuscript for the press.

Professor Gilbert Allen, my colleague at Furman University and my neighbor in Travelers Rest, South Carolina, provided many helpful suggestions, for which I thank him.

Norman S. Grabo, most recently author of *The Coincidental Art of Charles Brockden Brown*, views the novelist through optics sharply different from mine. This has not prevented him from sharing his ideas (and his page proofs), from promoting my project and encouraging me. It is a happy community of scholars that can claim such a citizen.

For good faith and criticism, exacting as it was enthusiastic, I am grateful to Professor Paul Seydor of the English Department at the University of Southern California. Paul has been an extraordinary friend to my book and to me.

Professor Wayne Franklin of The University of Iowa Department of English guided me through an earlier version of this study. To catalog his general and particular contributions to the present version would require more space and humility than I can spare. It must suffice to acknowledge that his judgment and generosity, no less than a host of his ideas, have enlivened every stage of the entire project. I thank him for being my teacher and my friend.

A Note on Texts and References

When this manuscript was being readied for the press, three volumes of the Kent State "Bicentennial Edition" of *The Novels and Related Works of Charles Brockden Brown* were available. As reference texts for this study I have used *Wieland; or, The Transformation: An American Tale* (1798), *Arthur Mervyn; or, Memoirs of the Year 1793* (1799–1800), and corrected page proofs of *Ormond; or, The Secret Witness* (1799—Kent, Ohio: Kent State University Press, 1977, 1980, 1982. For *Edgar Huntly; or, Memoirs of a Sleep-Walker* (1799), *Clara Howard; or, The Enthusiasm of Love* (1801), and *Jane Talbot* (1801) I used the David McKay editions (Philadelphia: 1887).

Brown edited three periodicals during his career: *The Monthly Magazine and American Review* (New York: Vols. 1–3, 1799–1800), *The Literary Magazine and American Register* (Philadelphia: Vols. 1–8, 1803–1808), and *The American Register, or General Repository of History, Politics, and Science* (Philadelphia: 1807–1811; Brown edited vols. 1–5). Footnote reference to these periodicals is by short title (*American Register*, etc.).

The following sources, to which I make frequent reference, are cited parenthetically in my text rather than in numbered notes:

Allen, Paul. *The Life of Charles Brockden Brown*. Facsimile of a printer's proof (ca. 1814). Delmar, N.Y.: Scholars' Facsimiles and Reprints, 1975. (Allen)

Bennett, Charles E. "The Charles Brockden Brown Canon." Ph.D. diss., University of North Carolina, 1974. (Bennett)

Clark, David Lee. *Charles Brockden Brown: Pioneer Voice of America*. Durham: Duke University Press, 1952. (Clark)

Dunlap, William. *Diary*. New York: Benjamin Blom, 1969. (Dunlap, *Diary*)

——— [and Paul Allen]. *The Life of Charles Brockden Brown*. Philadelphia: James P. Parke, 1815. (Dunlap, *Life*)

Poe, Edgar Allan. *The Complete Works*. Edited by James A. Harrison (1902). New York: AMS Press, 1965. (Poe)

Smith, Elihu Hubbard. *Diary*. Edited by James E. Cronin. Philadelphia: American Philosophical Society, 1973. (Smith)

Warfel, Harry R. *Charles Brockden Brown: American Gothic Novelist*. Gainesville: University of Florida Press, 1949. (Warfel)

Introduction

Prodigal no less than prolific, John Neal made little secret of his contempt for "unnecessary precision." The novelist and critic of the young Republic's literature is mistaken in practically every stroke of the portrait of Charles Brockden Brown he produced for an 1824 issue of *Blackwood's Edinburgh Magazine*:

> Brown's personal appearance was remarkable. He was a tall man —with a powerful frame—and little or no flesh. It was impossible to pass him, in the street, without stopping to look at him. His pale, sallow, strange complexion; straight black hair—"black as death;" the melancholy, broken-hearted look of his eyes; his altogether extraordinary face—if seen once—was never to be forgotten. He would be met, week after week—month after month —before he died, walking to and fro, in some unfrequented street of his native town, for hours and hours together—generally at a very early time in the morning—lost in thought, and looking like a shipwrecked man. Nobody knew him—nobody cared for him —(till WE took up his cause)—he was only an author—yet, when we have described him, everybody in Philadelphia will recollect him. After having walked, in this way, for several hours, he would return to his desolate, miserable, wretched family, and fall to writing, as if he had not another hour to live. We do not know his age—nor the time of his death, precisely. But it must have been about 1813—and he was not far from 35. He went off in a lingering consumption, with a broken heart—and a spirit absolutely crushed.[1]

There is no question that Neal's description, as an attempt to record fact, is just plain wrong. A glance at the thoroughly unimposing, even slightly effete, young man who sat for a pastel by James Sharples and an ivory miniature by William Dunlap tells as much.[2] Even the oil portrait reproduced as the frontispiece of this book, a recently discovered painting attributed to William Dunlap which depicts Brown very near the end of his life, does not resemble Neal's romantic word picture. Dunlap, who was one of Brown's closest friends, came in fact perilously near to describing the novelist as an ape. Writing to his wife, Dunlap reported that the husband of one Margaret Smith was "a little man [who] reminds one of C B B, but Brown has I think the air of a Philosopher, while S. looks like a Monkey turn'd Barber" (Dunlap, *Diary*, 385).

John Bernard, a British actor traveling in the United States, met Brown at the turn of the century and left an almost equally unimpressive picture of the young novelist:

> Brown gave very little idea of an imaginative writer in his appearance. He was short and dumpy, with light eyes, and hair inclining to be sandy, while the expression of his countenance told rather of ill-health than of intellect. The lines on his brow seemed to have been corroded by consumption, not chiselled by midnight meditations, and this was partly the case. A weak constitution had been his parents' legacy to him, and the ebullitions of his spirit proved too powerful for the vessel that contained it. Yet vividly in his countenance glowed the light of benevolence; that was his nature, and he could no more have suppressed its expression than he could have kept his eyes closed.[3]

Sharples, Dunlap, and Bernard had seen Brown; John Neal had not. Neal's childhood had been spent in Portland, Maine, where he began a would-be mercantile life at age twelve with successive clerkships in two firms that successively failed; thence he embarked upon a career first as an itinerant teacher of penmanship and, later, of portraiture as well. The seventeen-year-old Neal did not get anywhere near enough to Philadelphia or New York to lay eyes on Brown before the novelist died—in 1810 and at the age of thirty-nine.

But rather than dismiss Neal's egregious portrait as merely a lie, we should regard it as a work of fiction and an American tale. "Had [Brown] lived here [in England]—or anywhere, but in America," Neal observes in the paragraph that precedes his description of the novelist, "he would have been one of the most capital story-tellers—in a serious way, that ever lived" (425). Neal's picture of the solitary, forlorn Brown, whom no one knew and for whom no one cared, functions most immediately as an early chapter in The Tale of the Neglected American Author. This American tale was continued through Emerson's "American Scholar" through the careers of Poe, Melville, and, even to some degree, Hawthorne and Whitman; through the writings of Van Wyck Brooks, Waldo Frank, and others; and through the expatriations of Neal himself, James, Eliot, Pound, Hemingway, and Fitzgerald.

But it is not only as an archetypal American author that Neal depicts Brown. His portrait presents the novelist as an archetypal American, period. This becomes most apparent when we compare the *Blackwood's* article to a free plagiarism of it by the Philadelphia novelist George Lippard. Written twenty-four years after Neal's piece, "The Heart-Broken"[4] took the theme of the Neglected American Author from the earlier article, along with phrases like "Nobody knew him. Nobody cared for him" (Lippard, 22), the title "Heart-Broken," and the image of Brown wandering about Philadelphia rapt in melancholy meditation. Lippard must also have drawn upon the 1815 Allen-Dunlap *Life* of Brown (or the later British abridgment of it),[5] because a number of his facts are more accurate than Neal's; however, Lippard's physical description of Brown was clearly founded upon Neal's. We see the future novelist at age fourteen, "a pale-faced boy, with large grey eyes, flashing their vivid light from his sallow countenance" (Lippard, 20).

In his "borrowing" from Neal, Lippard betrays the lurid sensibility of his own sensational *Monks of Monk Hall*, dwelling on the withering and wasting effects of consumption. Yet, for all it owes to Neal, the portrait of Brown in "The Heart-Broken" ultimately conveys a very different impression. Whereas Lippard depicts a frail boy, Neal gives us a gaunt adult: "a tall man—with a powerful frame—and little or no flesh" (425). Although haggard and "heart-broken," Brown just might do as a backwoodsman similar to the "Down-Easter" Hayes in Neal's own short story "The Squatter"; or, minus the pallor, he would not even be out of place in the brutal wilderness of Neal's novel *Logan, a Family History.*[6] Whereas Lippard was interested in Brown only as an especially pathetic example of the Neglected American Author, Neal made much of the novelist's image as an American. Brown, Neal asserts, was "a sound, hearty specimen of Trans-Atlantic stuff . . . an American[7] to the backbone—without knowing it" (421), "a real North American" (425). Melancholy and solitary, neglected, forlorn as some gaunt wilderness figure in the midst of his country's principal metropolis, Brockden Brown, as John Neal saw him, is the very *type* of the American as writer. "If Brown deserved no other credit," Leslie Fiedler declares in *Love and Death in the American Novel*, "he should be remembered at least as the inventor of the American writer, for he not only lived that role but turned it into a myth, later developed by almost everyone who wrote about his career."[8]

It must be conceded that Fiedler overstates the mythic dimension of Charles Brockden Brown.[9] However, the novelist has long haunted American literature as a ghostly presence. A sketch by Nathaniel Hawthorne, "The Hall of Fantasy," suggests more precisely than Fiedler how Brown's nineteenth-century literary successors viewed him. Brockden Brown is the only American author Hawthorne places in the Hall, an imaginary shrine of fancy and genius, but he does not mention him by name. Referring to the novelist only as one "of our countrymen, the author of Arthur Mervyn," Hawthorne assigns a commemorative bust to "an obscure and shadowy niche," yet in company with likenesses of Homer, Aesop, Dante, Ariosto, Rabelais, Cervantes, Shakespeare, Spenser, Milton, Bunyan, Fielding, Richardson, and Scott. Given the nature of Brown's material, it is appropriate that he be placed in shadow and obscurity, but there is also satire in the American Hawthorne's at once audacious and self-effacing gesture of placing the American Brown among the most luminous writers of the Old World, yet in the recess of a shadowy niche.[10]

Although Brown is the only American writer in the hall, he is not the only American. Identifying the "peculiarly characteristic . . . genius of our country" with the "inventors of fantastic machines," Hawthorne peoples the Hall of Fantasy with a host of American inventors. Brown's ironic ensconcement in his shadowy niche suggests that his kind of "genius" runs counter to that of the country, something to which the Hawthorne of "The Custom-House" would be particularly sensitive. The precarious position of the "writer of story-books" in America is touched upon in another sketch that mentions Brown, "P's Correspondence," collected with "The Hall of Fantasy" in *Mosses from an Old Manse*. "P" suffers from a mental derangement that causes him to confound the dead with the living, so that, in a letter dated "February 29, 1845," he writes of meeting a portly, conservative, and eminently Victorian Lord Byron, who has just issued a self-bowdlerized edition of his works. "P" also sees, while strolling the streets of London, Robert Burns, aged eighty-seven; Shelley, who, reconciled to the Anglican Church, has taken orders; Coleridge, who has finally finished his *Christabel*; and Napoleon, whose exile on St. Helena has been exchanged for exile in London. Keats, too, is alive—but "P" hasn't seen him. Wordsworth has just died, and a fellow named Charles Dickens, having shown so much promise with a group of sketches called *The Pickwick Papers*, has been cut off in his prime, thus depriving the world of a successor to the ailing and elderly Walter Scott (who had actually died in 1832). "P" goes on to inquire of his American correspondent what there is "new, in the literary way" on the other side of the Atlantic, observing that "most of our writers of promise have come to untimely ends."[11] He cites Channing, Neal, Bryant, Whittier, and Longfellow (all very much alive in 1845, of course), adding:

> *P.S.* Pray present my most respectful regards to our venerable and reverend friend, Mr. Brockden Brown. It gratifies me to learn that a complete edition of his works, in a double-columned octavo volume, is shortly to issue from the press at Philadelphia. Tell him that no American writer enjoys a more classic reputation on this side of the water.

Through "P" Hawthorne suggests that Brown is a "classic," aesthetically "alive" and therefore superior to any number of contemporary authors, who, although literally living, have come to "untimely ends" as artists. These contemporary authors are nevertheless popular and esteemed in their own country. "P's" assessment of Brown's European reputation is actually accurate, but the case was quite different in Hawthorne's America.

Through much of the nineteenth century, Brown's work was far more celebrated abroad than in America, which means that the news about a fresh edition of Brown forthcoming from *Philadelphia* is an especially satirical product of "P's" derangement. Before its appearance in the 1846 *Mosses from an Old Manse*, "P's Correspondence" had been published in the April, 1845, issue of the *Democratic Review* (16, pp. 337–45). A year later an "Announcement of Complete Works of Charles Brockden Brown to be Published by William Taylor and Company" (of New York) did appear in the *New York Illustrated Magazine of Literature and Art* (2 [May, 1846], p. 64); however, only two volumes, *Wieland* and *Ormond*, were actually issued. At the time of "P's Correspondence" the latest complete reissue of Brown's novels was the 1827 Boston edition of S. G. Goodrich; the next complete set was not to come until 1857, from the Philadelphia press of M. Polock. Considerably more numerous at the time of Hawthorne's sketch were the British and French editions of Brown's novels.[12] Like Neal, then, Hawthorne pictures Brown as a Neglected American Author. "P" is as crazy to believe in a new Brown edition—especially in the popularly priced double-column octavo—as he is to have seen the dead alive and the living dead.

The figure John Neal depicted as a product of North America, a man of the wilderness walking the streets of Philadelphia, James Fenimore Cooper acknowledged as his own and his only predecessor in the depiction of things American. Still, there is something shadowy in Cooper's praise. Brown's work haunts the childhood memories of the "travelling bachelor" in Cooper's *Notions of the Americans* (1828). Having read *Wieland* "when a boy," the bachelor takes "it to be a never-failing evidence of genius, that, amid a thousand similar pictures which have succeeded, the images it has left still stand distinct and prominent in my recollection." Seven years before *Notions* appeared, however, Cooper seemed little moved by Brown's "pictures." Cooper acknowledges in the 1821 preface to *The Spy* Brown's early use of American material in the creation of literature, but he protests that, in the crucial "cave scene" of *Edgar Huntly*, Brown presents "an American, a savage, a wild cat, and a tomahawk, in a conjunction that never did, nor ever will occur." Cooper, who would himself so often neglect verisimilitude in order to create scenes of mythic intensity, fails to recognize the "conjunction" of elements in the cave scene as an icon strongly suggestive of quintessentially American rite and ritual.[13]

This failure to appreciate the cave scene seems even more ironic if we take seriously John Neal's accusation that Cooper plagiarized from Brockden Brown. Neal, in his *Blackwood's* series on American writers, may even have had in mind the allusion to *Edgar Huntly* made in *The Spy* preface when he accused Cooper, along with Irving *and himself*, of "purloining" from their common predecessor. Obliquely alluding to the scene in Chapter 28 of *The Pioneers* where Natty rescues Elizabeth Temple and her insipid companion Louisa Grant from a wildcat, Neal remarks: "The only catamount, that ever [Cooper] ventured upon, was a tame one, which had escaped out of Brown's clutches, first, with his nails paired [*sic*]'' (426–7).

As for Washington Irving, Neal charges that he "has purloined a head, and a scene, from Brown—probably, without knowing it" (426–7). A bit of hunting suggests that a "negro, looking over the rock" to which Neal specifically refers comes from "Adventure of the Black Fisherman" in Irving's *Tales of a Traveller*. Neal had probably just read the story, for it appeared in 1824, the year in which he was writing about Brown for his *Blackwood's* series. Sam, Irving's black fisherman, "his round black face peering above the edge of the rock, like the sun just emerging above the edge of the horizon, or the round-cheeked moon on the dial of a clock," is spying upon what he takes to be a gang of murderers burying their victim. " 'The murderers!' exclaimed Sam, involuntarily"—at which "The whole gang started, and looking up, beheld the round black head of Sam just above them. His white eyes strained half out of their orbits; his white teeth chattering, and his whole visage shining with cold perspiration."[14]

Neal charges that Irving made "*direct* use" of the head that is part of the "description of a murderer's face, appearing in a deserted house—at night" in *Wieland* (426–7). This must be the scene in which Clara Wieland, alone in a dark room, catches a glimpse of what turns out to be Carwin's face peering through the "aperture" of a doorway:

> Through this aperture was an head thrust and drawn back with so much swiftness, that the immediate conviction was, that thus much of a form, ordinarily invisible, had been unshrowded. The face was turned towards me. Every muscle was tense; the forehead and brows were drawn into vehement expression; the lips were stretched as in the act of shrieking, and the eyes emitted sparks, which, no doubt, if I had been unattended by a light, would have illuminated like the coruscations of a meteor (147–8).[15]

It is true that Irving did come into actual contact with Brockden Brown, who solicited from him in 1802 a contribution to the *Literary Magazine and American Register*. Brown also shared with Irving—in 1809—membership in the New-York Historical Society; and Irving biographer Stanley T. Williams suggests that Brown's journalism influenced Irving's *Salmagundi*.[16] However, the specific instance of "influence" to which Neal refers is neither very conclusive nor instructive. Despite some similarity in the straining of facial muscles, there is a great difference between the terror of Carwin's expression, his eyes emitting sparks, and the bug-eyed gaze of the moon-faced stock plantation "darky" Irving portrays. Whereas Brown employs the gothic in order to explore the extremity of terror, Irving exploits gothic trappings for their comic effect. Like the Cooper who, in *Notions of the Americans*, could appreciate the enduring shadows cast by *Wieland*, but who failed to acknowledge, in the preface to *The Spy*, the similar iconic intensity of *Edgar Huntly*, Neal develops a mythic image of Brown only to cite him as the "source" of a few dubious details of literary influence. Both Cooper and Neal do begin, and very tentatively, to suggest the outlines of what Leslie Fiedler asserts as the legendary or mythic stature of Brockden Brown in American literature. But neither of them articulates Brown's role with much precision.

The literary reputation of Charles Brockden Brown is fraught with paradox. In the American "Hall of Fantasy" he occupies a shadowy niche —yet in company with the very brightest luminaries of letters. Brown secured a dark but prominent place in the minds of John Neal, James Fenimore Cooper, and Nathaniel Hawthorne. Yet, among the writers who built the Great Tradition of America's nineteenth century, only Edgar Allan Poe owes Brown an extensive literary debt manifest in the details and major themes of his works. Herman Melville never even mentions Brown, at least not in writing.[17] Early reviewers of Brown were often patronizing and lukewarm, occasionally hostile, in their response to the novelist's works, even doubting their very "Americanness."[18] In contrast to this, later nineteenth-century commentators, such as William Hickling Prescott (1834) and George Barnett Smith (1878), cavalierly hailed Brown as one of the chief creators of an American literature, dubbing him a "pioneer."[19] Neither Prescott nor Smith develops this concept; in contrast, John Neal's 1824 portrait of Brown, which had also identified the novelist as a "frontiersman," did go beyond the simple pioneer label to define by evocation what we shall see as an important personal and cultural link between the gaunt and forlorn "frontier" novelist and the most profoundly American themes of his fiction. Unfortunately, it is the facile label rather than the rich image that has survived to inform two twentieth-century biographies of Brown: Harry R. Warfel's *Charles Brockden Brown: American Gothic Novelist* (1949) and David Lee Clark's *Charles Brockden Brown: Pioneer Voice of America* (1952). Granted, these are critically very naïve works, but the pioneer label is so pervasive that even a critic as astute as Harry Levin, in *The Power of Blackness* (1958), can let fall a phrase about Brown's "pioneering ingenuity."[20] Innocuous enough in any context other than an early American one, the danger of this label is that it simply ends discussion of Brown's literary and cultural identity. Summoning up such literal pioneers as Daniel Boone, it thrusts, *de verbo*, upon Brown a national significance, mustering the novelist without further argument into a virtually undefined American tradition.

Happily, critical discussions have become more sophisticated of late. Several recent studies of American culture and literary traditions have essayed definitions of Brown's place in the national literature. R. W. B. Lewis's *The American Adam* (1955), Richard Chase's *The American Novel and Its Tradition* (1957), Leslie Fiedler's *Love and Death in the American Novel* (1960, 1966), Richard Slotkin's *Regeneration through Violence* (1973), and William Spengemann's *The Adventurous Muse* (1977) are very useful. Nevertheless, focusing on a work or two at most and, at that, usually on a single aspect of a given work, these studies make only partial definitions in the solitary space of a chapter.

Finally, while four book-length studies devoted solely to the novelist have appeared before the present one, none of these is much concerned with Brown's Americanness. Donald Ringe's 1966 *Charles Brockden Brown* is a sturdy set of explications cast in the overly schematic Twayne format. Arthur G. Kimball's *Rational Fictions* (1968) and David Butler's *Dissecting a Human Heart* (1978) are specialized monographs, the first a Lockean reading of Brown, and the second a study of style. The most recent book, Norman S. Grabo's *The Coincidental Art of Charles Brockden Brown* (1981), is a major achievement. But even Grabo, concentrating brilliantly if narrowly upon motifs of plot and character doubling, chooses not to address questions of national identity and literary tradition.

What discussions we have of Brown's American identity, then, beginning with remarks by his literary colleagues and successors, as well as by his early critics, are tantalizing rather than fully revealing. Chapters in some recent general studies have been more suggestive, but books devoted exclusively to Brown have had little to say on the subject. The present study assumes that Brown is a significant *American* author. Indeed, it gives credence to Leslie Fiedler's assertion that the novelist approaches legendary dimensions; though if a myth is really at work here, it is very imperfectly formed, almost unmade—an underground myth. Most importantly, this study assumes that the great significance of Brown, as myth, as Emerson's "representative man," as writer, is inextricably bound up with his identity as an American. This is what John Neal hinted at in 1824, but, like the commentators on Brown who followed him, this is precisely what he failed to articulate, explore, and explain.

On the surface, there is little in Brown that makes him any more "American" than other writers of the period. He was not a prolific author. If, at thirty-nine years, his lifespan was brief, his career as a publishing fiction writer, spanning the three years between 1798 and 1801, seems almost abortive. Brown did publish in the magazines of which he was editor several pleas for a national literature free from the bondage of European models; he also proclaimed, in *Edgar Huntly*, the aesthetic and cultural significance of his having substituted in this American book the "incidents of Indian hostility and the perils of the Western wilderness" for the "[p]uerile superstition and exploded manners, Gothic castles and chimeras" of popular European fiction (4). But he never fulfilled his earliest literary dream of writing American epic poetry in the manner of Joel Barlow's *Vision of Columbus*. After writing novels for three years, Brown summarily turned to journalism (actually apologizing in one of his magazines for ever having written fiction), to political pamphleteering, to translation, and, at the close of his brief life, to geography. Of the six novels he published complete, only *Edgar Huntly* makes obvious and extensive use of the American wilderness, and only *Arthur Mervyn* (as well as *Ormond*, to a far lesser degree) fully exploits an American urban setting. Perhaps it was this paucity of obvious national material that led John Neal to contradict his statement that Brown was American to the backbone. Within the space of the very page on which he makes this judgment, Neal proclaims that Brown "had no poetry; no pathos; no wit; no humour; no pleasantry; no playfulness; no passion; little or no eloquence; no imagination." And after this catalog of impediments, the truly cutting blow: "He was . . . an imitator of Godwin, whose Caleb Williams made him" (*Blackwood's*, 421).

Neal did not acknowledge, much less explain, this contradiction; but we can do it for him. We shall see that Brown really did take very little interest in the American landscape, at least for its own sake, and that his fiction therefore is not much concerned with the surface of America. He resembles Edgar Allan Poe in his avoidance of what Poe himself called the "excessively opportune" subjects available to an American writer, the obvious physical facts of the national scene. Although his self-contradiction betrays a lack of self-consciousness, Neal, like Leslie Fiedler, had sensed a solid American backbone beneath the marginally American epidermis of Brown's fiction. Much of what follows in this book concerns itself with the tension between surface and core suggested by the contradiction in Neal's article. For it is actually no more true that a European novel "made" Charles Brockden Brown than that he relied exclusively on sources indigenous to America. Like any other American author, Brown drew upon both native and foreign materials for his work. But in the case of Brown, it is precisely the balance—tension is a better word—between the Old World and the New that is the crucial issue.

For Brown the wilderness was not the scenery of Pennsylvania's back counties, but rather what this scenery meant to his imagination. If he failed to paint the surface of the American scene as richly as Cooper, it is because the features of Brown's scene had little existence outside his own mind. We shall see that dreaming and writing were startlingly similar functions for Brockden Brown, and that, as in a dream, Brown's images do not so much evoke emotion as they are produced by it. The wilderness of Brown's fiction exists not so much as a record of a physical scene, but as a projection of what the novelist himself labeled a darker part of his being. But as the United States at the end of the eighteenth century was no longer simply a wilderness, so Brown recognized in himself what he called "a double mental existence," a dark self that emerged in writing, and a light self associated with society and civilization. America, with its Philadelphias fronting wilderness, became the ground upon which Brown acted out the drama of his identity between the dark and light within him. The script is at once private and public, personal and cultural, for Brown's fiction was wrought between two forces—the eastward pull of the Old World past, of light and civilization; and the westering lure of the New World future, dark and wild. The novelist's best work is the record and result of an effort to establish an American identity, to become what Crèvecoeur, also torn between the light and dark, called the "new man" in the New World.

Charles Brockden Brown's struggle to establish in his fiction union between the two halves of his double mental existence drew upon and reflected the culture of his countrymen as they attempted to create in America a United States. Brown's was by no means a unique effort. Quite the contrary, his project places him near the beginning of a succession of our most characteristic writers, whose works tend to weave the author's private fate into the public fabric of the nation's. What is both unusual and fascinating in the case of Brown is how the effort is at once hidden from obvious sight and yet peculiarly exposed. Brown's art was not adequate to reconciling fully the private and public functions of his novels. The most telling scenes and episodes are projections of inner conflict intensely felt, but they remain projections rather than finely finished objective correlatives. Too often the writing is abstract where concreteness is called for. Where Cooper would develop an image fully, Brown frequently supplies but half-images or even a single, though revealing, word. It is certainly not that Brown was more subtle than Cooper, but that he did not understand, consciously let alone self-consciously, the fullest implications of his materials and themes. Much of what is most interesting in a Brown novel is shaped with little intentional craft. Though this means that one must peer beneath a flawed surface in order to interpret the vision of a Brockden Brown novel, the imperfections are themselves often significant as signs of the personal and cultural tensions that produced them.

This study aims at a full appreciation of Brown's imperfect art, chiefly as it is embodied in his major fiction; indeed, it aims at a particular appreciation of the artist's very imperfections. Therefore, the discussion here is not confined to literary issues. Regarding the writer's works both as art and artifact, the chapters that follow consider the public culture in which Brown lived as well as the private world of his emotional and intellectual life. The object here is to explore the uneasy relation between Charles Brockden Brown and his native land, to assay something of the character of the early Republic as portrayed and even embedded in the productions of one of its literary citizens, and, by suggesting what place this author occupies in our literature, to discover some more general truths about writing in America.

CHARLES BROCKDEN BROWN

I

Irreconcilable Oppositions

The preface to *Edgar Huntly*, along with the subtitle "An American Tale" which Brown subjoined both to *Wieland* and to an early unpublished prototype of *Huntly* called *Sky-Walk*, seem unambiguously to proclaim their author's intellectual and aesthetic independence from the Old World. Pleas for the establishment of a national literature, commerce, and industry independent from Europe are to be found throughout the three magazines Brown edited.[1] Likewise, the national pride evident in a number of the notes he appended to his 1804 translation of the French traveler Constantin F. C. Volney's *Tableau du climat et du sol des Etats-Unis* would appear to be of a piece with the patriotic sentiment that motivated his bellicose 1803 *Address to the Government of the United States on the Cession of Louisiana to the French* . . . . In the face of such evidence, Brown has often been described simply as a patriot, nationalist, or "pioneer," descriptions that are justified as far as they go. But they do not go far: they begin to describe Brown's relation to the *United States*, but they do not touch upon his far more complex relation to *America*.

A good place to begin to distinguish between Brown's attitude toward the nation and his feelings about the continent is his *Address* on the cession of Louisiana. It is a curious work; and that it has received such little attention is surprising since it can be considered Brown's most ambitious piece of fiction. Published anonymously early in 1803, the pamphlet is a response to the secret Spanish cession of Louisiana to France in 1800 and to what was apparently Napoleon's plan of occupying New Orleans. In order fully to exploit the nation's outrage at the cession, especially in the wake of President Jefferson's refusal to take military action, Brown devoted most of the so-called *Address* to the divulgence of a "secret document," the report, presumably to Napoleon himself, of a French "counsellor [*sic*] of state" singing the praises of Louisiana, urging immediate French colonization, and denigrating the American people's willingness and ability to offer resistance. The document, like the councilor, is a fiction, a "hoax" in dead earnest. Had its intention not been obviated by the purchase of Louisiana negotiated by Jefferson's minister Monroe later in 1803, the

Address might have been instrumental in fomenting a war between France and the United States.[2]

The question of its morality aside, the creation of the French councilor allowed Brown not only to alert the American people to the dangers of French imperialism, but also to picture the virtues of Louisiana through the jealous eyes of Europe. In addition to providing a persona for an effective promotion tract, the councilor also serves as a mask from behind which Brown delivers a jeremiad against habits of self-interest rampant among the "jarring and factious citizens" of the United States, their passion for nothing but money, and their addiction to that "liquid poison called Whiskey."[3] Effective as this jeremiad might have been in galvanizing the national resolve, it is as a promotion tract that the *Address* is more interesting for what it suggests about the character of Brockden Brown. "Morass and forest," the councilor declares, "and a savage and naked race, have mostly disappeared. A Christian and European nation has sprung up in their place. That side of the sea has become a counterpart to this" (15). The rhetoric cuts two ways here. It is an inflammatory example of the "Frenchman's" colossal arrogance, asserting that Louisiana has been made valuable only insofar as it has been made European; and, because it has been made European in spirit, it by rights should become European in fact. Yet, its inflammatory purpose aside, the passage is also a blatant appeal to European standards as proof for Brown's American audience of the territory's value.

That the "Frenchman's" estimation of the territory's Europeanness is an exaggeration—Louisiana was of course largely an unexplored region at this time, before Louis and Clark—merely intensifies the ambiguity of "his" remarks. The estimation serves Brown on the one hand to mark the "Frenchman" as a foreigner, who sees in the territory what his imperialist eyes want him to see; but, on the other hand, the remarks value the territory only for its future civilized state. There is no attempt to argue the worth of the territory as wilderness; rather, in touting Louisiana for its civilization, the "Frenchman" is calculated to spur on the American settlers in their arduous mission of converting the American wilderness into a counterpart of Europe. Despite, then, his numerous pleas for artistic, intellectual, commercial, and, here, political independence from Europe, there is yet something in Brown that causes him to argue the contrary as well. Indeed, so successful is the "Frenchman's" European evaluation of Louisiana that Brown (as the anonymous patriot who introduces the "document" of the councilor, and who has the last word after it) leaves himself, awkwardly, with no ideological basis from which to argue the United States' right to the territory. All he can do is assert without argument that "we have a *right* to the possession. The interests of the human race demand from us the exertion of this right" (80). Brown finally invokes the deity for sanction:

We have looked on with stupid apathy, while European powers toss about among themselves the property which God and Nature have made ours. (86)

God and Nature may have destined the territory to belong to the United States rather than to Europe, but not as American *wilderness* so much as national *property*—which, of course, partakes of the Old World notion of ownership. So deeply ingrained is the European in Brown, that in asserting the Americans' right to Louisiana he can "argue" only from European premises.

The "Frenchman," it has been mentioned, is particularly contemptuous of the American willingness and ability to resist colonization. The nation's weakness, he argues, results from a lack of unity among a people who "call themselves one" even though "all languages are native to their citizens: All countries have contributed their outcasts and refuse to make them a people" (62). Although in 1886 Emma Lazarus would inscribe a sentiment proudly and perilously close to this on the base of the most famous French gift to our nation, in the earlier part of the century such words were well calculated to offend the national *amour propre*. Indeed, Brown was to comment on a point very like this in translating Volney's *Tableau* a year after the *Address to the Government* had appeared. Brown renders Volney's expression *Anglo-Américains* in an account of French settlements on the Wabash at Poste Vincennes with the simple term *Americans*, observing in a note that the "largest or most important *part* [of the population of the American continent] is naturally confounded with the *whole*, and the name of the latter bestowed upon the former." This, Brown continues, should be "a cause of pride and exaltation" for us:

We should exalt in the pre-eminence which this custom tacitly allows us, and ardently anticipate the period, when the extension of our empire will make the national appellation of *Americans* a strictly geographical and precise one.[4]

The anticipation of the doctrine of manifest destiny in this idea of present name as a prediction of future geography seems unambiguous here. Yet only four years earlier Brown had thought differently, observing that the "most suitable name imaginable for our country, would be that which is now appropriated to part of it: I mean *New-England*."[5] Such a name shows the same aversion to total independence from Europe evident in the ambivalence of the *Address*. The sense the name conveys, that the citizens of the United States are essentially European sojourners in America, is intensified by these further remarks on the notion of an *American* language:

The *name* of a language is, indeed, derived from the name of place, but not from that which the speakers may, at any time, chance to inhabit. . . . If our language ought not to be called

English, yet there is evident absurdity flowing from the same principles in calling it American, since this is not the language of *America*, a country which stretches nearly from one pole to the other, but of a small portion of its northeastern coast.

Brown considered schemes of an American language dangerous products of the "*amor patriae*," a "passion" that "can be approved, like other passions, [only] when strictly disciplined or limited. Its usual effects, like those of other passions, are, from the deplorable imperfections in human nature, absurd and pernicious." Of so great concern were the dangers of this "passion" that in an otherwise guardedly laudatory review of Noah Webster's *Brief History of Epidemic and Pestilential Diseases* Brown takes special pains to cavil not at Webster's theory of epidemiology but at his American orthography:

> Mr. W. will incur some censure in this respect, for while he is always and minutely careful to cut off a vowel from the end of some of his words, (*famin*, *determin*, &c.) which ordinary writers retain, he is unreasonably negligent in more important matters, and has failed to make his sentences coalesce fully with each other, or to harmonize with themselves.[6]

Umbrage over a few dropped vowels may seem trivial; but the anxiety apparent in Brown's overreaction to a scheme of an American language, of which Webster's orthography was of course a part, is genuine nonetheless. And its genuineness makes it seem all the more incongruous. From a man who tried to foster a national literature, who wrote in favor of national commerce and industry, and who was willing to go to war to defend national sovereignty over Louisiana, we should expect wholehearted support for a national language. Yet, Brown declares:

> Whatever may be said in favor of fostering the spirit of jealousy and animosity to foreign nations in a political sense, seems totally out of place in relation to science ["science," that is, in the more general eighteenth-century sense of "knowledge"]. Language is the vehicle of knowledge; but diversity of language is the greatest obstacle to its progress.

Political, commercial, even aesthetic independence from Europe is acceptable; but Brown balks at the most basic independence, which threatens the vehicle of knowledge itself, which threatens, more particularly, Brown's vehicle as a writer. Where, then, is the authority for the constitution of language to come from? Since "books are the only adequate authority for the use of words," Brown argues with a bullheaded circularity, and since the overwhelming majority of books in English come from England, "Whence, then, but from English books, from the writings of Englishmen, is the maker of an American dictionary to draw his material . . .?" ("On the Scheme of an American Language," pp. 1–2).

It is possible to argue that between 1800, when the articles on the scheme of an American language and on Webster's *Brief History of Epidemic and Pestilential Diseases* were written, and the period 1803–4, when the translation of Volney and the *Address* appeared, Brown had simply become a more ardent nationalist. But, true or not, this fails to explain the ambivalence in the juxtaposition of Brown's reactionary remarks on language with the pleas for political, commercial, and literary independence, pleas that were made *throughout* his career. Nor does it explain the basic ambivalence operating in the *Address* itself: the simultaneous allegiance to the United States and distrust of America. Nor, finally, does it adequately account for what must be called a sense of ambivalence in the translation of Volney's *Tableau*. Seizing upon a number of the notes appended to the translation, notes Brown intended as correctives to what he felt were some of Volney's mistaken notions about America, at least two critics have discussed what they judge to be Brown's diametric opposition to Volney's "anti-American stereotypes." [7] To be sure, Brown does frequently disagree with Volney, particularly as to the effects of the American climate and the virulency of American diseases; but he does not oppose Volney wholesale. Quite the contrary: Brown writes in his own preface to the translation that

> uncommon praise is due to Volney, for having produced a work so accurate and scientifical, with so little assistance from former publications, in relation to a country of such vast extent, and so much in the state of wilderness, and during so short a residence. Instead of reproaching him for the mistakes committed, we should grant him liberal applause for the truths he has attained. (*A View*, p. xxiv)

Brown praises Volney for the accuracy of his limited but firsthand knowledge based on actual observation rather than on the kind of "anti-American stereotypes" that dominated, for instance, Buffon's opinions about an America he had never bothered to see for himself. The fact remains, however, that a great many of Volney's views are not flattering to America, and Brown, all too easily pictured as the unthinking nationalist, translated these views for his countrymen, differing with them frequently, but, on the whole, praising and commending the book.

While none of these works is among Brown's major accomplishments, they are all important for what they tell us about his ambivalence toward America. Although the articles, the *Address*, and the translation were written after *Edgar Huntly*, they *seem* only the adumbration of and prelude to its theme, worked through obsessively and unconsciously. In this novel, for the first and last time in his career, Brown sent a character to the frontier, and with him explored the meaning of America in the extremity of its wilderness.

All but the most faithful subscribers to D. H. Lawrence's injunction to trust the tale and not the teller must read Cooper's remarks on the cave scene of *Edgar Huntly* with surprise and disappointment. Cooper, who made himself an easy target for Mark Twain by progressively sacrificing verisimilar for symbolic truths (so much so that Lawrence described the Leatherstocking cycle in the order of its composition as "a *decrescendo* of reality, and a crescendo of beauty"[8]) cavils at the improbability of the cave scene. We have seen that he cites the very constituents of a ritual iconography—"an American, a savage, a wild cat, and a tomahawk"—only to ignore their power as symbols when he remarks the unlikelihood of their "conjunction." Today, even the cursory reader of *Edgar Huntly* is quick to appreciate the ritual initiatory aspects of the cave scene and what follows it, just as such a reader does not overlook the ritual resonance in *The Deerslayer* when Cooper has Natty kill his first Indian. Indeed, there is a great temptation to define Brown's place in our literature simply by seizing upon the fact that both Cooper, whose role in American literature has been extensively defined, and Brown, whose role has yet to be fully understood, created ritual wilderness scenes. But once we label two such scenes "ritual" or "initiatory" it is all too easy to neglect the crucial differences between them, precisely those differences from which we learn most about Brown's relation to America.

The greatest difference is between Hawkeye and Huntly. If, as D. H. Lawrence suggested, Hawkeye was in part a projection of the white Cooper's Indian unconscious, at least the character Cooper projected was in himself a thoroughly conscious being who is acutely aware of what he is doing, never more so, certainly, than at the moment of his "initiation" in *Deerslayer*. Edgar Huntly, in contrast, is a sleepwalker. His literal unconsciousness reflects Brown's inability to reconcile the white "European" values of the United States with those of the Indian's wilderness America, whereas the supremely self-conscious figure of Hawkeye is the very means through which Cooper reconciles discrete white and Indian identities. Cooper was able to dramatize the contradictory demands of civilization and wilderness in a character whose career ran through five American novels. In the only complete novel Brown set extensively in the wilderness, ambivalence, rather than sharply defined contradiction, is the source of drama.

Although the genre of the Leatherstocking series is closer to elegy than to epic, Hawkeye, like the hero of the elegiac *Beowulf*, emerges as something of an epic figure. Displaced by the very civilization his efforts in the wilderness have made possible, Hawkeye nevertheless retains his identity. Cooper could cherish apart from quotidian society the heroic memory of Hawkeye even while he felt the need in society for the more prosaic Mordaunts and Littlepages of *Satanstoe* and its sequels. But Huntly, whose initiation begins when he is unconscious and lost in the wilderness, returns from his adventure largely bereft of identity, disoriented and dispossessed. Written with the density of a dream, the cave scene begins a complex definition of Edgar Huntly's encounter with America. The scene vividly concentrates Huntly's ambivalence toward Old World and New; and his ambivalence, we shall see, is an implicit function of Charles Brockden Brown's.

It is in a long letter to his fiancée Mary Waldegrave that Huntly relates his experience in the cave—really a pit inside a cavern—along with the adventures that precede and follow it. He has taken it upon himself to investigate the death of Mary's brother, who, he comes to believe, has been murdered by one Clithero Edny, an Irish immigrant employed as a farm laborer by a man named Inglefield. Discovering that Clithero is subject to nocturnal wanderings, Huntly stalks him through the Pennsylvania wilds as a hunter stalks his prey. Fascinated to find that the mysterious farmhand is a sleepwalker, Huntly overtakes him one night and persuades him to relate the particulars of the life he led in Europe. After so doing, Clithero disappears into the woods.

On succeeding nights Huntly, with a quiet obsessiveness, continues his pursuit. Catching sight of Clithero on one occasion, he gives chase only to lose him again when a panther intervenes. It leaps at Huntly, who is saved from certain death when the animal falls into a chasm. Huntly returns home, and the narrative is taken up for three chapters with the mysterious disappearance of some letters left by the murdered Waldegrave and the story of a man, Weymouth, who lays claim to Mary Waldegrave's inheritance. But suddenly, in chapter 15,[9] Huntly turns to the bizarre account of how, safe at home, he had fallen asleep as he lay "stretched upon a down bed" in a "lightsome chamber," only to awaken, dazed, "upon a rugged surface and immersed in palpable darkness" (153):

> I emerged from oblivion by degrees so slow and so faint, that their succession cannot be marked. When enabled at length to attend to the information which my senses afforded, I was conscious for a time of nothing but existence. It was unaccompanied with lassitude or pain, but I felt disinclined to stretch my limbs or raise my eyelids. My thoughts were wildering and mazy, and, though consciousness was present, it was disconnected with the locomotive or voluntary power. (152)

That Edgar Allan Poe borrowed from Brockden Brown is well known and has been fairly well documented.[10] "The Pit and the Pendulum" echoes the passage quoted, as well as others from the cave scene, not only in the use of certain words and phrases but also in the central motif of the protagonist's gradual coming to consciousness. Although we shall fully explore in Chapter 2 the affinity between Brown and Poe, particularly as revealed in the parallels between the cave scene and "The Pit," it is important to anticipate a bit of that discussion here. While Poe did borrow a number of Brown's words to describe his victim's dazed efforts to orient himself, he did not adopt the one term—"wildering"—which makes

Huntly's internal state a resonant sign of his external condition. The absence of this figure of speech suggests Poe's recognition that, in the European setting of "The Pit and the Pendulum," the word would be without the significance it has in Brown's American world. "Wildering" is a verbal link to the wilderness in which Huntly and his thoughts are, quite literally, bewildered. It links the external reality of the New World to the corresponding psychological state that world evokes. The figure of speech, we shall see presently, emphasizes aspects of Huntly's experience which are wonderfully representative of numerous other encounters, in works by other writers, with a New World that has similar psychological dimensions. It also points to the ways in which Huntly's confrontation with America was also Brown's own.

Huntly must confront first, however, not so much a world, "New" or otherwise, as the apparent absence of one. Like the victim of Poe's "Pit," Huntly finds upon opening his eyes that "the darkness" is "as intense as" it was when they were closed. Like the character in Poe, Huntly brings reason to bear against the darkness:

> The first effort of reflection was to suggest the belief that I was blind: that disease is known to assail us in a moment and without previous warning. This, surely, was the misfortune that had now befallen me. Some ray, however fleeting and uncertain, could not fail to be discerned, if the power of vision were not utterly extinguished. In what circumstances could I possibly be placed, from which every particle of light should, by other means, be excluded? (153)

Whereas Poe's victim assumes that he has been immured alive or is perhaps "experiencing" the nothingness of death itself, Huntly first thinks less sensationally, seeking a less radical explanation of his plight. Yet both characters respond to situations that partake similarly of a universal horror. Confronted with circumstances without parallel in the experience of either man, each assumes that a common, though dire, transformation has taken place within himself—death or sudden blindness—rather than admit the possibility that such radically uncommon extremity actually exists outside himself. Huntly, in fact, would sooner question his senses than entertain the possibility of so intense a darkness in the world.

But there are places in the world, in the "New" World of Huntly's pit, where such darkness does exist. An "adventurer" in the caves of Kentucky, John Filson observed in 1784, "will have a perfect idea of primeval darkness"[11]—which not only suggests how at least part of Huntly's experience is rooted in one kind of New World fact, but also illustrates the paradoxical "newness" of what James Russell Lowell's Hosea Biglow called a "strange New World, that yit wast never young" (Lowell, *Complete Writings* [New York: AMS Press], vol. 11, p. 140). The darkness that caused Huntly to question his senses is, like the darkness in Filson's

Kentucky caves, "primeval." Huntly's attribution of the darkness to sudden blindness proceeds from the kind of intellectual egocentricism typical not only of Brown's fictional heroes but also of the European adventurers who called the primeval world they had landed upon "New." It was of course new only to the experience of those born into the "lightsome chamber" of a manmade European civilization.

Edgar Huntly finds it impossible to account for the sudden, it would seem magical, translation from his own lightsome chamber to the darkness of the wilderness pit. Huntly has not yet discovered that he, like the strange man he stalks, is a sleepwalker. All he does know is that he lay down to sleep on his own bed and in his own room only to awaken into absolute darkness and utter strangeness. With this imperfect knowledge, he can attribute the transformation of his condition only to some external malevolent—and gothic—agent. "What dungeon or den," Huntly asks, "had received me, and by whose command was I transported hither?" (153); and again: "Methought I was the victim of some tyrant who had thrust me into a dungeon of his fortress, and left me no power to determine whether he intended I should perish with famine, or linger out a long life in hopeless imprisonment" (154). Appropriate to Poe, the dungeon image seems as foreign to the world of *Edgar Huntly* as "wildering" is foreign to that of "The Pit and the Pendulum." One is, moreover, tempted to declare that *Brown* borrowed this all—a passive victim in the dungeon of some shadowy Inquisitorial tyrant—from Poe. Here is an instance of what Harold Bloom calls "apophrades," a situation in which the chronology of literary influence is to all appearances reversed: the work of a later writer shows the influence of his precursor not as though the precursor had written the work of the later writer, "but as though the later [writer] himself had written the precursor's characteristic work."[12] The precise nature of the relation this image bears to Poe will be taken up later, but it is important now to recognize that the image, however out of place in the American wilderness, is no conventionally gothic slip of Brown's pen.

The intrusion of the dungeon is highly appropriate to Huntly's emotional and intellectual state because it is the product of an attempt to attenuate the horror of the unfamiliar by invoking that of the familiar. Sudden blindness is horrible, to be sure, but Huntly can understand it as he cannot understand the unfamiliar phenomenon of absolute darkness. Similarly, horror expressed in a familiar image of an Old World dungeon is less overwhelming than unfamiliar terror expressed in terms more obviously suited to the New World. Poe's character performs a similar evasion in "The Pit and the Pendulum" when he tells us that he stepped through the utter darkness of his dungeon "with all the careful distrust with which certain antique narratives had inspired me" (Poe, 5:72). Antique narratives are like Huntly's dungeon: although frightening enough, they counteract the radical unfamiliarity of whatever torment the Inquisition may invent by bringing the experience within the pale of "antique"—and therefore assimilated—history.

But there is a telling difference between Brown and Poe even on this point. Set in the wilderness of America, the dungeon imagined by Brown's Huntly is representative of a specific kind of New World experience. Washington Irving, in the course of his tranquil *Tour on the Prairies* (1835), drew on a European stock of images in order to make himself more at home on his American journey. Despite his anticipation of Thoreau's notion of the "wild," the rejuvenating effect of the westering experience, Irving is loath to relinquish the world east of the Atlantic. "We send our youth abroad," he declares, "to grow luxurious and effeminate in Europe; it appears to me, that a previous tour on the prairies would be more likely to produce that manliness, simplicity, and self-dependence, most in unison with our political institutions."[13] But looking out upon the "new," the primeval prairies, Irving observes that they "appear to have been laid out by the hand of taste; and they only want here and there a village spire, the battlements of a castle, or the turrets of an old family mansion rising from among the trees, to rival the most ornamented scenery of Europe" (108). The "hand of taste," defined by the context of the passage as the hand of the *European* artificer, is also present in Irving's perception of the Osage Indians as "so many noble bronze figures" with "fine Roman countenances" (21–2), and in his description of a stand of trees:

> We were overshadowed by lofty trees, with straight, smooth trunks, like stately columns; and as the glancing rays of the sun shone through the transparent leaves, tinted with the many-colored hues of Autumn, I was reminded of the effect of sunshine among the stained windows and clustering columns of a Gothic cathedral. Indeed there is a grandeur and solemnity in our spacious forests of the West, that awaken in me the same feeling I have experienced in those vast and venerable piles, and the sound of the wind sweeping through them, supplies occasionally the deep breathings of the organ. (41)

Irving's purpose here may be consciously patriotic, a demonstration that "our" scenery is as fine as any in Europe; but it is nonetheless more significant that Irving's emotion among American trees should duplicate what he feels in a European cathedral. Where Huntly—or Brown—imports a dungeon to temper the newness of a distinctively New World horror, Irving draws upon European-born emotion to define and contain his sense of an American sublime.

Like Brown's more benighted traveler, Irving is unable or unwilling to meet the New World entirely on its own terms. He repeats the "error" William Carlos Williams discusses at the outset of "The American Background," a marvelously concise appreciation of the impact America had on the epistemology of the Old World. The earliest English settlers, Williams points out, saw birds with rusty breasts and called them robins. Thus, from the start, an America of which they could have had no inkling drove the first settlers upon their past. They retreated for warmth and reassurance to something previously familiar. But at a cost. For what they saw were not robins. They were thrushes only vaguely resembling the rosy, daintier English bird. Larger, stronger, and in the evening of a wilder, lovelier song, actually here was something the newcomers had never in their lives before encountered. Blur. Confusion. A bird that beats with his wings and slows himself with his tail in landing.

"They found they had not only left England," Williams continues, "but that they had arrived somewhere else. . . . The most hesitated and turned back in their hearts at the first glance."[14]

Read in the context of others' experience in the New World, Huntly's dungeon image cannot be dismissed simply as inappropriate. Nor, however, is it likely that the image is the product of conscious art. For, in his address "To the Public" prefacing *Edgar Huntly*, Brown declared his conscious intention to exclude from his American novel the "Gothic castles and chimeras" of European fiction (4). Consciously, Brown intended to fashion an American story from American materials, but, like the Washington Irving of *A Tour on the Prairies* and the Englishmen of William Carlos Williams's essay, Brockden Brown hesitated in his project and turned back in his heart.

Since Hawthorne, we have come to recognize that *heart* in American literature is a heavily freighted word. And as we shall see, Brown regarded the wilderness as the territory of the heart rather than of the head, of individual instinct rather than social rationality. By no means is Brown's view of the American wilderness and its frontier unique. Quite the contrary, it is so pervasive that Ralph Ellison, a writer apparently far removed from the concerns of Crèvecoeur, Brown, Irving, Cooper, and Hawthorne, once defined himself as a resident of the "American frontier": a territory that functions implicitly "to encourage the individual to a kind of dreamy wakefulness, a state in which he makes—in all ignorance of the accepted limitations of the possible—rash efforts, quixotic gestures, hopeful testings of the complexity of the known and the given."[15] As we explore the cave scene further, we will find that Huntly probes his own frontier, rashly, quixotically, hopefully, and ignorantly, until he reaches just beyond the accepted limitations of the possible.

For Brown's Huntly, sleepwalking across the frontier, the wilderness is literally a territory of dreamy wakefulness. The specific image of the dungeon comes to him during a delirious "wakeful dream" (154), and the entire landscape of *Edgar Huntly*, reached via sleep, becomes a frontier between waking and dreaming, a disputed territory in which waking reality is often nightmare and in which sleep brings yet more dreams of the environing wilderness. Disputed too is the frontier that should separate

Brockden Brown from Edgar Huntly, the author from his creation. Physically and factually inaccurate as it is, John Neal's description of the novelist as a melancholy, forlorn young man dreaming his dark dreams through the streets of Philadelphia rings with psychological truth—at least for the youthful Brown of 1796. Whether the air of gloom in which he immersed himself was part of a fashionable Wertherian pose or the genuine product of deep-seated depression, it was sufficiently disturbing both to worry and annoy two of Brown's closest friends. Writing on behalf of himself and William Dunlap, Elihu Hubbard Smith complained to Brown about the portentous obscurity of his melancholy letters. "The man of Truth, Charles! the pupil of Reason, has no mysteries. . . . The pen of poesy, Charles, is not often that of Philosophy & Truth" (Smith, 164). The criticism of his two friends seems to have cut him deeply, for Brown took their remarks as an accusation of deliberate and habitual lying. Brown's reply to Smith is lost, but a draft of Smith's response to that reply does survive. From it we can gauge the depth to which Brown had taken offense:

> Here are no doubts expressed of your veracity [Smith wrote]. Here is no more than a plain intimation of an erroneous manner of communicating information, which those who love you regard as a misfortune,—as an error—persisted in you, thro' ignorance, & capable of being remedied by you . . . your style of composition . . . was charged with certain defects . . . & we endeavoured to make you sensible of them. We were unsuccessful. (Smith, 171)

Most of the "defects" Smith goes on to list are examples of the kind of circumlocution that still irritates the reader of Brown's major novels; but there is yet another "defect" that, Smith's disclaimer to the contrary notwithstanding, does bring Brown's "veracity" into question:

> That the example of J. J. Rousseau had too many charms in your eyes, not to captivate you, & incite you to imitate him; & that you were pleased to have others believe those misfortunes to be real, which you knew so eloquently to describe. The transition is natural—& to a mind of sensibility almost unavoidable: you began to fancy that these fictions were real; that you had indeed supposed, enjoyed, known, & seen, all that you had so long pretended to have experienced; every subsequent event became tinctured with this conviction & accompanied with this diseased apprehension: the habit was formed; & you wandered in a world of your own creation. (Smith, 171)

Clearly, these remarks could have done nothing to soothe Brown's wounded feelings. Smith must have realized as much, for a few pages after the draft appeared in his *Diary* he noted that "I never sent the letter which

I wrote, on the 27th of May, to Charles B. Brown. To-day I composed a new one—in which part of the former was incorporated." But the remarks are revealing just the same. They suggest that from a point very early in his career, Brown's "habit" had been to inject himself, naturally, automatically, unawares, into his fictions, perhaps (as Warner Berthoff has suggested) even channeling into his mature novels the "irrational melancholy" with which he had formerly burdened Dunlap and Smith.[16]

That Brockden Brown made an especially dreamlike identification with Edgar Huntly is suggested by Leslie Fiedler's quip that the novel was "not so much written as dreamed."[17] There is more than casual truth to the observation, for Brown himself once described his method of composition as something very like dreaming. When John Bernard, whose physical description of the novelist was quoted earlier, commented to Brown on the surprising contradiction between the "sombreness of his writings" and the engagingly "cheerful" quality of his social self (a "very cheerful if not . . . entertaining companion"), Brown replied:

> I am conscious . . . of a double mental existence. When I am sufficiently excited to write[,] all my ideas flow naturally and irresistibly through the medium of sympathies which steep them in the shade, though the feelings they bring are so pleasing as to prevent my perceiving it. The tone of my works being thus the necessary result of the advancement of those truths or discoveries which lead me to composition, I am made so happy by it for the time as to be ignorant of its real effect upon my readers. This I term, therefore, my imaginative being. My social one has more of light than darkness upon it, because, unless I could carry into society the excitement which makes me write, I could not fall into its feelings. Perhaps . . . the difference of the two may be thus summed up: in my literary moods I am aiming at making the world something better than I find it; in my social ones I am content to take it as it is.[18]

As in a dream, the novelist yields to images and ideas involuntarily. Like Huntly, Brown conceives himself the passive "victim" of his own adventure, a dream dark enough to be called nightmare, but which serves something like Freud's pleasure principle as well. Steeped in the "shade" as Brown's ideas are, "the feelings they bring are so pleasing" as to keep the writer from realizing the gloom of their shady frame. As dreaming is for us all a natural function essential to maintaining waking existence, so writing had a biological urgency for Brockden Brown:

> As soon . . . as I could put two ideas together I felt a craving to invent, which required certain trains of thought to be daily put in action in order to get rid of a surplus of daily generated ideas. This employment was just as necessary to my mind as sustenance to my

frame. It was synonymous with a vital function. Fame I have longed for, certainly; and sympathy from my friends, much more than from the world; but, had I been exiled to Kamschatka [Kamchatka], I must have written as a mental necessity, and in it have still found my highest enjoyment.

Like dreaming, writing seems to have served Brown as a purgation. But writing, even as it enabled Brown to live in society by purging antisocial impulses, actually subverted the idea of society. Brown equates the private melancholy that motivates his writing with a state of pleasurable excitement and "highest enjoyment," while social cheerfulness is compatible only with insufficient excitement. He appreciates approval for his writing, but he could just as well work in the egocentric isolation of Kamschatka. Even as it served Brown's public self, composition staked out a private reserve of dream territory apart from the measured social tracts of waking reality. In the case of *Edgar Huntly*, to write meant to explore the wilderness, and both writing and wilderness exploration were accomplished as "dreams."

Like his creator, Huntly led a double mental existence. His was divided between the lightsome chamber of civilization and the dark pit of the wilderness as Brown's was between the light mood of society and the dark one of literary composition. Brown's remarks to John Bernard suggest a neat balance between the two moods, but they are actually in a state of tension. The mission of Edgar Huntly, as Brown's dreamer-proxy, was not only to sleepwalk into a dark landscape beyond those "limitations of the possible" accepted and imposed by a waking civilization, but also to explore the frontier between Old World and New, the frontier between the two halves of Brown's—and his nation's—double mental existence. The intrusion of the dungeon into the wilderness is only one of the many interpenetrations of civilization and wilderness values that betray the tension between what we might call Brown's Old and New World selves. The dungeon image alerts us to the meaning of the cave scene as evidence of Brown's richly "bewildered" American vision. It is with this ambivalent image in mind that we continue the explication of the cave scene.

After Edgar Huntly has fully regained consciousness, he attempts a strictly mechanical exercise of reason. Like the victim of "The Pit and the Pendulum," Huntly tries to gauge the dimensions of his "dungeon," groping for a wall and feeling his way along it in absolute darkness. Poe's character admits "little object—certainly no hope—in these researches" prompted merely by a "vague curiosity" ("Pit," 73); but Huntly embarks upon his own blind "researches" so single-mindedly that he dismisses a tomahawk he stumbles over as something affording "no hint from which [he] might conjecture [his] state" (*Huntly*, 154). He is forced at last to deem his exercise "fruitless" when, his faculty of reason little availing him, he is "overpowered" by fears. Now—like Poe's victim—he considers that he may have been buried alive. It is with this notion that Huntly's sense of removal from the familiar world becomes most acute, so that he is for the moment "full of tumult and confusion" but, oddly, neither terrified nor spurred on in his "efforts at deliverance." He seems to himself not only removed from the world but from its time as well, perhaps like the explorer in one of Filson's primevally dark caves:

> There is no standard [Huntly writes] by which time can be measured but the succession of our thoughts and the changes that take place in the external world. From the latter I was totally excluded. The former made the lapse of some hours appear like the tediousness of weeks and months. (155)

Passivity and the sense of time's suspension come to an end when "a new sensation" recalls Huntly from his "rambling meditations." Like Poe's character, he suddenly feels the "cravings of hunger" and is overtaken by the fear of "a tedious and lingering death" which might result from starvation. Once again he is prompted to exercise reason and again performs a kind of measuring task. He listens for sounds, trying to get an idea of the dimensions of his "dungeon" from the echoes. The noise of something like "wind sweeping through spacious halls and winding passages" (an extension of the gothic dungeon image) suggests to Huntly that the pit may not be completely sealed off: "I now exerted my voice, and cried as loud as my wasted strength would admit. Its echoes were sent back to me in broken and confused sounds from above. This effort was casual, but some part of that uncertainty in which I was involved was instantly dispelled by it" (155). It occurs to Huntly that this is the very cavern through which he had previously passed during an earlier pursuit of Clithero:

> In passing through the cavern on the former day, I have mentioned the verge of the pit at which I arrived. To acquaint me as far as was possible with the dimensions of the place, I had hallooed with all my force, knowing that sound is reflected according to the distance and relative positions of the substances from which it is repelled.
> The effect produced by my voice on this occasion resembled, with remarkable exactness, the effect which was then produced. Was I, then, shut up in the same cavern? (155-6)

Whether he realized it or not, Brown created in this juxtaposition of pedantic accoustical physics and the absolute horror of total darkness, imminent starvation, and living burial an acutely ironic icon of reason literally crying out in the wilderness. The "cry," born of reason, results in irrational panic as Huntly realizes what his soundings have told him: "The sides of the pit were inaccessible; human footsteps would never wander into these recesses. My friends were unapprized of my forlorn state. Here I should continue till wasted by famine. In this grave should I linger out a few days in unspeakable agonies, and then perish forever'' (156). Driven to ''frenzy,'' Huntly now not only abandons reason but also abrogates the authority of his senses, which surely ''were fettered or depraved by some spell'': ''I was still asleep, and this was merely a tormenting vision; or madness had seized me, and the darkness that environed and the hunger that afflicted me existed only in my own distempered imagination'' (156).

This latest response to extremity is as egocentric as the earlier conclusion that he had gone suddenly blind, that darkness so intense was not possible in the world; but this time the response produces something more, an action and a feeling that have ramifications not only for Brown personally, but for experience in the New World generally. Huntly described himself as ''forlorn''—not merely despairing, but abandoned, lost, doomed, forgotten. This sense of divorce from the known world, coupled with a ferocious hunger, elicits what is in a New World context a particularly desperate but revealing act. After trying unsuccessfully to assuage his hunger by tearing and swallowing bits of his shirt, Huntly almost considers self-cannibalism: ''I felt,'' he reports, ''a strong propensity to bite the flesh from my arm.''

Now cannibalism was nothing new to the American scene or to the European experience of America. Perhaps Brown's ''favourite pursuit,'' his lifelong interest in geography,[19] had led him to read Hakluyt's ''Voyage of M. Hore and divers other gentlemen, to Newfoundland, and Cape Briton, in the yere 1536 and in the 28 yere of king Henry the 8,'' or any of a number of similar narratives of American exploration or Indian captivity.[20] The Hakluyt account relates how certain of the ''gentlemen'' roaming the desolate coast ''grew into great want of victuals'' and sought herbs and roots; but,

> the famine increasing, and the reliefe of herbes being to little purpose to satisfie their insatiable hunger, in the fieldes and deserts here and there, the fellowe killed his mate while he stooped to take up a roote for his reliefe, and cutting out pieces of his bodie whom he had murthered, broyled the same on the coles and greedily devoured them. [Upon hearing of this,] the Captaine found what became of those that were missing, & was perswaded that some of them were neither devoured with wilde beastes, nor yet destroyed with Savages: And hereupon hee stood up and made a notable Oration, containing, Howe much these dealings offended the Almightie, and vouched the Scriptures from first to last, what God had in cases of distresse done for them that called upon him, and told them that the power of the Almighty was then no lesse, then in al former time it had bene.[21]

The unwieldy Elizabethan prose imparts to this scene an unintentional tone of deadpan black comedy that yet serves to underscore the tragic newness of an experience for which Hakluyt's language is pathetically inadequate. There is a twofold irony at work here, for the voyage, made in the expectation of plenty, yields only "famine," which compels the good English Christians, who may have heard tell of a native population of "anthropophagi, and men whose heads / Grew beneath their shoulders," to become cannibals themselves. The "notable oration" the captain delivers upon learning of the cannibalism among his men is described by Hakluyt with headings appropriate to any commonplace sermon one might hear back in England. Its doctrine is the benignity of God's providence—"for them that call upon him"—and, more significant for the New World experience, the omnipresence of God, even in Newfoundland: the power of the Almighty was "then no lesse, then in al former time it had bene." This European-style sermon with its message that the God of Europe is also God of the New World serves a purpose similar to the intrusion of a dungeon into Brown's American landscape, or of cathedrals, castles, and bronze Indians in Irving's. Like these, it is an attempt to preserve a European identity in the face of American extremity.

Yet it is important to note how this "sermon" in a sense betrays itself, underscoring rather than ameliorating the radical displacement and extremity that prompted cannibalism among the Hore party. For although the alienation from European and Christian codes is a function of displacement in space—a voyage to a distant world—the captain's "sermon" translates the displacement into temporal terms by arguing that God is no less powerful now than "in al former time." This translation is not merely a symptom of Hakluyt's uncertain command of language but an emphasis on the sense that the new *place* has wrought a change in the character of European Christians as profound as any that *time* might bring about.

"Cannibalism," as Richard Slotkin points out, "had traditionally been associated with the Indians of America since the discovery of the New World by the men of the Renaissance" (*Regeneration*, 90). The incident among the men of Hakluyt's account, like the self-cannibalistic gesture Huntly contemplates, betokens an abrogation of European values and at least a partial acceptance of values thought to be native to America. But there is of course one essential difference between these two instances of cannibalism. Huntly's gesture is a cannibalism of the self, a literally self-defeating means of survival, whereas the cannibalism Hakluyt reports is a practical expedient, whatever its emotional, moral, and metaphoric value.

The English captain recalls his cannibal crew of potential Indians to their Christianity and Englishness by reminding them of the operation of providence even in this alien world, but it is the wilderness itself that forestalls the self-cannibalism to which it had incited Huntly in the first place. For a new image occurs to him at this point, one drawn not from Europe, but from the kind of wilderness Thoreau would philosophize upon at the beginning of the "Higher Laws" chapter of *Walden*. Huntly's heart overflowed with cruelty, he reports, as "I pondered on the delight I should experience in rending some living animal to pieces, and drinking its blood and grinding its quivering fibres between my teeth" (156). But this thought passes or, rather, is transformed. Taking up the tomahawk he had ignored while intent on the reasonable task of measuring his dungeon, Huntly thinks about plunging it into his own heart, "delighted to consider that the blood which would be made to flow would finally release me, and that meanwhile my pains would be alleviated by swallowing this blood" (157). This is, if anything, an even more intense impulse toward self-cannibalism than the mere thought of biting his arm had been, but the notion has undergone a change away from egocentrism. Before, he merely would have bitten himself—an act of self-sustenance, for all its violent paradoxes—but Huntly now is prepared to use an Indian weapon against his own life, thus becoming an almost ritual enemy to himself, an enemy indigenous to the alien wilderness. What is more, this new expedient makes him, by its juxtaposition in the text to his thoughts of "rending some living animal to pieces," both wilderness man and wild prey. This complexly double identification of Huntly with the wilderness is, as well, an echo of the common practice for the Indian hunter to merge with his prey, or the Indian warrior with his enemy (cf. *Regeneration*, especially p. 385). Huntly has begun to renounce the lightsome chamber and identify himself with the dark wilderness.

But he fortunately delays driving the tomahawk into himself long enough to grope for and finally to find footholds, by means of which he climbs at last to the verge of the pit:

> The darkness was no less intense than in the pit below, and yet two objects were distinctly seen. They resembled a fixed and obscure flame. . . . These were the eyes of a panther. . . . The desperateness of my condition was, for a moment, forgotten. The weapon which was so lately lifted against my own bosom was now raised to defend my life against the assault of another. There was no time for deliberation and delay. (158–9)

This new menace with which the wilderness threatens Huntly is also the means of his salvation. The panther forces Huntly both to turn from self-cannibalism and to override his civilized habit of reason. And this time the result is not the paralysis that had earlier accompanied his dreamlike torpor. With no "time for deliberation and delay," he acts on unmediated instinct, like the stereotyped Indian or like the panther itself: "No one knows the powers that are latent in his constitution. Called forth by imminent dangers, our efforts frequently exceed our most sanguine belief" (159). Hurled with unconscious dead aim, the tomahawk finds its mark between the panther's glaring eyes.

Some five years after *Edgar Huntly* appeared, Brown would find occasion to carp (though not without his customary ambivalence) at the

French traveler Constantin F. C. Volney for what he took as an implication in the manner of Buffon that the American climate has a degenerative effect on organisms, including man. Brown endeavored to "correct" such notions in a number of notes he appended to his 1804 translation of Volney's *Tableau du climat et du sol des Etats-Unis*. To take one instance, Volney remarked on the baneful influence of the "dreaded" northeast wind in America, which "oppresses the brain, and produces torpor and headache." Since "the physical and moral constitution of man is greatly influenced by the state of the air," Volney reasoned, we may in some measure attribute to climate "diversity . . . in the character of nations, some being distinguished by lively wit and keen perception, and others by torpor and feebleness of mind." Brown counters that the severity of the American climate actually hardens "the constitution of those exposed to [it] from birth," and that "this evil influence [which Volney attributes to climate], therefore, is only to be dreaded by weak and effeminate forms, which a mild and serene climate is more likely to produce than a bleak and churlish one."[22]

Like Irving in *A Tour on the Prairies*, Brown in his note associates Europe with effeminacy; but whereas Irving speaks of the "luxurious and effeminate" cultural influence to which American young men were commonly exposed during their European *Wanderjahre*, Brown intends something more elemental. Volney himself had reiterated the commonplace assertion that climate influences not only the physical but also the moral and intellectual self,[23] and it is highly probable that Brown was familiar with the work of Dr. Benjamin Rush, the early American researcher in what today would be called psychosomatic medicine. If he did not know Rush's work directly, then certainly he must have heard of it from his close friend Dr. Elihu Hubbard Smith, who had studied under Rush at the University of Pennsylvania. In "An Oration Delivered before the American Philosophical Society, Held in Philadelphia on the 27th of February, 1786" Rush addressed himself to the question of the "Influence of Physical Causes upon the Moral Faculty," observing that among a host of physical influences

> the effects of CLIMATE upon the moral faculty claim our first attention. Not only individuals, but nations, derive a considerable part of their moral, as well as intellectual character, from the different portions they enjoy of the rays of the sun. Revenge —levity[—]timidity—and indolence, tempered with occasional emotions of benevolence, are the moral qualities of the inhabitants of warm climates, while selfishness tempered with sincerity and integrity, form the moral character of the inhabitants of cold countries.[24]

With such ideas in mind we can appreciate both the seriousness of Brown's note on Volney's remarks about the American climate, and part of the cultural context in which Edgar Huntly's physical transformation in the cave scene must be placed. The "lightsome chamber" and "down bed" from which Huntly is so mysteriously transported, like the mild and serene climate of Volney's France, demand little, so that a life confined to such a chamber and such a bed, or to the physical (if not the political) climate of Volney's France, might be expected to produce the "weak and effeminate forms" Brown implies are indigenous to Europe. Had Huntly passed all his life in the comfortable "climate" of his house, had he never been tested by the "rugged surface" and "palpable obscurity" of the pit, the tough American qualities of his constitution, shaped by the rigors of a "bleak and churlish" climate, would not have developed. In Richard Hakluyt's account of Hore and his gentlemen, an experience of the New World's physical extremity produces only horror at the transformation brought about in English Christians; but the chain of trials that leads Huntly to the verge of cannibalism and to the actual killing of the panther produces a gratifying realization of his physical prowess. The pride evident in Huntly's remark that no one knows the powers latent in his constitution until they are called forth by imminent danger is the same pride that motivated Brown's note on Volney. The wilderness nearly kills Huntly, but it also sends in the nick of time an avatar of all its horror and threat—the panther—to save him by transforming him.

Alas, it is not only Huntly's physical being that is transformed by the experience in the pit. The captain in Hakluyt's account of the Newfoundland expedition reacted not so much to the physical horror of cannibalism as to the religious apostasy it signified. Similarly, as he retails the story to his fiancée, Huntly's pride in his prowess changes to ambivalence oscillating between boastfulness and shame. This moral transformation can be understood best in terms of the religious and emotional implications of Huntly's extreme acts. After killing the panther, and finding that "all fastidiousness and scruples [were] at an end," Huntly devours the animal —raw. He writes to his fiancée about this with circumspection and regard for a female sensibility bred to the niceties of a lightsome chamber: "I will not shock you by relating the extremes to which dire necessity had driven me. I review this scene with loathing and horror." Indeed, returned to the familiar comforts of home, Huntly finds his recollection of the panther feast unreal, "some hideous dream . . . some freak of insanity" (159–60). Huntly's delicate bearing toward Mary Waldegrave cannot alone explain this sense of unreality or the deep confusion evident in his attempt to justify what he had done. "If this appetite"—Huntly's incongruously genteel term for starvation—"has sometimes subdued the sentiments of nature, and compelled the mother to feed upon the flesh of her offspring, it will not excite amazement that I did not turn from the yet warm blood and reeking fibres of a brute" (160).

He justifies an act he now regards as unnatural by invoking the precedent of nature itself, couching the whole grotesque defense in the politely periphrastic negatives ("that I did not turn from") of eighteenth-century syntax. By its contrast with the material it embraces, this syntax serves only to emphasize more strongly such lurid details of physical sensation as the beast's "yet warm blood and reeking fibres." That the action had some particular appeal both for Brown and for Huntly, despite his protestations to his fiancée, is suggested not only by the close attention to physical detail, something rare in the characteristically abstract Brown, but also by repetition. This is really the second occurrence of these images; "the delight . . . in rending some living animal to pieces, and drinking its blood and grinding its quivering fibres between my teeth" (157) had already been fantasized by Huntly a few pages before he actually eats the panther. The apology written for the benefit of his fiancée must be seen, then, as a mixture both of contrition and of a savoring of fulfilled fantasy. Huntly's report to Mary Waldegrave, which observes even as it violates social propriety, is like a Brockden Brown novel in miniature, steeped in the shade of private fantasy even as it is delivered into the genial and public light of society.

We strike an even richer vein of this duplicity in Huntly's account of the effects produced by eating the panther. He becomes so ill immediately after gorging himself that he wishes he were dead. Ultimately, however, he is the better for his grisly meal:

> Gradually my pains subsided, and I fell into a deep sleep. I was visited by dreams of a thousand hues. They led me to flowing streams and plenteous banquets, which, though placed within my view, some power forbade me to approach. From this sleep I recovered to the fruition of solitude and darkness, but my frame was in a state less feeble than before. That which I had eaten had produced temporary distress, but on the whole had been of use. If this food had not been provided for me I should scarcely have avoided death. (160)

At first reading, this dream seems an unambiguous expression of the frustration inherent in Huntly's situation. Suffering in the wilderness, he dreams of a promised land not of milk and honey, but of streams and banquets. Yet some anonymous malevolent power, corresponding to the "agent" he thinks of as having brought him into captivity in the first place, prevents his approaching the longed-for streams and the banquets. A straightforward dream of wish-fulfillment frustrated.

But not quite straightforward. For this is not the first occurrence of the word *banquet*. It is used just a few paragraphs earlier in a very different context when Huntly relates his self-disgust at the memory of having eaten the panther: "The whole [episode] appears to be some freak of insanity. No alternative was offered, and hunger was capable of being appeased even by a banquet so detestable" (159–60). The word is hardly appropriate here, of course, as incongruous as the stilted syntax in that description of "warm blood and reeking fibres." One might see a conscious attempt at irony, but the prevailing tone of the narrative is anything but ironic and, in any case, verbal playfulness is something for which Brown can seldom be given credit. Perhaps the inappropriateness of the word should simply be judged a symptom of Brown's haste and lack of sensitivity to nuance. It is more useful, however, to interpret the word as the product neither of accident nor design, but, like the earlier dungeon image, as the result of Brown's intimately ambivalent identification with the frontier.

Brown's ambivalence causes *banquet* to bear an ambiguous definition. A distinctly civilized word, *banquet*, as used in the dream, suggests Huntly's longing for the familiar world of his lightsome chamber. Applied to the waking reality of having devoured raw panther flesh, the word may be taken, like the image of the dungeon, as an attempt to ameliorate with an Old World expression the horror of the New. Considered this way, then, *banquet* is a verbal means of escaping the wilderness. But the word appears first in the description of the grisly wilderness meal and then, a few paragraphs later, in the dream. By calling the panther feast a banquet, Brown has made Huntly charge the word with a new and specifically American meaning that contradicts the accepted definition of a formal, civilized, "European" meal. When the word reappears in the dream, then, we cannot know whether the conventional or the new *ad hoc* definition is operating. Thus we cannot be sure—as neither Huntly nor Brown is sure—whether the dream expresses a wish to return from the wilderness or to remain in it. It is unclear whether the "power" that forbids approach to the dream banquet is the same one Huntly had earlier imagined as the malicious agent of his translation from chamber to pit, or whether it is the conscience that occupies the lightsome domain of civilization itself.

The tangle of guilty emotion evident in the ambiguous meaning of "banquet" finds psychosomatic expression in the physical torment Huntly suffers after gorging himself on the wild beast:

> One evil [starvation] was now removed, only to give place to another. The first sensations of fulness had scarcely been felt when my stomach was seized by pangs, whose acuteness exceeded all that I ever before experienced. I bitterly lamented my inordinate avidity. The excruciations of famine were better than the agonies which this abhorred meal had produced.
>
> Death was now impending with no less proximity and certainty, though in a different form. Death was a sweet relief for my present miseries, and I vehemently longed for its arrival. (160)

We have already seen that Brown almost certainly knew something about Dr. Benjamin Rush's work in psychosomatic medicine. We cannot, of course, declare with certainty that Brown intended Huntly's violent reaction to his first wilderness meal as a symbol—literally, a symptom—of his guilty and vacillating attraction to the wild. However, one of Rush's observations does have particular bearing upon the case of Edgar Huntly:

"EXTREME HUNGER produces the most unfriendly effects upon moral sensibility. . . . The Indians in this country whet their appetites for that savage species of war, which is peculiar to them, by the stimulus of hunger."[25]

Suggesting that extremity of physical circumstance overrides moral scruples, this statement corroborates Huntly's justification of his wilderness banquet. More importantly, it begins to suggest that the identification with wilderness values implicit in eating the panther is more than symbolic. Physical and emotional extremity, of which "EXTREME HUNGER" is one variety, is a property of the wilderness. It is this extremity that elicits the "savage" act which tends to identify the hitherto civilized Huntly with the values of the wild realm into which his sleep has taken him. The Indians of Rush's observation, for whom wilderness life is a state of waking existence, consciously draw upon the extremity of their world by deliberately starving themselves in order to "whet their appetites" for a species of warfare particularly abhorrent to the "civilized" sensibility. Huntly partakes unconsciously in the psychosomatic rite which Rush's Indians consciously embrace. By eating the panther, Huntly, like those white European Christians who dined on one another in Newfoundland, begins to transform himself unawares into what white European Christians call a savage.

Like Hakluyt's account of the Newfoundland expedition, Huntly's adventure in the pit demonstrates how the physical conditions of the wilderness urge, even force, a spiritual and moral identification with "Indian" values and, as a consequence, the renunciation of Old World identity. Indeed, Richard Slotkin writes of cannibalism (closely associated in the European mind with the American Indian) and the Indians' partaking of a freshly killed forest beast as "eucharists," symbolic acts by which the individual establishes communion with the wilderness:

> Eating a bit of one's slain enemy . . . was to primitive men a ritual means of taking on the strength of that enemy. For the same reason they would cut a piece of a just-killed bear or wolf and eat it raw, believing that they were thus taking on the bear's strength or the wolf's cunning. (*Regeneration*, 90)

Edgar Huntly is, in part, a story of wilderness initiation in which the cave scene, culminating in the wild eucharist, figures as the central rite of passage. But it is an initiation story only in part. Slotkin calls Huntly's experience a "quest . . . a hunt for his identity among the choices offered him by the American wilderness" (*Regeneration*, 390). What this assessment ignores is the ambivalence at the core of the character Brown created. The degree of consciousness Slotkin's notion of a "quest" or "hunt" implies is more appropriate to the case, say, of Natty Bumppo, who, no matter what "Indian" activity he takes part in, is always aware of allegiance to his white "gifts." Whereas we can appreciate Natty's killing the Indian who names him "Hawkeye" in *The Deerslayer* as part of an unambiguous initiation into further knowledge of the wilderness, Huntly's wilderness eucharist leaves us, as it leaves Huntly himself, with disturbing and confusing emotions. Natty recognizes in himself a dialectic between his white gifts and his life in an Indian's wilderness, a dialectic he fully understands and often dilates upon. Huntly, however, is torn by the cultural opposites Natty Bumppo is able to reconcile.

The division of self Huntly suffers is projected symbolically in two ways. First, as Richard Slotkin points out, we see that, in hunting Clithero Edny, Huntly actually pursues his wilderness double. Like an Indian hunter, Huntly identifies himself with his "prey," projecting, albeit unconsciously, a part of himself into Clithero. Equally significant is the second way in which Huntly demonstrates his disturbing doubleness: the flirtation with self-cannibalism that precedes his encounter with the panther. It is not only that the physical extremity of the wilderness forces Huntly to act against himself, but, as with the other instances of extremity we have considered, self-cannibalism entails emotional and moral consequences. It is yet another assault on white, Christian, Old World identity.

We turn again to Richard Slotkin: it was a "common Indian torture . . . to cut off some part of a man's anatomy—an ear, a strip of flesh, a finger—and force the victim to eat it" (*Regeneration*, 124). How this practice figures in the pattern of a wilderness eucharist is illustrated most astonishingly by the captivity of Father Isaac Jogues, a French Jesuit ministering to the Hurons in the late 1630s and early forties. One of many tortures Jogues endured during his captivity among hostile Mohawks was the singularly horrific experience of having his thumb amputated:

> Then, taking in my other hand the amputated thumb, I offered it to Thee, my true and living God, calling to mind the sacrifice which I had for seven years constantly offered Thee in Thy Church. At last, warned by one of my comrades to desist, since they might otherwise force it into my mouth and compel me to eat it as it was, I flung it from me on the scaffold and left it I know not where.[26]

Jogues wants to consecrate the amputated thumb to his Christian God as, perhaps, a kind of reverse eucharist, an offering of his own body and blood to the heaven he serves even in the wilderness. Warned that he may be made to eat the thumb himself, thus partaking in the cannibal eucharist of the Indians, Jogues casts it into the unknown wild. Just as he later refuses to eat some venison given him by his captors, because it "had been offered to the Devil" (48), Jogues will not be forced to an act of cannibalism signifying apostasy from his Christian identity. Huntly's contemplation of very nearly the act Jogues most desperately seeks to avoid is naturally due to intense hunger, but it also testifies to an essential confusion of identity. The Jesuit has as clear a sense of his white Christian "gifts" as Natty Bumppo, but Huntly has already in some measure identified himself with the Indian wilderness.

The experience in the pit is not so much an initiation or a quest as it is a surfacing of latent ambiguities in Huntly's identity. "Called forth by imminent dangers," he writes his fiancée, "our efforts frequently exceed our most sanguine beliefs." There is, as has been suggested, a pride in this realization, but, given the long train of bloody events that will follow Huntly's killing the panther, one can hardly resist a pun, or parapraxis, in that word *sanguine*. Having eaten the raw flesh of a forest beast, Huntly stalks and kills many an Indian before the story ends. Could the white Christian, when he set out to investigate the murder of Mary's brother, have believed himself capable of becoming so "bloody," bloody as any stereotype paints the "savage"? After killing the Indian in *Deerslayer*, Natty gains a firmly realized identity as Hawkeye, a white man who can live successfully in the wilderness; but Huntly, after his extended and bloody encounter with that wilderness, is left neither white nor Indian—or, rather, neither Indian enough to live in the wilderness nor any longer white enough to dwell without ambivalence in the lightsome chamber.

Huntly writes Mary Waldegrave that he is "conscious to a kind of complex sentiment of distress and forlornness that cannot be perfectly portrayed by words" (152). Safely returned home, Huntly describes his emotional state with the very word he had previously used to describe his situation in the pit. There he had been "forlorn"; now, taking up his pen at his own desk and in his own bright room, he feels "distress and forlornness." There can be little wonder why he had felt lost, hopeless, abandoned in the strange new world of the pit. However, that the emotion persists in the familiar light of his old world conveys a more enduring sense of dislocation, dislocation from the familiar and a failure to possess the new. Certainly, *forlorn* was a common enough word with "gothic" and "graveyard" writers during the latter years of the eighteenth century. But, in Brown's America, it was also preeminently a word of the frontier. It was as "a kind of forlorn hope, preceding by ten or twelve years the most respectable army of veterans which came after them" that Michel Guillaume Jean de Crèvecoeur's Farmer James described the backwoods pioneers.[27] "Forlorn hope" is military jargon for the advance guard or shock troops who are calculatedly sacrificed to secure a position for the main body of soldiers, that "most respectable army of veterans which [come] after them." Crèvecoeur uses the term to define the melancholy and degenerate state of the frontiersmen, whose laziness and shameless immorality he blames on their having forsaken idyllic agrarianism for brutish hunting ("Eating of wild meat . . . tends to alter their temper") and on their long separation from the civilization for which, ironically, they are securing the wilderness. No longer white enough to be considered civilized, the backwoodsmen are yet too white to be called Indians.

For Huntly the frontier is no simple geographical demarcation. It defines his identity now as a wanderer in a spiritual no-man's-land, the disputed border between old and new worlds. A citizen of neither, Huntly is forlorn. And it is with this notion of loss and abandonment that the identification of the novelist with his character, implicit in the unconscious quality of Brown's prose and in the dreamlike nature of his habits of composition, becomes dramatically explicit. John Neal had fancifully described Brown as a powerfully built though spare man who, but for his pallor, might be taken for a woodsman, a "sound, hearty specimen of Trans-Atlantic stuff." But Neal's North American Brown is heartbroken as well, his "spirit absolutely crushed." Indeed, Neal might just as well have been describing Edgar Huntly in his *Blackwood's* article. Like Neal's Brown, Huntly is forlorn, physically strengthened by his wilderness sojourn, emerging from his ordeal a "sound, hearty specimen of Trans-Atlantic stuff," but broken in spirit. Remote as it is from the facts of Brown's actual appearance, Neal's portrait is emotionally accurate. Brockden Brown and Edgar Huntly are both uneasy frontiersmen.

It is only in *Edgar Huntly* that Brown allows one of his characters prolonged and meaningful exposure to the literal frontier of the New World; but emotional, intellectual, and moral frontiers, shaped by the geographical one, figure in all of the novelist's work. The interest, the success and failure, the "Americanness" of Brown's novels turn upon a single constant in his vision: ambivalence. Although Brown was rarely able and little concerned to establish the settings of his novels realistically, *Wieland*, *Ormond*, and *Arthur Mervyn*, novels into which the literal wilderness *seems* hardly to intrude, are unmistakably set along a figurative frontier. *Edgar Huntly*, then, is unique among Brown's novels only in that its action takes place along a frontier of literal as well as figurative dimensions. All of Brown's novels occupy the emotional, intellectual, and cultural territory of Janus, looking forward into the darkness of the private self and backward into the public light of society; ahead into the wilderness and back into civilization; west toward a New World, east toward an Old. Within the novelist there is this Janus, too. But if the "double mental existence" Brown described to John Bernard enabled him to glimpse worlds dark and light, it failed, we shall discover, to tell him which of the two he might call home.

II

Metaphysic Wilderness

Except for the novel fragment *Stephen Calvert*, in which the title character lives on the shores of Lake Michigan, *Edgar Huntly* is the only fiction Brown set explicitly in the literal wilderness. Even so, there is little vividly detailed scene-painting in the novel. We have seen, for example, that rather than fully depict the physical details of the pit into which Huntly sleepwalks, Brown more simply has his hero label it a dungeon. Lacking immediate and overt connection with the wilderness, the dungeon is, in effect, so portable that Edgar Allan Poe was able quite handily to move it into a story set not in the wilds of America, but in the Spain of the Inquisition. Granted that Brown wrote during an age not yet fully emerged from the shadow of Dr. Johnson's dictum that the artist's task is not to number the streaks of the tulip; but even that critic would have objected to a degree of abstraction great enough to permit such wholesale transplantation of particular devices.

Brown's habit of translating the scene around him into an intellectual shorthand is an artistic failing. We have already seen, though, how one "failure"—Brown's inability to resolve the ambivalence created by his allegiance to both Old World and New—is actually a principal source of the novelist's enduring significance. The failure to render the concrete and particular in the American landscape likewise warrants investigation for what more it tells us about Brockden Brown's relation to the native place that was never quite his home, and for what it suggests about his role in the making of an American literature. The discussion in the preceding chapter focused on the emotional dimension of Brown's uneasy American stance; the discussion that follows attempts to define the intellectual dimension.

For a novelist, Charles Brockden Brown took remarkably little interest in the physical features of the world around him. When John Davis, British novelist, traveler, and sojourner in the United States, called at Brown's "dismal room in a dismal street" in New York City, he asked the author what effect his surroundings had on his work. Brown's window opened on a bad view of an unprepossessing street, so that Davis wondered

whether a view of nature would not be more propitious to composition; or whether he should not write with more facility were
his window to command the prospect of the Lake of *Geneva*.
—Sir, said he, good pens, thick paper, and ink well diluted,
would facilitate my composition more than the prospect of the
broadest expanse of water, or mountains rising above the clouds.

And when Davis "mentioned this reply of Mr. *Brown* to one of the most
distinguished literary characters now living[,] Sir, said he, this *American*
Author cannot, I think, be a man of much fancy."[1]

The distinguished character's reply, considering his emphasis on
Brown's nationality, was probably motivated in part by British anti-
American snobbism; yet the indifference to place and the details of landscape is sufficiently startling to prompt our own doubts about the writer's
powers of "fancy." Some remarks Brown published—and likely wrote—in
his *Literary Magazine* about his country's literary resources do seem to contradict what he reported to Davis. Surprised and dismayed at the slumber
of the American muse, Brown protested that:

We have skies, which give us the varied and kind returns of seasons;
we have winds, which one would think would blow the spark of
genius into flame; we have waters, which should allure to their
banks the vagrant foot of enthusiasm; and we have mountains
which furnish us with all that is grand and elevating in prospect.[2]

Ironically, this landscape inventory, abstract and formulaic, itself exhibits complete indifference to the particular details of the American
scene. The physical features of his country did intrigue Brown sufficiently
for him to take in 1801 a boat tour up the Hudson into the semiwilderness
of upstate New York as far as Albany, traveling overland as well through
parts of Connecticut and Massachusetts. But it turned out to be little more
than a casual sightseeing excursion among "sweetly picturesque" scenes. If
the pitted and craggy landscape (what there is of it) in *Edgar Huntly* owes
something to Edmund Burke's notion of the Sublime, the landscape
Brown "saw" along the Hudson could have been drawn according to
Burke's Beautiful: "I had heard much of the stupendous and alpine
magnificence of the scenery. We entered it this morning, with a mild
breeze and serene sky, and the prospect hitherto has been soft and beautiful. Nothing abrupt, rugged or gigantic."[3]

And there was nothing to excite Brown's imagination as he dutifully
recorded such scenes in a journal. The Hudson tour was popular at the turn
of the century—six or eight vessels "like our own, have been constantly in
sight, and greatly enliven the scene"—but by the time he reached North-
ampton, Massachusetts, on the overland leg of his excursion, the novelist
was depressed, lonely, perhaps a bit forlorn, but mostly bored. Brown
complained that he and his traveling companion William Coleman (who

was shortly to found the New York *Evening Post*) knew "nobody and [could] therefore seek employment and amusement only in ourselves, in the fields, and in the outside of houses."

> We might have had letters introducing us at every considerable town in the course of this journey, but proposing to fly rapidly, we omitted to apply for them. I think we erred, as a friend, for even a half hour is of some value.

At one juncture on the Hudson, Brown simply conceded his inability to render the "passing scene" into words:

> I have gazed at the passing scene from Stony Point to West Point, with great eagerness, and till my eye was weary and pained. How shall I describe them. I cannot particularize the substance of the rock, or the kind of tree, save oaks and cedars. I am as little versed in the picturesque. I can only describe their influence on me.

This passage not only proclaims the writer's capitulation to the recalcitrant facts of the landscape, it also conveys his testy impatience with them: he has gazed until his eyes hurt. What *does* interest Brown, or, at least, what he claims to be able to describe, is the "effect" of the landscape upon him. That is, for the novelist, particular rocks and trees, oaks and cedars, have little interest or meaning in themselves. Only their "effect" promises genuine fascination, only their status in the mind and imagination. True, Brown seems generally to have been incapable of rendering visually concrete detail, but the abstractness of his American "landscapes" is not due solely to inability. Brown perceived and recorded landscapes not for what they presented in themselves, but for what they represented in himself. Details of a scene figured abstractly, not as objects but as tokens of thought and imagination.

Indifferent as he was to the details of landscape, Brown steeped his creative being so deeply in the wilderness that each of his novels, even those most remote from a native setting, draws upon the wilderness for both crucial and casual images and figures of speech. We shall examine many of these as we discuss the novels in the following chapters, but the habit of abstracting the wilderness into images and figures was present near the very beginning of Brown's literary career, before he wrote any fiction. Although it was not published until 1808, Brown composed "Devotion: An Epistle" in 1794. It is a kind of intellectual verse autobiography, a *Prelude* of sorts, composed before Wordsworth's, writ small by comparison, but competently. At one point the poet speaks of his relation to "Plain Nature," who

> in her flow'ry paths, has long
> Detain'd me, lost in her enchanting maze

Awhile; anon, delighted more to trace
The footsteps of Linnean guide, and out
Of such sweet prison wind me, by the clue,
Spun by Upsalian [*sic*] hands, conducted safe
Through pleasant paths: and long has been the march
And weary, through the thorny tracts that lead
To nothing in the metaphysic wilderness.[4]

Foremost in evidence here is Brown's uneasiness in the midst of *plain* nature, the natural scene in and of itself. Enchanting and pleasant, the "flow'ry paths" nevertheless detain the poet, who feels himself "lost" in a "maze." The only way out of the "sweet prison" is to intellectualize it by studying Linnaeus (a native of Uppsala, Sweden), who provides an abstract codification of its particulars. It is in Linnaeus's annotation of nature, and not in plain nature itself, that Brown takes delight.

Reliance on Linnaeus is neither the only nor most important evidence in this passage of Brown's penchant for abstraction. The idea of nature's "pleasant paths," punctuated with a colon in the seventh line of the passage, introduces another kind of "path," this one wholly figurative. The poet speaks of his early intellectual pursuits as a long and weary march "through thorny tracts"—punning here on forest tracts encumbered by literal thorns and thorny tracts written by abstruse philosophers—"that lead / To nothing in the metaphysic wilderness." It is as if the colon separates the two halves of an equation in which a literal discussion of the wilderness yields a figurative—"metaphysic"—one.

In examining *Wieland* in the next chapter we shall see exactly in what sense exploring the metaphysic wilderness led Brown to "nothing." For now, considering Brown in 1794, we might conclude that the young poet-philosopher intended a confession that his poring over thorny tracts had borne no fruit. The chief problem of Brown's intellectual youth seems to have been a difficulty in harnessing an overly exuberant mind. In the verse paragraph that follows the passage about the metaphysic wilderness, the poet writes of tracing "the secrets of mysterious mind"; however, his thoughts are "frolicsome and wild" despite the "unwonted fetters" of "analytic power." Like the literary ideas Brown would describe to John Bernard—ideas that, unbidden, overwhelm the novelist during composition—the youthful writer's "wild" thoughts are "Link'd and unlink'd at random, starting now / A thousand leagues awry; eluding long / The yoke; which to impose my task enjoined." The important thing to note is how this discussion of "wild" thoughts begins with the poet's experience in the "metaphysic" wilderness, which in turn is preceded by an account of his relation to a literal, physical scene in nature. The sequence is one of progressive abstraction.

In the poem, Brown attempts to impose order on his wildering thoughts by means of two incongruous images. The young man would become captain of his ideas, training them

> to range, in firm phalanx, and form
> The mystic dance spontaneous, and to move
> Their files in beauteous order, quick to spy
> Error, their lurking foe, or ardent wield,
> In war with Sophistry, indignant arms . . .

The impossible mixture of metaphors—of "phalanx," "files," "order," and the other military figures with the "mystic dance spontaneous"—betrays the poet's ambivalence. Even as he insists on the necessity of disciplining his thoughts, he would have them dance with mystical abandon. Drawn to an indulgence of the unbidden and wild products of what he would later call his dark, literary self, Brown nevertheless recognizes a duty to avoid the *mazy paths* of a metaphysic wilderness in order to

> beat with indefatigable heels,
> Th' *highway* which Reason's oracle directs
> The traveller to tread, who meditates
> A journey from his own to other worlds. (italics added)

The mental landscape of "Devotion: An Epistle" is at once the simplest and most complete we find in Brown's work. Seductive but hazardous wilderness paths beckon to imagination even as "Reason's oracle directs" the mental traveler to tread the straight and civilized "highway." Brown's early poem is valuable not so much for what it tells us about his "double mental existence"—the novels tell us much more—but for its demonstration of how readily, even automatically, the writer appropriated his physical environment for the purposes of intellectual autobiography. He would continue this project with less completeness but more complexity in his major novels.

But the project was conducted at a sacrifice: while the novelist's double mental existence was in significant measure shaped by the corresponding dichotomy of his culture and country, his works reveal little of the American surface and scene. Missing from Brown's fiction are what William Carlos Williams called "the peculiarities of an environment," a phrase that is part of Williams's assessment and celebration of Edgar Allan Poe: "This is culture, in mastering them, to burst through the peculiarities of an environment."[5] For the very "defect" we have been exploring in Brown, Williams pays homage to Poe as the first fully matured *American* writer. This figure, whom the traditional, if superficial, view would set beside Washington Irving as among the most European of the young nation's writers, Williams sees as a literary frontiersman whose "greatness is in that he turned his back and faced inland, to originality, with the identical gesture of a Boone" (226). Poe's "originality," Williams asserts, is a solid thing that "goes back to the ground," because his was "a genius intimately shaped by his locality and time" (216).

No statement could seem more contrary, arbitrary, or absurd to those who subscribe to the traditional view most succinctly expressed by Van Wyck Brooks, that Poe, "having nothing in common with the world that produced him, constructed a little parallel world of his own," diaphonous and private, "of mist and twilight," so that he emerged a "supersensual enigma, who might have lived with equal results in Babylon or Sioux City."[6] What Brooks's view requires of Poe is the manifest solidity of the "realist" impulse that set the boot-soles of even the transcendentally inclined Whitman firmly on American soil. The single time Poe tried seriously to exercise such an impulse he produced *The Journal of Julius Rodman*, or what there is of it, a hopelessly dull wilderness "adventure" fragment.

It is for the opposite gesture, the steadfast refusal to copy the peculiar features of a particular America, that Williams calls Poe a writer of the New World: "He abhorred the 'excessively opportune.'·"

> —Of course, [Poe] says, to write of the Indians, the forests, the great natural beauty of the New World will be attractive and make a hit—so he counsels writers to AVOID it, for reasons crystal clear and well chosen. (See *Fenimore Cooper*). His whole insistence has been upon method, in opposition to a nameless rapture over nature. He admired Claude Lorraine. Instead of to hog-fill the copied style with a gross rural sap, he wanted a lean style . . .

". . . a lean style," Williams continues, using a metaphor drawn deliberately from Boone's American wilderness: "rapid as a hunter and with an aim as sure" (227). It was not the choice of any subject peculiar to the surface of America that made Poe an American writer. It was, rather, an immersion in the New World so thorough that the *act* of writing became a frontiersman's skill.

Brown's immersion in the New World likewise took him beneath America's "excessively opportune" surface. Neither Brown nor Poe wrote much about their nation's literal frontier, but, as Edwin Fussell asks in his *Frontier: American Literature and the American West*, "Who shall say precisely where the Western frontier was in 1844?"

> It is not so much Poe who is bizarre as we who have read him without understanding. In his restless patrol along the lines between the senses, between waking and sleep, between sanity and insanity, between order and disorder, between sentience and insentience, between the organic and the inorganic, between life and death, between good and evil, between Heaven and earth, he was the typical American of his age, eccentric primarily in the boldness and determination with which he carried forward his investigations.[7]

Like Brown, Poe appropriated the "frontier" as metaphor, a mental territory in which a divided self shaped by what Richard Chase called, in his *American Novel and Its Tradition*, a "culture of contradictions" had squatter's rights.

The insights of Williams and Fussell suggest that Poe's affinity for Brown, especially evident in Poe's borrowing from the cave scene of *Edgar Huntly*, was neither an accident nor a case of one "gothic" writer filching effects from another. Instead, Poe came to Brown as one American writer to another, not to commandeer peculiarities of an environment in order to write a handful of stories, but to transform them in order to fashion an artifact of American culture. Fussell begins his discussion of Poe as a frontier author by cataloging the evidence of his fascination with the literature of the West, with travel accounts, and works of local colorists, and then shows how frontier metaphors worked their way even into such a manifestly non-American tale as "The Masque of the Red Death." Significantly, though, he does not base his argument primarily upon Poe's having read a good deal of Western material. Instead, like Williams, he sees American life during the early years of Western expansion as a frontier experience, regardless of where a given individual actually made his home. Bringing such a life to expression of necessity involved thinking as well as writing in metaphors of the frontier, whether the writer was wholly conscious of them or not. Precise knowledge of the frontier, whether gained through reading or by actually living out West, was of less consequence than an imaginative identification with the frontier *idea*. Indeed, the great literature of the "frontier"—including the works of Poe, Hawthorne, and Melville, as well as the more obvious instances of Cooper, Thoreau, and Whitman—did not come from Westerners. Fussell convincingly argues that so apparent a frontier author as Thoreau actually held the historical West in contempt as a vast tract exposed to spoliation by men whose desperation was anything but quiet. And when Whitman, in his later years, embraced a literalist, Greeley-esque vision of an imperial West, he mouthed the clichés of a poetry become flaccid and formulaic.

Brown belongs with Poe in the tradition of America's "frontier" writers. It is not possible to say with certainty more than this—to declare that the influence of Brockden Brown is responsible for Poe's abstracted and rarified frontier vision. It is a fact, though, that Poe was an inveterate borrower, that his was a transforming genius, requiring the catalyst of literary precursors. It is a fact, too, that Poe borrowed significantly from Brown, especially from the cave scene of *Edgar Huntly* for "The Pit and the Pendulum." The influence is worth examining not just for the sake of literary history, but, in a study of Brown, for what it reveals about the earlier writer's role in the intellectual grain of America's literature. Poe's borrowing constitutes an extraordinarily acute critical reading of Charles Brockden Brown.

In the documents they have left us, James Fenimore Cooper and Nathaniel Hawthorne each mentions Brown twice, Melville mentions him not at all, but Poe refers to him at least five times, going so far as to promise an essay on the novelist.[8] Some of the earliest commentators on Poe, including his first translator, E. D. Forgues, have recognized his affinity with Brown, and better than a half-dozen more recent articles have treated some particulars of Brown's influence on Poe.[9] The most detailed of these articles is the 1929 "Sources of Poe's 'The Pit and the Pendulum,'" in which David Lee Clark tallied the debt that "The Pit" owes to Brown's cave scene: the situation of an unconscious protagonist whose awakening is a gradual and literal return to this senses followed by labored self-reflection on his physical state; the protagonist's initial inability to move or to see (Poe's victim, like Huntly, wakes into total darkness) followed by attempts to diagnose his condition; his fear that he has died and is somehow doomed to "experience" the nothingness of death; the horror of living burial; the protagonist's determined but fruitless exploration of the chamber by groping along its walls; and the great hunger and thirst that provoke gorging on a "provided" meal followed by a deep sleep.[10]

Clark even noted such details as a similarity between the glaring eyes of the ravenous rats that infest Poe's dungeon and the "fixed and obscure flame" of the panther's eyes; and that Poe's victim estimates the dimensions of his cell to be one hundred paces around, while it is one hundred feet from the rim of Huntly's pit to the mouth of the cavern that contains it. The critic might have added at least two other bits of minutiae to his catalog. The "demon eyes" of the gargoyles that adorn the iron walls of the Inquisitorial cell glare "with the lurid lustre of a fire" that resembles the flame of the panther's eyes at least as much as the rats' eyes do (Poe, 5:85). One might also note that both Huntly and Poe's character use sound and echo to gauge the depth of their respective pits. Huntly cries out from the bottom of the pit into which he has fallen, while the prisoner of the Inquisition lets drop a small fragment of stone dislodged from the rim of the one he has so narrowly escaped falling into.

More importantly, Clark might have taken note of the similarities between the cave scene and *The Narrative of Arthur Gordon Pym*, which began serial publication in 1837, five years before "The Pit and the Pendulum" first appeared. The motif of premature burial is found twice in *Pym*, first when Arthur is stowed away in an iron-bound box in the hold of the *Grampus*, and again toward the end of the novel when Arthur, Dirk Peters, and Wilson Allen (who does not survive the ordeal) are buried beneath a mountain. These two scenes have a great deal in common with the pit motif in "The Pit and the Pendulum," as well as with the cave scene in *Edgar Huntly*. In all three scenes the protagonist is shown returning to consciousness, awakening to a darkness that prompts him to doubt his senses. There is a literal physical groping in all three scenes—a thrusting out of hands to find walls—that parallels the gropings of reason confronting darkness and irrational terror. Awakening in the hold of the

Grampus, Arthur, like Huntly, is tormented by a terrible hunger and thirst that add to his terror. He soon becomes aware as well of a presence in the darkness: the "paws of some huge and real monster pressing heavily upon [his] bosom." He nearly dies from "sheer fright" before discovering that the "monster" is nothing more terrible than his own Newfoundland dog, which bears the comically dreadful name "Tiger" (Poe, 3:28).

Given the other echoes of the cave scene, the appearance of Tiger may be taken as a burlesque quotation from Brown; but Tiger's similarity to the panther of *Edgar Huntly*, whose eyes resemble "a fixed and obscure flame" (158), becomes anything but funny a few pages later when the dog lives up to his wild name. Crazed with hunger and thirst, "his eyeballs flashing fiercely," Tiger really does attack Arthur (Poe, 3:43). Not only did Poe apparently draw upon *Edgar Huntly* some years before writing "The Pit and the Pendulum," but, two years after this story appeared, he made use of Brown's novel once again. Boyd Carter, in "Poe's Debt to Charles Brockden Brown," argues that Poe's 1844 "A Tale of the Ragged Mountains" imports its "aborigines" from *Edgar Huntly*.[11] And G. R. Thompson, in *Poe's Fiction: Romantic Irony in the Gothic Tales*, suggests that the story, with its "punning, hoaxing, burlesque atmosphere," is Poe's self-conscious parody of Brown.[12]

The evidently enduring interest in Brown and, most particularly in *Edgar Huntly*, suggests that Poe did not merely rifle the novelist and his book for a few effects. After all, a central motif in the cave scene, premature burial, has come to seem such an obsessive trademark of Poe that it would be presumptuous to declare that he simply lifted it from Brown. Poe did not merely regard the earlier novelist as a mine of gothic devices, but rather as something of a kindred spirit, who had seen, felt, and thought much as Poe himself. Bearing in mind Fussell's reading of Poe, and Brown's preoccupation with a metaphysic wilderness, we might conclude that in Brown's "frontier" Poe recognized his own. *Edgar Huntly*, ostensibly set in the wilderness of Pennsylvania, and "The Pit and the Pendulum," ostensibly set in Spain during the Inquisition, are products of American personalities. Partly because it is removed from the "excessively opportune" setting of a literal America, Poe's story, as it has borrowed from *Edgar Huntly*, helps us to define the artifacts of culture in Brown's work that have burst through the peculiarities of environment.

We have already discovered that the darkness into which Huntly wakes is native to the New World. Like that primeval darkness, the other motifs entailed by premature burial—the living death and the experience of nothingness—are also phenomena of frontier extremity, although the "frontier" need not be located literally in America. The same distortion of time's passage Huntly suffers in the dark pit of the New World cavern ("the lapse of some hours appear[ed] like the tediousness of weeks and months" [155]), Poe's victim experiences in the dungeon of the Inquisition. "I could take but imperfect note of time" (Poe, 5:78), he says, although Poe has with vicious irony secured him beneath the razor-edge of a pendulum swung from "the painted figure of Time" itself (5:77). Down the scimitar blade swings, steadily down, creeping toward its victim's heart "with the stealthy pace of the tiger" (5:80–1), if not of Huntly's panther —though we might recall that Poe had previously translated the panther of Huntly into Arthur Gordon Pym's Newfoundland dog named Tiger.

Turning to *Pym*, we find that Poe was concerned with yet another phenomenon associated with the extreme conditions of a New World. The cannibalism that figures as a crucial though shadowy presence in *Edgar Huntly* is on prominent display in Poe's novel when, threatened with starvation while adrift after shipwreck, Pym, Augustus Barnard, Dirk Peters, and one Parker draw lots to determine who will be sacrificed for the sustenance of the others. When the field has narrowed to a contest between Pym and Parker, who was about to draw his lot, "all the fierceness of the tiger" (note well) possessed Pym's "bosom, and I felt towards my poor fellow creature, Parker, the most intense, the most diabolical hatred." Parker draws the unfortunate lot and "I must not dwell upon the fearful repast which immediately ensued," Pym demurs, using language that recalls Huntly's circumspect relation of his own wilderness "banquet."

> Such things may be imagined, [Pym observes,] but words have no power to impress the mind with the exquisite horror of their reality. Let it suffice to say that, having in some measure appeased the raging thirst which consumed us by the blood of the victim, and having by common consent taken off the hands, feet, and head, throwing them together with the entrails, into the sea, we devoured the rest of the body, piecemeal, during the four ever memorable days of the seventeenth, eighteenth, nineteenth, and twentieth of the month. (Poe, 3:128–9)

Like Huntly, Pym follows his demurral with most of the disgusting details anyway. The tension between professed reticence and lurid particulars related with relish is interesting for what it suggests about the sensibilities of Huntly and Pym as well as of their creators. More significant is the symbolic, even ritual, role disgust plays in wilderness literature. Whether embodied in a "eucharist," such as cannibalism, or in devouring a freshly killed panther, the particulars of disgust define the literal and symbolic frontier which a civilized white Christian would, in all but the most dire circumstance, never cross.

An extremity similar in magnitude to that of *Huntly* and *Pym* compels the narrator of "The Pit and the Pendulum" to cross a frontier through an action about as disgusting as any peculiar to the eucharist of the actual wilderness. As Huntly had contemplated cannibalizing himself in order to relieve the pains of thirst and starvation, so the victim of the Inquisition, bound beneath the sweep of the pendulum, hits upon the stratagem of making himself bait for the rats. He reaches with his partially free hand into the platter of food his tormentors have provided him (the rats frequently fastening their sharp fangs into his fingers as he does so) in order to smear the "surcingle" that binds him with "particles of the oily and spicy viand." The rats, attracted by the meat, are to set him free by gnawing through his bonds:

> The measured movement of the pendulum disturbed them not at all. Avoiding its strokes they busied themselves with the annointed bandage. They pressed—they swarmed upon me in ever-accumulating heaps. They writhed upon my throat; their cold lips sought my own; I was half stifled by their thronging pressure.

And then the telling word: "disgust, for which the world has no name, swelled my bosom, and chilled, with a heavy clamminess, my heart" (5:83). For "world" we may read the familiar world, the one made up of all the "lightsome chambers" this side of the frontier.

The horror of the frontier, like that of the gothic, has its source in something closely allied to what Poe once named "The Imp of the Perverse." Both the gothic world and the frontier environment provoke irrationality and perversity, often forcing the self to act seemingly against itself. Thus Huntly, seeking to avoid a wasting death by starvation, nearly falls to devouring himself; and Poe's victim, among whose greatest fears are the horrors of the tomb, makes of himself a living corpse to be crawled over, nearly devoured, even kissed by vermin. The terms of gothic and frontier experience are therefore to a surprising degree interchangeable. Poe uses as least two words appropriate to the wilderness—"abyss" and "chasm" (5:74)—in describing the pit of the dungeon. Brown, for his part, uses the conventional terms of gothic horror to describe the situation of the pit set in the American wilderness: "dungeon or den" and "wind sweeping through spacious halls and winding passages" (153-5). That both authors share the more neutral term "pit" further confirms the essential similarity of the events they depict. *Edgar Huntly* shows that the frontier experience is gothic; "The Pit and the Pendulum" shows how the gothic partakes of the frontier.

David Lee Clark left out of his catalog of Poe's borrowings from Brown the least obvious and perhaps the most suggestive item: the idea of the Inquisition itself. Not only may Poe have located the foundation of his Spanish dungeon in Brown's America, but, in Huntly's depiction of himself as the helpless victim of some nameless, faceless "tyrant" or "author" of distress (155-6), Poe may also have found his Inquisition. Found—not borrowed. The Inquisitors are only subliminal presences in Brown's novel, implicit in Huntly's offhanded figures of speech. Yet, looking forward to "The Pit and the Pendulum" from the vantage point of *Edgar Huntly*, it does appear that Poe's victim actually inhabits the very metaphor Huntly had used merely to describe his dire situation. In the adumbrated Inquisition of *Edgar Huntly*, Brown predicted what Poe created in the literal

Inquisition of "The Pit": the metaphorical language for a vision of an irrational universe. "I had none but capricious and unseen fate to condemn" (156), Huntly writes of the pit's horrors, anticipating the kind of "intangible malignity" Captain Ahab posits as the central feature of his universe. Like Ahab, too, Huntly does not allow the malignity to remain intangible. As Ahab translated it into the preeminently visible white whale, so Huntly ascribes "capricious and unseen fate" to the operation of a horrible but comprehensible (tangible) tyrant and author of distress. For Poe's narrator, too, the decree of the Inquisitors "was Fate" (5:68), though, as we see at the very end of "The Pit and the Pendulum," even the Inquisitors cannot govern the cosmic "perverse," an ultimate intangible Poe's victim inadequately understands by the word "Fate."

It is all too easy to dismiss "fate" as a hackneyed theme of conventional gothic romance. But its use in *Edgar Huntly* and in "The Pit and the Pendulum" is particularly and carefully motivated. It should be seen as shorthand for what Poe's character and Huntly experience at the "frontier," a loss of intellectual egocentricism resulting from an encounter with something beyond the knowledge of civilization. Huntly's initial reaction to the darkness into which he awakens is dramatically egocentric. Such absolute darkness cannot exist in the world beyond himself, he reasons, therefore he *must* have gone suddenly blind. The next phase of his response, in which he pictures "fate" in the conventionally gothic terms of an Inquisitorial tyrant tormenting an innocent and helpless victim, still partakes of an egocentric orientation. In using the grotesque but familiar gothic images, Huntly refuses consciously to acknowledge the newness of the frontier, so alien to himself. Yet, these images are the language by which he defines "fate"; so that, in effect, Huntly does concede something of the alien quality of his new environment as a place where reason holds little sway. It is a place where "fate" signifies the essential powerlessness of a self bred on civilized modes of thought. When Huntly, without stopping for reflection, kills and eats the panther, he leaves reason behind and, with it, his old conception of self. His becoming almost a "savage," with a grisly penchant for the bestial aspects of savage life, defines the horror of crossing the frontier.

At least the frontier, as defined by Huntly's experience of it, would horrify one who had not crossed it—Mary Waldegrave, say, or the part of Huntly that has neither forgotten nor forsaken the lightsome chamber. But we have seen that Brown's frontier is productive of something more than horror. The wilderness summons powers in Huntly that lay dormant in his civilized life. It is on this point that the "frontiers" of Brown and Poe differ, and the difference derives from degree of abstraction. While Brown does abstract the elements of the frontier to a considerable degree, Poe abstracts them thoroughly. His story is completely severed from its American sources. Brown's, on the other hand, still grounded in the literal fact of the frontier, allows the ambivalent development of both the horror and the fulfillment offered by the wilderness. In appropriating the Inquisition and its dungeon from *Edgar Huntly*, Poe took the metaphors of the only phase of frontier experience that could serve any purpose in a story not actually set in America. He could take only the metaphors of Huntly's immediate horror because there is literally no *place* in Poe's tale for anything more of the frontier experience. Whereas the instruments of the wilderness's menace become the very means of Huntly's salvation, the Inquisitors' paraphernalia are never more than instruments of physical and psychological torment. The wilderness is present in Brown's novel as a space into which Huntly can be "initiated"; Poe's claustrophobic tale, though it draws upon Brown's frontier images, offers its protagonist no equivalent space.

Without an actual wilderness space, the frontier metaphor provides Poe only with a set of irrational extremes to be met by his protagonist's sheer reason. When Huntly kills and devours the panther, it is not reason that prompts him, but an instinct summoned by the threatening wilderness. The parallel action Poe's victim performs when he entices the rats to gnaw him free is, however, born entirely of reason. Although both he and Huntly share in a paradoxically self-destructive instinct for survival, the stratagem with the rats is not only a deliberate stroke of conscious invention, it actually represents the triumph of reason over a deeply instinctual disgust. This victory is both short-lived and ironic. "For the moment, at least, *I was free*," declares Poe's protagonist, only to undercut himself with: "Free!—and in the grasp of the Inquisition!" (5:84). The iron walls now glow, beginning to close him in, pushing him to the brink of the pit. Reason, finally, has gained him no measure of self-determination. He lives suspended in the kind of Inquisitorial metaphor Huntly pinned to implacable and intangible fate.

Nor will Poe's victim ever be free. His *deus ex machina* rescue from the edge of the pit is not a symptom of the sudden failure of Poe's imagination. The absurd abruptness of the denouement results from a vision of the universe absurdly grotesque and arabesque. As when the prisoner had narrowly escaped falling into the pit because he tripped on his torn garment, so the arrival of General Lasalle is a strictly fortuitous event. Had the General taken Toledo a few minutes earlier, Poe's victim would have been spared his most exquisite torments; a few minutes later, he would have suffered a horrible death. As the unfortunate man had found himself helpless at the hands of a seemingly all-powerful Inquisition, so now "the Inquisition was in the hands of its enemies" (5:87), turn and turn about. "Revolution" had been on his mind when they sentenced him: the "dreamy indeterminate hum" of the judges' voices "conveyed to my soul the idea of *revolution*—perhaps from its association in fancy with the burr of the millwheel" (5:67). Recalling the medieval iconography of fortune's wheel, the image is appropriate for a universe whose workings are as ineluctable as they are absurd.

Beyond this, we might well be reminded that Antoine Charles Louis, comte de Lasalle, the young general who marched into Toledo in 1808, and whom Poe calls to the rescue of his protagonist, served under that most extraordinary product of revolution, Napoleon Bonaparte. In the further revolution of history, of course, Napoleon, too, would find himself in the hands of his enemies and, whether Poe knew it or not, General Lasalle would fall in battle but a year after the imagined events of "The Pit and the Pendulum."[13]

The idea of revolution is of a piece as well with the apocalyptic cosmogony Poe outlined in *Eureka*, the maelstrom descent into the nothingness of original unity that will inevitably reverse the expansion of matter away from itself. In every sense, then, the rescue from the pit is but the most temporary of reprieves in a universe subject to "laws" beyond reason or human government. While the best Poe can do for his protagonist is to snatch him from the jaws of the pit by means that simply confirm the absurdity of which the Inquisition is only a part, Brown allows Huntly not only to escape from the pit, but to emerge from it in a manner reborn. By the conclusion of the tale, Poe's pit comes to symbolize the imminence of universal annihilation, against which we can bring only our impotent reason. The claustrophobia of Poe's dungeon, its walls forcing the victim to his death, is *the* condition of existence itself. There is no real space in Poe's universe beyond this dungeon, which General Lasalle enters from an absurd universe that amounts to another dungeon only a little larger.[14] But beyond the pit in the cavern Edgar Huntly finds the physical and psychological space of the American wilderness.

Edgar Huntly and "The Pit and the Pendulum" share the immediate horrors of their common "pit"; but Brown's novel develops another, subtler horror as well. Frightening as Huntly found the wilderness while he was lost in it, returned from it he found that civilized existence held terrors as well. In spite of his fears and over the protest of his civilized sensibilities, Huntly had become a formidably efficient wilderness man, having encountered a panther and killed it, hostile Indians and killed them. Whereas Poe's protagonist is only momentarily effectual, Brown's realizes in himself powers he had never known before. Returned from the wilderness, however, Huntly finds himself as ineffectual as the victim of Poe's Inquisition. As we shall see in the final chapter, his efforts to redeem Clithero Edny not only fail, but—the typical result whenever a Brown character tries to do a good deed—actually cause injury and death. Only in the wilderness, where the universe's intangible "Inquisitors" are immediately manifest as panthers and savages, does Huntly enjoy a measure of effectual heroism. It is true that there the savage lurks and the panther crouches; but there, in the moment of the attack and the leap, reason must give way to an act of instinct with an unambiguous and immediate result. Civilized life offers few such direct encounters. Conventions, laws, and institutions mediate reality, imposing between it and the individual a Daedalian maze. In *Edgar Huntly*, where abstract wilderness figures are grounded in a literal space, the territory offers not only images of confusion and terror but also the opportunity for fulfillment of innate powers and prodigious action.

A territory beyond the variegated mazes of civilization, the wilderness seems to offer the revelation of truth itself. At least it was a desire to see life outside the mediation of civilization that sent Thoreau to the woods: "to front only the essential facts of life." Thoreau's frontier, like that of Brown or Poe, is more metaphorical than literal; however, like the frontier of *Edgar Huntly*, it is also grounded in geography. Still, Walden was hardly America's literal frontier when Thoreau went to live there. It was, rather, Thoreau's own—for, as he had explained in *A Week on the Concord and Merrimack Rivers*, the frontier exists wherever a man "fronts" a "fact."[15] This idea of fact, and of a frontier as the "place" where one confronts it, defines both Brown's and Poe's intellectual use of the wilderness. For Thoreau, a frontier meant confronting the extremity of truth, a "fact" unmediated by social convention, ego, will, or reason (but not, in the Transcendentalist formulation, divorced from the Coleridgean conception of imagination). It is what Emerson called the "not-me." "Fact," then, as Thoreau used it to explain "frontier," is the extremity of extremity itself, the place (or "place") of ultimate confrontation.

When we have survived everything, Emerson wrote, when we have found no grief inconsolable, no truly ultimate grief—not even in the loss of a son—then "nothing is left us now but death. We look to that with a grim satisfaction, saying, There at least is reality that will not dodge us."[16] Thus we may define death as Edgar Huntly and Poe's victim face it: death as "fact," the extremity of truth. Death, of course, is not unique to the frontier, but both Brown and Poe are concerned with the knowledge of death, with the paradoxical situation of experiencing death—which means that both authors explore the frontier between life and death. The prospect of cannibalism, especially self-cannibalism, associated with the literal frontier, forces a special self-consciousness of death. Even more dramatically paradoxical is the motif of living burial. Edgar Huntly and Poe's victim each wake into the image of death—indeed, into its nonimage, absolute darkness. Huntly, like so many of Poe's characters, is brought to the territory between being and nothingness, brought to the verge of experiencing what no man can experience. Almost certainly without knowing it, Brown had predicted in "Devotion: An Epistle" the meaning of his project in fiction. He imagined a "metaphysic wilderness" whose "thorny tracts" literally led to "nothing."

Waking into absolute darkness, Poe's protagonist fronts the fact in this way: "I still lay quietly, and made effort to exercise my reason" (5:71), and, acting upon the promptings of reason, he gropes along the walls in order to measure his prison. Huntly does much the same thing at first, exercising reason until the exigencies of the wilderness, in the immediate form of a panther, force him to act upon instinct. Although, then, for a time Huntly abandons a mode of being associated with civilization, he cannot wholeheartedly embrace a wild life of instinct. Nor is he allowed to dismiss the lesson of the pit, of reason's impotence against irrational darkness. This confrontation, abstracted from its wilderness setting, follows Huntly out of the pit and back to his lightsome chamber; he is afflicted with a chronic sense of the forlorn. "Possibly," Huntly writes, "the period will arrive when I shall look back without agony on the perils I have undergone. That period is still distant." For the conditions of the pit cannot be evaded, even in the midst of civilization:

> Solitude and sleep are now no more than the signals to summon up a tribe of ugly phantoms. Famine, and blindness, and death, and savage enemies, never fail to be conjured up by the silence and darkness of the night.

He does not speak directly of panthers and Indians now, but, more periphrastically, of a *tribe* of ugly phantoms and of *savage* enemies, indicating that the specific horrors of the wilderness have assumed for him a new reality apart from a particular space and time. "Tribe" and "savage" are drawn directly from the wilderness, of course; but the "ugly phantoms" and "enemies" to which these terms are joined occupy the mind's own ubiquitous territory. Referring to these phantoms and enemies, Huntly continues: "I cannot dissipate them by any efforts of reason" (151). We recall how reason had failed to vanquish the "fact" of darkness at the actual frontier as it now fails against the frontier metaphors lingering in Huntly's mind. Where civilized reasoning fails, Huntly turns to the more mechanical artifices of civilization: "My cowardice requires the perpetual consolation of light. My heart droops when I mark the decline of the sun, and I never sleep but with a candle burning at my pillow."

But he is not afraid of nightmares alone: "If, by any chance, I should awake and find myself immersed in darkness, I know not what act of desperation I might be suddenly impelled to commit" (151). At the frontier Huntly discovered what Thoreau would call the "essential facts of life": just what deeds of prowess and of savagery he is capable of, despite will and reason. As Brown identified the darkness of his literary imagination with the wilderness, so Huntly, returned from the literal frontier, carries with him the disturbing knowledge of his inner frontier. The lightsome chamber itself has become a place of darkness now, as subject to horror as any other "environment."

It is not in the wilderness that the primal qualities of *Edgar Huntly* inhere, but in the dialectic of the frontier. What Poe recognized in Brown's novel was the emotional depth of a fully dramatized intellectual problem. He saw the primal confrontation of thought with "fact." The absolute darkness into which Huntly awakens is immediately evocative of terror as well as emblematic of an epistemological problem; but its most enduring and disturbing impact has a more personal and primal origin. The immediate emotion of horror evoked by darkness, and the more abstract problem of knowledge it suggests, seem to have been intimately connected in Brown's imagination.

Young Charles was living in New York during the autumn of 1796.

He had just experienced the second of four major yellow fever epidemics he was to live through when he took up his pen on October 25, 1796, to write a reassuring letter to his brother James.

> I believe the yellow fever has taken its final leave of us, at least for the present season. Not even the name of it has been mentioned in my hearing, nor the idea of it, scarcely occurred to my mind, since I last wrote you. When you talk of the necessity of circumspection to escape its ravages, I can not but admire the exaggerations of rumor, and the multiplying and enlarging efficacy of distance. Physical objects are diminished by distance, and even vanish altogether as we go farther from them. Not so the yellow fever and the like imaginary spectacles which cling closer, grow into gigantic dimensions, in proportion to their actual distance from us.
>
> Plague operates by invisible agents, and we know not in what quarter it is about to attack us. No shield, therefore, can be lifted up against it. We fear it as we are terrified by dark in which tho much of our panic be, doubtless, owing to the influence of education, and may be removed by habitual exposure to it, yet our defenseless condition and the invisible approaches of danger may contribute to our alarms. I am not even wholly uninfected by this disease, because strong is the influence of early association; when in the dark, if an unlucky incident calls my attention to the imperfect gleam which may be darted from a neighboring lamp along the ceiling, or to that more imperfect glimpse which will be produced by the faintest starlight when reflected from irregular polished surfaces, I find myself seized by unwelcome shrinkings and hasten to the asylum which sleep, or light, or company, or abstract meditations may offer me. I have never had recourse, in this phantastic distress, to the best expedient, but when all others fail me, that is, the endeavor to *reason down* my perturbations, and dispeople by mere energy of argument the aerial work of "calling shapes and beckoning shadows dire!" (Clark, 156)

The parallel is striking not only between Brown's and Huntly's attempts to vanquish darkness by reason but also between their similar couching of the irrational in the precise, even pedantic, language of reason. But, as in *Edgar Huntly*, this kind of language serves only to heighten the sense of the irrational, widening the gulf between intellect and emotion.

Yet more curious is the occasion of the confession of his fear. His brother had apparently written him out of legitimate concern over a real and terrible danger. With uncharacteristic bravado, Brockden Brown likens James's trepidations to a childish fear of the dark. The result, however, is not so much a diminishment of the yellow fever's terror as it is a hyperbolic heightening of the fear of darkness. After all, the comparison

of a very understandable dread of a deadly disease with a simple fear of
darkness is absurd. More fantastic is the verbal equation Brown makes between darkness and deadly disease when he admits that he is not "wholly
uninfected" by the "disease" of fearing the dark. Like so much in Brown's
writing, the equation seems to have come to him unbidden, surprising the
author himself by welling up from some shady region of his "literary self."
Following a brief speculation on the early influence of education in shaping such fears as his own dread of darkness, Brown jolts himself, as it were,
back into full consciousness: "But how came my pen to make this wide excursion into the mysterious regions of conjuration and necromancy? I remember; I was talking of the yellow fever, or rather of the plague" (Clark,
156). Having formulated, in his letter, yellow fever as an epitome of the irrational terror against which man brings his poor reason, Brown, with scant
self-consciousness, translates the situation into a confrontation of reason
and darkness. Born of a childhood fear and nurtured in images of the
wilderness, absolute darkness became for Brown the least geographically
bound and therefore the most enduring definition of frontier horror.

    Poe's borrowing from *Edgar Huntly* amounts to a reading of Brown. It
allows us to see beneath the superficial effect of gothic terror to the
epistemological assumptions upon which the terror is founded. In reading
Brown intellectually, Poe reveals something of the American quality in the
earlier writer's works that critics since John Neal have surely sensed but
have weakly articulated. The abstract intellectual dimension Poe un-
covered in Brown's horror-effects is very much of a piece with Richard
Chase's description of the American literary "romance." As important as
the genre's melodramatic structure and tone, Chase argues, is its intellectual orientation and tendency toward abstraction, qualities peculiar to the
American brand of romance writing. That the classic form of American fiction is preeminently intellectual is borne out by the host of recent critical
works that address epistemological issues in our literature. One thinks of
Charles Feidelson's *Symbolism and American Literature* and John Lynen's
The Design of the Present, in which epistemology is a central concern; and
of F. O. Matthiessen's *American Renaissance*, Edwin Fussell's *Frontier*,
Richard Slotkin's *Regeneration through Violence*, and William
Spengemann's *The Adventurous Muse*, in which such considerations are
vitally implicit, despite the authors' diversity of approaches.
    Of course, one need only read in the volumes that compose the Great
Tradition of American fiction to remark the profundity of concern that
Poe, Hawthorne, Melville, Stephen Crane, James, and Faulkner manifest
toward basic questions about the nature and perception of reality. Where
the European novelist of the nineteenth century often doubts social,
political, and theological propositions about reality, the American novelist
is skeptical about a reality he confronts without social, political, or theological mediation. He questions, that is, the very nature of the relation

between subject and object, returning again and again to a stubborn perspectivalism. If the American novelist is not always a confirmed "naysayer," he is at best a resolute "maybe-sayer," a skeptic. The out-and-out "yea-sayers"—Emerson, Thoreau, Whitman—also address themselves to the nature of the subject-object relation. The very source of their "yea" is found in the subject-object dialectic, the relation between "me" and "not-me." Reality resides in the *act* of perception, they say, the moment of the subject-object relation. Later writers as different as Ernest Hemingway and Wallace Stevens inherit both strains of this American epistemology. The theologically inspired cosmogony of the Transcendentalists is no longer fully available to either of them, of course; yet in his project of restoring to language something of its origin in the act of perception, Hemingway recalls the Emerson of *Nature*. The hero of *A Farewell to Arms*, in the unreality of a very real war, describes the project for Hemingway when he observes that "abstract words such as glory, courage, or hallow were obscene beside the concrete names of villages, the numbers of roads, the names of rivers, the numbers of regiments and the dates," much as Emerson had decried the modern devaluation of language from original "bullion" to a mere "paper currency."[17] And Wallace Stevens's location of the value of reality in the necessarily creative act of perception recalls, as far as the twentieth century permits, the Transcendentalists' assignment of reality itself to the relation between subject and object.

It is certainly reasonable to locate the origin of this American epistemological tradition in the collocation of a Calvinist religious heritage (with its highly wrought self-consciousness about perception and the allegorical nature of reality) and the philosophical idealism of the Romantic age, in which the major phase of American literature was launched. But the examples of Brown and Poe, and of the so-called yea- and nay-sayers of the nineteenth century, suggest that a more specific and contemporary feature of American life motivated our most characteristic authors' fascination with epistemological themes. For Brown and, as Edwin Fussell demonstrates, for Poe, Hawthorne, Thoreau, Melville, and Whitman, the idea of the frontier figured centrally as a metaphor of the confrontation between subject and object. Commenting on a section from *Walden's* "Where I Lived, and What I Lived For," the passage that begins "I went to the woods because I wished to live deliberately," Fussell argues that Thoreau's frontier is "epistemological-aesthetic," a "frontier between subject and object."

> As nature and civilization meet and interpenetrate—either in a general way or in specific encounters between the pioneer and his new environment—losing their ostensible antithesis in a new unity, so the "I" . . . and the "facts of life" meet and interpenetrate for an equally creative and transcendent end.[18]

When Thoreau abstracted the frontier from geography, "placing" it wherever a man "fronts" a "fact," he made explicit a paradigm that had informed the likes of Brown and Poe and was yet further to inform the vision of some of our most representative writers. If a Romantic self-consciousness about the nature of perception and knowledge was in the nineteenth century's air, it was the frontier that drew it so particularly into the American soil.

In the process of American discovery, of which, we have suggested, Brockden Brown's work is a part, the abstract notions of subject and object, self and other, "me" and "not-me" find their figurative equivalents in phenomena of the Old and New Worlds. The frontier, as the encounter of Old and New, and what each of these represents, was readily, even unconsciously, translated into metaphor. Through this metaphor, developed in the cave scene, Brown's Huntly struggled to reconcile the familiar with the radically unfamiliar; civilized values with those perceived in the wilderness; security with a risky self-fulfillment. That Huntly awakens in the wilderness forlorn and returns the same way indicates that he struggled with little success.

Others in our literature have also used the frontier as a means of creating identity, fashioning what Crèvecoeur called the "new man" in the New World. Thoreau, for example, was content neither with a geographical frontier nor with an entirely figurative one. By Walden Pond, well east of the national frontier, he cultivated something more concrete than a metaphor. His bean-field was neither civilized farm nor wild growth, but rather "the connecting link between wild and cultivated fields; as some states are civilized, and others half-civilized, and others savage or barbarous, so my field was, though not in a bad sense, a half-cultivated field."[19] As the physical evidence of civilization fronting the wilderness, subject fronting object, self fronting fact, the bean-field figures as a synecdoche (partaking of both the purely literal and the purely symbolic) through which the frontier dialectic finds expression. It is a formal means of expressing both the "me" and the "not-me," preserving the integrity of both, just as Thoreau's sojourn at Walden was not a return to nature but an attempt to allow both wilderness and higher laws true expression beyond the distortions wrought by civilized convention and artifice. The bean-field is the notation of an urgent intellectual experiment, a précis of the frontier experience.

While Thoreau brought to self-conscious expression the frontier as a means of reconciling the extremes of civilization and the wilderness, such metaphorical use of the territory was present even in our earliest literature. Richard Slotkin demonstrates that, for the Puritans, the

> Indian wars proved to be the most acceptable metaphor for the American experience. To all the complexities of that experience, it offered the simplicity of dramatic contrast and direct confrontation of opposites. It became a literary means of dealing with all

sorts of social tensions and controversies—between English and American Puritans, between classes and generations within American society, and between political and religious controversialists.[20]

The extremes of experience at the frontier made that territory the Puritan's precursor of the American romance. Indeed, in *The Adventurous Muse*, William Spengemann casts back further still, beginning with the letters of Columbus and the accounts of early travelers, in which he sees the origin of the American novel's shape and distinctive concerns in a more universal confrontation of opposites. The New World gave rise to a "poetics of adventure," which was to come into "open conflict" with an Old World "poetics of domesticity." This tension of extremes, present in our earliest fiction, would become "a continuing dialogue" in the work of Hawthorne, Melville, Twain, and James.[21] In effect, the American novel, as the space in which Old World fronts New, is itself the frontier.

Thoreau's bean-field, the Puritan's literary "frontier," and the tension between adventure and domesticity provide a context that greatly enriches Chase's notion of the American "romance." Although the literal frontier is for Chase only one aspect of the "culture of contradictions" that produced the romance, the other oppositions he cites as endemic to American culture—the "Manichean quality of New England Puritanism" and the American's divided allegiance between Old and New World values—are readily subsumed under the concept of the frontier as an *idea* that shapes perception.[22] Like the frontier, the romance expresses the "radical disunities" inherent in American life (7). "The English novel," Chase explains, "has been a kind of imperial enterprise, an appropriation of reality with the high purpose of bringing order to disorder." On the other hand, the American novel

> has usually seemed content to explore, rather than to appropriate and civilize, the remarkable and in some ways unexampled territories of life in the New World and to reflect its anomalies and dilemmas. It has not wanted to build an imperium but merely to discover a new place and a new state of mind. (4–5)

While Chase's description of the American romance is especially valuable for what it suggests about how the New World environment shaped our fiction, it does represent an overstatement of the American novel's "newness." In denying any imperial purpose in the American novel, Chase contradicts his own picture of the romance as a vehicle of tension, a tension here between the impulse of the vulnerable explorer and that of the implacable imperialist. Chase does, in fact, acknowledge that the romance, though it suffered an extensive American conversion, is of venerable European origin. Leslie Fiedler, in *Love and Death in the American Novel*, is even more insistent: not only was the American novel cast in European molds, but those molds have yet to be broken. Because American fiction does not exist independently from European origin and influence, in the New World it must be to some degree an imperial enterprise. This is not true just because the novel carries Europe into America. Chase points out the tendency of the American romance to become self-consciously symbolic (to the point of allegory), intellectual, and abstract. This intellectual appropriation of New World matter is as imperialist a gesture, say, as Brown's attempt to vanquish darkness by reason.

Our study of Brown and Poe, as well as Fussell's comments on other writers, suggests that the frontier's greatest literary impact was not as a geographical locale to be explored, but as a phenomenon to be appropriated (and perhaps subdued) imaginatively and intellectually. Significantly, Brown's own definition of romance writing turns precisely upon its intellectual quality. The novelist explained in "The Difference between History and Romance," in the April 1800 issue of the *Monthly Magazine*, that the "historian" observes and records the world as an "experimentalist," objectively portraying only the appearance of phenomena, whereas the romance writer "adorns these appearances with cause and effect."

> An historian will relate the noises, the sights, and the smells that attend the eruption of Vesuvius. A romancer will describe, in the first place, the *contemporary* ebullitions and inflations, the combustion and decomposition that take place in the bowels of the earth. Next he will go to the origin of things, and describe the centrical, primary, and secondary orbs composing the universe, as masses thrown out of an immense volcano called *chaos*. Thirdly, he will paint the universal dissolution that is hereafter to be produced by the influence of volcanic or internal fire.
>
> An historian will form catalogues of stars, and mark their positions at given times. A romancer will arrange them in *clusters*, and dispose them in *strata*, and inform you by what influences the orbs have been drawn into sociable knots and circles.[23]

Unlike the historian, who is content merely to discover "what is," the romancer makes of physical reality an idea, establishing in the midst of what he sees an "imperium" of the intellect.

In *The American Novel and Its Tradition*, Richard Chase was content to argue that American fiction, born of "a culture of contradictions," does not synthesize innate disunities but expresses and preserves them. A year later, in *The Democratic Vista*, Chase modified this argument subtly but significantly and most suggestively. He argued that Van Wyck Brooks's plea for an American "middlebrow" culture to mediate the extremes of high- and lowbrow culture is misguided. It runs contrary to the genius of America, which was born of and lives through contradiction. As he had asserted in the *American Novel*, Chase claims here that American art does not unify disunity, but—he continues in *The Democratic Vista*—neither does it serve only as a vehicle of contradiction. Rather, its mission is to bring disunities into the confrontation of dialectic. This, we would add, is precisely the function of a "metaphysic" American frontier. Chase himself acknowledges the link between romance and frontier when he comments in his *American Novel* upon Hawthorne's classic description of romance as "a neutral territory, somewhere between the real world and fairyland, where the Actual and the Imaginary may meet, and each imbue itself with the nature of the other." Chase seizes upon the frontier metaphor of "neutral territory," commenting that "romance is . . . a kind of 'border' fiction." He cites the tales of Cooper and William Gilmore Simms as romances of the literal geographical frontier, "the neutral territory between civilization and the wilderness." But for "Hawthorne and later romancers, the field of action is conceived not so much as a place but as a state of mind—the borderland of the human mind where the actual and the imaginary intermingle" (18–9). The romance, F. O. Matthiessen declared, "raises its material to the level of contemplation."[24] In the work of Brockden Brown, and even in that of Poe, Hawthorne, and Melville, the "material" so raised is the frontier itself.

If we consider the romance as an enduring intellectual monument to the American frontier, the epistemological interpretation of Brown and of other major American writers takes on historical, as well as theoretical and aesthetic, significance. The idea of symbol Charles Feidelson discusses in his theoretical and "ahistorical" *Symbolism and American Literature* becomes not only a borderland between the "me" and "not-me," but also a frontier space in which those extremes of perception function in dialectic. In John Lynen's *The Design of the Present*, it is the present itself that serves as symbol, a frontier in which the moment and eternity "front" one another in an oxymoronic but synthetic opposition that reveals the temporal dimension of the American author's deepest philosophical interest.

A concern for the nature of knowledge is by no means solely the province of American literature. It is implicit in all significant literature and, in the twentieth century particularly, figures as the principal theme of much important writing. Plato's cave, although geologically no more venerable than any in the New World, was discovered—and became an object-lesson in the study of knowledge—long before Edgar Huntly's. Nor is fiction of the borderland to be found only in America. Sir Walter Scott (at best a grudging admirer of Brown[25]) habitually set his romances along disputed frontiers, and his Highlanders were, often enough, compared to the "natives" of that other wild world across the ocean. But for Scott and Europe the borderland was simply a stage for dramatic conflict, while in America it became a distinguishing fixture of the literary mind. Again and again our writers, Charles Brockden Brown among them, front intellectual extremity, framing a dialectic of subject and object, of self and fact, according to what seems a tacitly understood model of the frontier. In the next chapter we examine *Wieland; or, The Transformation*—the novel Brown called "An American Tale"—as an early example of American epistemological fiction. We shall study it as the product of the novelist's own ambivalent frontier consciousness, as well as of a larger national culture of intellectual, moral, and religious contradictions. We shall read it as an artifact of the New World.

III

New World Genesis,
or the Old Transformed

James Yates, known to the community of Tomhannock, New York, as a naturally gentle man, industrious, sober, and kind, threw his Bible into the fireplace, deliberately demolished his own sleigh, killed his wife, his four children, and his horse shortly after nine on a December evening in 1781. That afternoon, a Sunday, there being no church nearby, several neighbors had gathered at Yates's house to read Scripture and sing psalms. So cordial were his spirits that he persuaded his sister and her husband to remain until nine, long after the others had left. They engaged in serious, interesting, and affectionate conversation, Yates addressing his wife in more than commonly endearing terms. He spoke of his happy home and of how, tomorrow, he would treat his wife to a sleigh ride as far as New Hampshire. Before his sister and her husband left, they all sang one more hymn.

Upon his capture and interrogation Yates told how he took his wife upon his lap and opened the Bible to read to her. Their two sons, a five- and a seven-year-old, were in bed. Eleven-year-old Rebecca sat by the fire, while the baby, a daughter aged six months, slumbered at her mother's bosom.

"Instantly a new light shone into the room," and two Spirits appeared before Yates, one at his right and the other at his left. The latter bade him "destroy all his *idols*, beginning with the Bible." Although the Spirit at his right hand attempted to dissuade him, Yates obeyed the first, calling it his "good angel," and cast the book into the flames. Bolting from her husband's lap, Mrs. Yates snatched the Bible from the fire, but before she had time to utter a word, Yates threw it in again, holding his wife fast until the book was completely consumed.

Seizing an axe, Yates ran out the door and broke up his sleigh. He ran to the stable and killed one horse, striking another, which, however, escaped. When he returned to the house to tell his wife what he had done, the "good angel" reappeared: "You have more idols, (said he) look at your wife and children." Without a moment's hesitation, Yates ran to the bed of his two sons, caught the older one up in his arms and threw him against the wall with such force that he "expired without a groan." He next seized the younger boy by the feet and dashed his "skull in pieces against the fireplace" before the child could even awaken.

Seeing that his daughter and wife had fled with the baby, Yates again took up his axe "in pursuit of the living." His wife was running with the baby to her father's house half a mile away. Yates called to her, but she only screamed, redoubling her pace. Within thirty yards of her, Yates hurled his axe, gashing the woman's hip and causing her to drop the baby girl. Gathering the infant in his own arms, Yates threw her against a log fence. He had now lost sight of his wife, though the track her bleeding hip left in the snow was easy enough to follow.

Within eyeshot of her father's house—inexplicably—she turned and ran across an open field back to Yates's own door, whereupon all her husband's "*natural feelings*" welled up within him: "Come then, my love (said I) we have one child left, let us be thankful for that—what is done is right—we must not repine, come let me embrace you—let me know that you do indeed love me." With that, she embraced Yates in her "trembling" arms, pressing her "quivering" lips to his cheek.

"This is also an idol!" a voice spoke behind him, and breaking instantly from her, Yates wrenched a stake from the garden fence. He leveled her with a single stroke. Realizing that the blow might only have stunned her, he struck again and again until he himself could not recognize one feature of her face.

Then he heard moans and sobbing coming from the barn. It was Rebecca, who begged her father's mercy so affectingly that once again "*natural pity*" took possession of Yates. He thought now "that to destroy *all* my idols, was a hard task." So, taking her by the hand, he asked her to sing and dance for him. And while she danced and sang, Yates pondered: this pity and these feelings were not "in the line of my duty." Convinced of his momentary error, he caught up a "hatchet that stuck in a log." Presently, Rebecca's forehead was "cleft in twain."

Theodore Wieland's ritual murder of his family had its genesis in the James Yates tragedy. Brown suggested in his prefatory "Advertisement" to *Wieland* that "most readers will probably recollect an authentic case, remarkably similar to that of Wieland." As early as 1801 a reviewer recognized this as an allusion to the murders in Tomhannock, a case (Carl Van Doren concluded in a 1914 article for *The Nation*) indeed familiar to Brown's contemporary readers. Perpetrated in 1781, the Yates atrocity was not news by July of 1796 when it first reached print as a complete account in *The New York Weekly Magazine*. However, it did excite sufficient interest among the public to merit reprinting a month later in the *Philadelphia Minerva*.[1]

In his *Nation* article, Carl Van Doren cataloged enough parallels between the Tomhannock and *Wieland* tragedies to confirm the 1801 reviewer's speculation that the actual case had inspired the fictional one. In addition to the generally parallel situations of "divinely inspired" murder, *Wieland* shares with the Yates atrocity such details as the murderer's extended confession, a wife killed with her four children (two boys and two girls—the baby, in each case, a girl), and the mangling of a corpse beyond recognition (Yates's wife and Wieland's foster daughter Louisa Conway). Both Yates and Wieland protest their innocence not of the deed, but of crime, insisting that they obeyed the will of a superior Being. Both are cast into dungeons and loaded with chains: Yates escapes twice and is recaptured, while Wieland also twice escapes and is twice retaken, only to escape a third fatal time. Wieland attempts after his third escape to kill Clara, as Yates had attempted to kill his sister immediately after the slaughter of his wife and children.[2]

An outline Brown apparently drew up shortly before the composition of *Wieland* reveals the influence of the Yates murders in even greater detail than the finished novel.[3] We first note that, in the outline, Theodore is called Charles, and, like James Yates, he has a wife and four children. Like the Theodore of the finished novel, he also has an adopted daughter. His conversation with his family on the night he kills them is "affectionate, solemn, foreboding misfortune," as Yates's conversation had been "grave . . . but interesting and affectionate." At midnight Charles hears "vocal sounds" and sees a "light" and a "figure," much as "a new light [had] shone into the room" when Yates looked up to behold "two Spirits." The "figure" Charles sees "forewarns against Idolatry"—echoing the idol motif that is very much a part of the Tomhannock murders, although absent at least in explicit form from *Wieland*. Then Charles (433):

. . . Destroys 1 some favourte [*sic*] in-animate object. an organ.

	2. greyhound.	
		200.
	3. children 2.	
omen	4. -Wife- Ward.	
Command	5. -Ward- Wife.	
Repugnan[c]e	6. Sister.	

Resolute
-Interval-of-
Repenting

Yates had conducted himself similarly, destroying (1) his sleigh, (2) a horse, (3) two children, (4) his infant daughter and his wife, and (5) his older daughter. He ended (6) by attempting to murder his sister. Twice Yates faced his "Command" with "Repugnan[c]e" and had intervals of at least near repentance. But he is finally and fatally "Resolute."

More significant than the details Brown drew from the account of the Yates atrocity is the central thematic concern *Wieland* shares with the Tomhannock murders; these murders, like Brown's novel, dramatically manifest the complex effects of New World extremity. *Wieland* bears two subtitles. The first, "The Transformation," reflects the horrible change Theodore (like Yates) suffers, turning from a civilized, gentle family man to, from all appearances, a monster. What we shall be exploring now is how this transformation reflects the national environment and culture: the "American Tale" that is the second subtitle.

James Yates, the Charles Wieland of Brown's outline, and Theodore Wieland in the finished novel each delivers, upon capture, confessional narratives aimed at justifying the transformation they have undergone. James Yates exhibits nothing but contempt for his accusers. After coolly relating his deeds, he refuses "to confess his error or *join* in prayer," praying instead to a deity he addresses as "Father": "My father, thou knowest that it was in obedience to thy commands, and for thy glory that I have done this deed." This seems to have impressed Brown, who, in sketching Charles's confession, elaborated upon Yate's contempt, particularly emphasizing its intellectual ramification:

> Thou, omnipotent & holy! Thou wast the prompter of my deed. My hands were but the instruments of thy will. I know not what is crime. Of what action caused [?] evil is the ultimate result. Thy knowledge as thy power is reverenced[?]. I lean[?] upon thy promise I cheearfully [*sic*] sustain the load of pain of [infaming] hatred wh[ich] erring [?] men lay upon me. In thy arms of thy protection I entrust my safety. In the fullness of thy justice I confide for my reward.

Charles now addresses judge and jury:

> You say that I am criminal, Presumptuous man! Thou deservest
> that the arm of vengeance righteous [?] should crush thee. Thus impiously to usurp the prerogative of thy creator! To count thus rashly on the comprehension of thy views: on the fall [frail?] pervading property of thy foresight! (437)

Having acted at what he believes the behest of God, Charles sees himself placed far above the faulty "comprehension" and "foresight" of presumptuous mankind. While much of Charles's outline confession finds its way into *Wieland* substantially unchanged (see pp. 176–7), the intellectual significance of revelation is further developed in the finished novel. Theodore Wieland's religious mania is depicted as the result of an intellectual errand, a quest for absolute truth. Theodore testifies:

> My days have been spent in searching for the revelation of [God's] will; but my days have been mournful, because my search failed. I solicited direction: I turned on every side where glimmerings of light could be discovered. I have not always been wholly uninformed; but my knowledge has always stopped short of certainty. (165)

Having isolated the intellectual dimension of the Yates-Wieland murders, we may decide that they are not so much "American" as biblical. It is as if both Brown *and* Yates had drawn upon Genesis, the twenty-second chapter, in which Abraham, hearing the voice of God command the sacrifice of his son Isaac, obeys, like Yates and Wieland, without hesitation. Abraham puts aside the dictates of what James Yates called "natural feelings" (for Isaac is his only son, whom he loves) in obedience to what he perceives as an absolute truth transcending them. It is this leap of faith, of course, that inspired the epistemological fable Søren Kierkegaard, in *Fear and Trembling*, embroidered upon Genesis, chapter 22. The self, a vessel of "natural feelings," is itself the means through which the absolute truth of God's command contrary to those feelings must be apprehended. Like Abraham, Yates and Wieland believe implicitly in their ability to apprehend divine truth. The transformation from loving husband and father to murderer they see as a transformation from the state of fallible mortality motivated by the relative truths of nature to an infallible state of divinity as agent of God's truth. Pondering the mortal consequences of his divine deed, Yates for a moment considers dragging all the dead into his house, setting it afire, and attributing the carnage to Indian massacre. "I was preparing to drag my wife in, when the idea struck me that I was going to tell a *horrible lie*; and how will that accord with my profession [that the killings were an act of divine truth]? . . . No, let me speak the truth, and declare the good motive of my actions, be the consequences what they may" (28). Absolute truth must not be pleaded with lies before the relative justice of men.

The manner in which the Abraham and Isaac story became an American tale is complex, likely involving more than the direct use of "native" materials. This we shall examine presently; but first, and more simply, we should observe that Brown's version of the biblical episode is a grotesque criticism of the intellectual blindness behind the Abrahamic leap of faith. This critical view is abetted by—may even have been inspired by—the extremity of wilderness life. Although Brown may have been familiar with Michel Guillaume Jean de Crèvecoeur's observation that vast wilderness space fosters among Americans a (healthy) "religious indifference" because zeal cannot be transmitted over any great distance,[4] the novelist would have seen that, in the case of James Yates, precisely such wilderness conditions nurtured fanatic notions. Yates's Tomhannock, remote from city and established church (Yates was accustomed to conducting impromptu services himself) concentrated in itself the newness of the New World. Yates's act, like Theodore Wieland's, was born of that world, a wilderness isolated from the emotionally and intellectually tempering influence of city civilization and organized religion. Their immediate environment helped make antinomians of Yates and Wieland, each of whom is convinced that he enjoys an original relation to the absolute.

If the wilderness offers nothing to check a misguided leap of faith, it does, ironically, provide a model after which the tragic consequences of the leap may be fashioned. The blackest irony of James Yates's action is that in performing what he sees as God's will he commits an atrocity worthy of the stereotyped "godless" American Indian. His project of slaughter bears more than a casual resemblance to a particular account of Indian atrocity written by a young gentlewoman named Ann Eliza Bleecker. Her *History of Maria Kittle* ("A Pathetic Story Founded on Fact")[5] was popular enough to go through two printings before 1800. Set in Tomhannock, the hometown both of Mrs. Bleecker and of James Yates, the story relates with pornographic zeal the lurid details of cruelties practiced by Indians upon Maria and her household. The Indians attack primarily with their "tomahacks," cleaving in twain as handily as Yates the foreheads of their victims. Not content with a single deadly stroke, they beat their victims' corpses beyond recognition. Maria's pregnant sister-in-law falls victim to a "tomahack" blow between her eyes:

> Her fine azure eyes just opened, and then suddenly closing for ever, she tumbled lifeless at [her attacker's] feet. His sanguinary soul was not yet satisfied with blood; he deformed her lovely body with deep gashes; and, tearing her unborn babe away, dashed it to pieces against the stone wall. (35–6)

The Indian's "tomahack" can be readily recognized in the axe Yates uses to destroy his sleigh, kill his horse, and wound his wife, before battering her lifeless face beyond recognition with a fence stake. The hatchet he drives between his daughter's eyes is even more closely identifiable with the Indian weapon. (The word is of French origin, but the *OED* indicates that *hatchet* was almost automatically associated with the Indian by the end of the eighteenth century.) When he does not resort to hatchet, axe, or fence stake, Yates dashes members of his unfortunate family against the nearest wall or fireplace. Recall, too, that after he surveyed the slaughter, Yates contemplated blaming it on Indians, as if to certify the completion of his "savage" transformation.

As a group of phenomena, the Yates case, *Maria Kittle*, and *Wieland* do not so much represent a chain of influence as they do a web of culture. Mrs. Bleecker might have drawn the violence of *Maria Kittle* directly from examples of Indian hostility in upstate New York; or she may even have modeled her book's violence on the crime of her white Tomhannock neighbor, who proved himself so precocious a student of Indian-style mayhem. Beyond doubt, Mrs. Bleecker knew Yates and knew of the murders. Bound with *Maria Kittle* in Bleecker's *Posthumous Works* (1793) is a letter dated December 1781 to Miss Susan Ten Eyck, the person to whom the epistolary *Maria Kittle* also is addressed. "JAMES YATES," Mrs. Bleecker writes, "a few nights ago murdered his wife, four children" and (as she reports it) more than one horse as well as a cow. Mrs. Bleecker further remarks that "by all appearances [Yates] is a religious lunatic" (151). Though she forbears to relate to Miss Ten Eyck the particulars "of cruelty too horrid to mention'' (unwonted reticence from the author of *Maria Kittle*!), she had apparently seen Yates at close quarters after the murders. The *New York Weekly Magazine* account of the murders mentions that after his capture Yates was held some time at the house of a ''Mrs. Bl-----r,'' and a year after the murder a ''Mr. Bl-----r'' (note that there are enough blanks for the ''eecke'') sent some fruit to Yates in his Albany ''dungeon.''

We may speculate on how conscious Brown was of the profound implications of the Yates story when he appropriated it for *Wieland*. Did he realize, consciously and articulately, that Yates had partaken of that ''eucharist'' Richard Slotkin described, the act betokening New World transformation through ''communion'' with the wilderness? Brown does make Clara Wieland say, after she has read the first part of her brother's confession, that Theodore's deed ''was worthy of savages trained to murder, and exulting in agonies'' (174). Advised to leave the country because Theodore will not rest until he has killed her along with the others, Clara protests: ''I live not in a community of savages; yet, whether I sit or walk, go into crouds, or hide myself in solitude, my life is marked for a prey to inhuman violence'' (189). The white residents of James Yates's Tomhannock were entitled to similar protests, no doubt. But the town's very name sounds like ''tomahack.''

While the evidence is very convincing that Brown was familiar with the Tomhannock murders and used them in *Wieland*, Edwin Fussell suggests that the book also owes a debt directly to *Maria Kittle*.[6] And it is true not only that the *Posthumous Works* of Mrs. Bleecker were published by T. and J. Swords, the firm that was to print much of what Brown wrote, but also that Ann Eliza's nephew, Anthony Bleecker, was a member with Brown of the intimate New York Friendly Club.[7] In this manner Brown must have found himself caught up in a complex web of influences that made up the conditions of existence in his nation and that caught him up in the writing of an American tale. Brown's outline for *Wieland* suggests that he was not moved to compose his tale directly. The invention of an American Abraham proceeded along a circuitous route, apparently, via Yates and *Kittle*, the Bible, of course, but also through Europe in the form of a minor poem by the novel's namesake, Cristoph Martin Wieland. By recalling what Brown told John Bernard about his habits of composition, how literary ideas worked in his mind unbidden and practically divorced from consciousness, and by examining the outline for *Wieland*, we can speculate on how the novelist wove the variegated strands of multiple influence into the fabric of his book.

Preceding Brown's outline proper are columns of more than one hundred names, among which we recognize Conway, Bedloe, Lorimer, Dudley, Pleyel, Edny, Wyatte, Inglefield, Carwin, and Welbeck as characters in Brown's fiction. Not ''Wieland,'' but ''Weyland'' appears twice in the list. ''Weiland'' occurs in a shorter list near the end of the outline, and ''Wieland'' appears twice in a list of book titles. The columns are a quarry sufficient to supply a dozen novels with character names. We know from Elihu Hubbard Smith's diary that Brown was fond of drawing up plans and programs for literary projects, and perhaps the name lists were part of such a plan. Indeed, following the names in the outline is a list of titles, quite possibly drawn up as a prospectus for a literary career:

Sky-walk, or the man unknown to himself
Wieland, or, the Transformation
-Carwin. or [subtitle obliterated]
Bedloe. or the self devoted
Gower, or The dead recalled

More remarkable is this catalog of themes found at the end of the outline:

Tales. passions poutrayed.
Hallucination
     ulation
Somnamb. | Mimicry
⎰ person. Simil | --personal-Similitude--
⎱ Melanaema* |
Hallucinat. | Ventriloquizm
Love of Country | Dissimulation

Although a penchant for drawing up lists and literary programs tends to contradict the impression of spontaneous composition Brown conveyed to Bernard, the lists themselves exhibit a kind of "automatic" writing. They are neither systematic nor wholly random. Such alliterative clusters as "Barwell / Bertrand / Carew / Caster" occur frequently and even suggestions of imperfect rhyme, as in "Heene / Mayne." "Welbeck" follows "Beckworth," and the sound of "Car" seems particularly to have appealed to Brown:

Carrington	Caring
Carling, —	Carey.
Charlton,	Carton.
Carlingford.	Carford.
Carlington.	—Carfield
Carbourg.	
	Carobury
Carsey	
	Carlosteen
Carlette. Carney	

*Melanaema: "A condition of suffocation in which the blood throughout the body assumes a dark or black color" (*OED*).

Carwin.   Carhill
Carrell.   Carlhurst
Cardale.
Carville.
Carhuyson.
Carry.
Carborough.

One of the names Brown recorded struck in him a conscious intellectual chord. The "Weyland" of the name list is transformed into the title list's "Wieland," a name familiar to Brown (and to most of literary America and Europe) as that of an enormously popular and influential German pre-Romantic poet.[8] Early in his novel (7), Brown has Clara Wieland acknowledge her family's literal kinship with Christoph Martin Wieland (1733–1813). Best known to Brown and his contemporaries as the author of the epic poetic fantasy *Oberon* and several novels, Wieland appealed to Brown (and to many another nascent Romantic) for both aesthetic and political reasons. Attuned to the ideas of Rousseau and Godwin, C. M. Wieland was also an intellectual idealist whose Platonism was filtered through Shaftesbury. One student of the poet's work sees his career as a "continual struggle for certitude, for the right answers," suggesting further that "epistemology is the key to a deeper understanding of Wieland's personality and accomplishments."[9] Given what we have already determined about Brown's place in the intellectual tradition of the American novel, it is little wonder that the novelist's freely flowing thoughts should have paused at Wieland's name. For Brown, like Christoph Martin Wieland —and Theodore Wicland, like his German namesake—was engaged in continual struggle for certitude.

At least two other German sources—Friedrich Schiller's *Der Geisterseher* and an imitation of it by Cajetan Tschink, bearing the same title— also probably figured in the composition of *Wieland*;[10] but an early effort of Christoph Martin Wieland seems to have exerted the greatest influence. *Der Gepryfte Abraham*, a minor verse epic retelling the Abraham and Isaac story, appeared in 1754 and was translated into an English prose version, *The Trial of Abraham*, issued by the Norwich, Connecticut, press of John Trumbull in 1778. Like *Wieland*, *The Trial of Abraham* is to a large extent an intellectual elaboration upon Genesis, chapter 22, probing the psychological and moral consequences of absolute obedience born of absolute faith. Like Theodore Wieland and James Yates, C. M. Wieland's Abraham consciously subdues "natural affection" to the command of divine will. Natural affection is real, but revealed truth transcends it. While C. M. Wieland's Abraham pondered God's awful command, "his musing soul in a scale of speculation ascended from truth to truth, till it brightened up, that every painful sentiment dissolved in the radience [*sic*] of inspired wisdom."[11] Still, like Yates and Theodore, Abraham consciously has to suppress the immediate promptings of nature. In order to

achieve certitude a man must attain the realm of pure thought, which (in
C. M. Wieland's Platonic cosmogony) is the realm of God. "Silence,
Nature," bids the loving father of Isaac. "My will is dedicated to God"
(35).

There is a striking psychological and intellectual similarity not only
among *The Trial of Abraham*, *Wieland*, and the Yates atrocity but also
among the physical phenomena associated with the moment of "divine"
revelation in each case. James Yates reported the presence of "a new light"
as the two "Spirits" appeared before him. The display to which C. M.
Wieland treats his Abraham is more spectacular:

> And now a sudden effulgence diffuses itself over the hill, and
> with increasing radiancy, like a cloud of light, moved through the
> azure sky: Abraham lifted up his eyes, felt the presence of the
> Deity; an angel, by God's intuitive [?] command, descended in-
> visible, to strengthen the patriarch's eyes: At one look, for only of
> one is the human soul capable, he saw the divine glory through
> inconceivable ranks of adoring angels, between them Jehovah in-
> throned on cherubs; celestial scene, which verbal description
> would obscure! (3)

None of this is present in the austere description of the scene in
Genesis, chapter 22; however, most of the elements C. M. Wieland includes are also to be found in Theodore Wieland's confession. He tells the
court how he entered his sister's house, its total darkness requiring caution
in descending the stairs. As Theodore reached for the balustrade—

> How shall I describe the lustre, which, at that moment, burst
> upon my vision!
> I was dazzled. My organs were bereaved of their activity. My
> eye-lids were half-closed, and my hands withdrawn from the
> balustrade. A nameless fear chilled my veins, and I stood motion-
> less. This irradiation did not retire or lessen. It seemed as if some
> powerful effulgence covered me like a mantle.

As with Abraham's vision, the revelation is too intense to be borne by mortal senses.

> I opened my eyes and found all about me luminous and glowing.
> It was the element of heaven that flowed around. Nothing but a
> fiery stream was at first visible but, anon, a shrill voice from be-
> hind called upon me to attend.
> I turned: It is forbidden to describe what I saw: Words, indeed,
> would be wanting to the task. The lineaments of that being,
> whose veil was now lifted, and whose visage beamed upon my
> sight, no hues of pencil or of language can pourtray. (167–8)

For Theodore Wieland, as for the German poet's Abraham, the experience of the absolute is beyond words.

Whatever the order in which Brown read *The Trial of Abraham* and read about Yates, it is the American situation—and Brown's own deepest ambivalent response to it—that drew Abraham and Isaac, Christoph Martin Wieland, Theodore Wieland, and James Yates together. Indeed, despite its remote origins in the German poet's fatherland and in the biblical land of Moriah, *The Trial of Abraham* employs the very epistemological metaphor most immediately available to the American writer. On the eve of the day appointed for his sacrifice, Isaac relates to Abraham and Sarah an adventure that befell him and his friend Abiasaph in the wilderness of Haran. The youths, wandering along the frontier, spy a beautiful bird, its song the sweetest music, its wings a rainbow. Isaac would capture it as a present for Ribkah (Rebecca, his future wife), and with Abiasaph he follows the bird into the forest. Oblivious to all but the gorgeous bird, they are soon lost. Worse, they wander into the domain of Tidal and Gog, grandsons of Nimrod, who plan to sacrifice the youths to their god Adramelech. There is little hope, until Elhanan, Isaac's guardian angel, intervenes, rescuing both young men.

Isaac and Abiasaph's adventure in the wilderness, far more a product of C. M. Wieland's imagination than of the Old Testament, is crucial to the poet's intellectual reinterpretation of the Abraham and Isaac story. The bird that the boys blindly follow is a metaphor of sublunary sensual reality. Lured by "too much love to God's creatures" (in both his attraction to the bird and to Ribkah, for whom the bird is intended), Isaac forgets himself and is lost in the creature's realm, a chaos of sensuality ruled by a deity who, appropriately, demands actual, physical sacrifice, rather than the ideal, symbolic sacrifice finally enjoined by Abraham's God. The moral of the parable is found in Abraham's words to Sarah as he and Isaac embark for Moriah: "Yet, oh guard thine heart, lest too much love to God's creatures insensibly stifle the thoughts of God" (30). Intellectually considered, the wilderness of *The Trial of Abraham* is a version of Plato's cave. By no means is Brown's American wilderness so one-dimensional as the German poet's, but something like it does figure in the precarious balance of Brockden Brown's ambivalence toward civilization and the wild.

The Yates murders served as the American nexus upon which other "sources" converged. Yates became an Abraham, flourishing tragically in the isolation and violence of a New World frontier town. And Abraham, through Christoph Martin Wieland, became an actor in a drama of epistemology. In Brown's work, the Old World is repeatedly tested by the New World as, compulsively, certitude falls before skepticism, doubt, error, and the frailty of human perception. Recall that Brown, in his outline for *Wieland*, identified himself with two seekers of certitude: he named his first Wieland "Charles," having drawn "Wieland" from his list of names likely because it resonated so tellingly with the surname of a German poet engrossed in themes of knowledge and knowing. The American nexus of the Yates tragedy, then, became for Brown the correlative of an intensely felt intellectual conflict.

What *Wieland* wonderfully illustrates is how Brown's American subjects serve to focus and concentrate his "wildering" thoughts into an artifact of culture burst through the mere peculiarities of an environment. The essence of Brown's "Americanism," of his relation to his time and place, consists precisely in his uneasy command of both Old and New World sources. *Wieland* suggests that, for Brown, to be an American, especially an American author, meant a life lived in emotional conflict born of restless skepticism about the truth of thought and perception. The novelist found that what had been a comfortable confidence in one's "eastern" mind could become an agonizing doubt as one forced consciousness to a "western" frontier. Brown carried a great deal of the Old World into his New World fictions, using the Bible and *Der Gepryfte Abraham* to translate the Yates murders into the tale of Theodore Wieland.

The creation of Theodore's father required even more of the Old World.

The man who would become the father of Clara and Theodore Wieland, smothered by seven years of spiritual aridity as apprentice to a London trader and charged with a zeal born of radical religious reading, was overwhelmed one day by an awakening of the religious affections, which prompted him to leave England for the banks of the Schuylkill outside Philadelphia. His intention (for so he believed God had commanded) was to preach to and convert the Indians; but fear of the Indians, which had tormented him even before he left Europe, was "revived [upon reaching America], and a nearer survey of savage manners once more shook his resolution" (10). Cheap land and black slaves "gave him who was poor in Europe all the advantages of wealth," so that for fourteen years, setting aside the zeal of youth, he prospered as a farmer. Having earned a degree of leisure, he took up Scripture and theology once again until "his ancient belief relative to the conversion of the savage tribes, was revived with uncommon energy" (10). Missionary labors, undertaken at last, "were attended with no permanent success." A minor spiritual victory here and there was poor compensation for the derision and insults to which Wieland was subject. The extremities of wilderness life, fatigue, hunger, sickness, and solitude also took their toll. "The license of savage passion, and the artifices of his depraved countrymen, all opposed themselves to his progress" (11).

Discouraged, essentially broken by his wilderness missionary sojourn, Wieland came back to his family. Eschewing conventional and social religion, he worshiped in complete solitude daily at noon and midnight, building for this purpose "what to a common eye would have seemed a summer house" (11). Slight and airy, it "was no more than a circular area, twelve feet in diameter, whose flooring was the rock, cleared of moss and shrubs, and exactly levelled, edged by twelve Tuscan columns, and covered by an undulating dome'' (11). We shall see in a later chapter that this "temple" is of a piece with Palladian designs Brown sketched in fragmentary manuscripts that are probably parts of a youthful and abortive utopian project. This does not explain, however, the incongruity of having the senior Wieland conduct his "gothic" religious exercises in a monument to the neoclassical sensibility.

The picture Clara Wieland paints of her father's religious beliefs is grimly fanatical. It was the chance reading of "a book written by one of the teachers of the Albigenses, or French Protestants" that sent the senior Wieland on his ill-fated mission to America. A consideration of this religious background figured in the earliest stages of the composition of the novel. Wieland "contracted a gloomy & religious spritt [sic]," Brown noted in his outline, "from the perusal of the works of the first reformers. He built up a system of his own. The Savoyard protestant faith was his. See Chambers Cyclopaedia" (427).

Ephraim Chambers's *Cyclopaedia* does not have an article on "Savoyard protestants," nor are they mentioned under the main "Protestant" entry. Perhaps Brown intended a reference to the entry under "Waldenses" in Chambers, since these Protestants were "Savoyards," residents of the Savoy Piedmont. The religious persecution they perpetually suffered culminated in the "massacre" of April 24, 1655, that is the subject of John Milton's Sonnet 18. But this resolutely independent yet simple and mild sect hardly seems a likely source for a "gloomy," let alone fanatical, religious spirit. The Waldenses were, however, often confused with their neighbors to the east, the Albigenses, with whom, theologically, they had very little in common. Chambers's *Cyclopaedia*, in its article on the Albigenses, stresses the sect's Manicheanism. Their belief was in "two Gods, the one infinitely good, the other infinitely evil . . . the good God made the invisible world, and the evil one that which we live in." Some later commentators have observed that the Albigenses were actually a direct outgrowth of the Persian Manichees. Chambers enumerates additional Albigensian heresies, including a belief in two Christs (one good, the other evil), no resurrection of the body, the uselessness of baptism and other holy rites and sacraments, the absence of confession and penance, and the belief that marriage is both unholy and unlawful. Later writers mention the Albigenses' fanatical asceticism, which may culminate in suicide among the sect's "perfected" as a means of evading mortal sin. For once an Albigensian has been initiated through a laying on of hands known as the "*consolumentum*," a single sin of the flesh forfeits eternal salvation. Suicide was generally by starvation.[12]

Melancholy, foreboding, fanaticism, self-loathing, deprecation of the physical and elevation of the spiritual: Brown could have found enough of these in the Albigensian doctrine to supply two generations of Wielands. Why, then, attenuate the gothic effect of such a religion by having its American disciple worship in the bright product of the age of reason? The incongruity is made the more striking by the sedate temple's location "on the top of a rock whose sides were steep, rugged, and encumbered with dwarf cedars and stony asperities" (11), a "sublime" landscape that antici- pates *Edgar Huntly*. If the admixture of classical restraint with fanaticism and the sublime is a product of Brown's incongruous nature, it was an in- congruity he shared with his culture. As conspicuously out of place in the American landscape as the "dungeon" Edgar Huntly projects into it, Wieland's temple has its source in a similar reaction to the extremity of wilderness experience. Wieland, all but destroyed by his missionary en- deavors, erects a symbol of classical order at the edge of the wilderness that had debilitated him. Upon the Albigensian passion that sent him into the wilderness in the first place, he imposes a symbol of passionless order; and where once he had worshiped in limitless American wilds, he now confines religious meditation daily behind twelve Tuscan columns at noon and at midnight exactly. The rage for order Edgar Huntly and the senior Wieland manifest is part of the impulse that led the "gothic novelist" himself to sketch drawings of Palladian buildings. And these designs, like the "dungeon" and "temple" Huntly and Wieland respectively project into the wilderness, may be located along the same cultural continuum that moved a Thomas Jefferson to build Monticello.

If the senior Wieland's architectural reaction to the wilderness can be accounted typically American, his religion, despite its familiar missionary element, seems quite alien. It is initially puzzling that Brown failed, say, to tap the rich vein of Puritanism Hawthorne would later discover. After all, as Larzer Ziff has suggested, in *Wieland*, "Brown . . . penetrates beneath the principles of the optimistic psychology of his day, and recognizes the claims which Calvinism makes on the American character. . . . Beginning consciously in the camp of the benevolent Philadelphians of the American Philosophical Society . . . Brown ends his journey through the mind by approaching [Jonathan] Edwards' camp." Brown "was the first [American novelist] to face the confusion of sentiment and optimistic psychology, both of which flowed through the chink in the Puritan dike, and to represent American progress away from a doctrine of depravity as a very mixed blessing indeed."[13]

While Ziff is correct in remarking the similarity of intellectual tone be- tween *Wieland* and Puritan theology, it is an oversimplification to declare that Brown sided with the Puritans in order to attack facile optimism. It is true that the novel explores the horrors of an irrationality against which reason proves powerless; and it is also true that in the blind fate of Wieland, father and son, and in the motiveless malignity of the "bilo- quist" Carwin, we do see a species of "depravity." However, if Brown can be said to attack anything, it is fanaticism; and the novelist must have seen that neither of the Wieland men could be literally Puritans. Required were solitary figures whose religion, like that of James Yates, had developed in isolation. Puritanism, for all its potential extremity (especially as it might have been popularly perceived), was simply too social an institution, providing too many of the checks and balances of rational civilization to serve the novelist's purpose.

While Albigensianism, a long-dead schism originating in medieval Toulouse, may at first seem a gratuitously exotic choice for the Wieland religious background, the sect can be seen as a caricature of the more sulfurous aspects of Calvinist doctrine. The Albigensian's Manichean cosmogony of absolute good and evil and its rigorous doctrine of natural depravity resonate powerfully with the kind of religion that would appeal to the literary sensibilities of Hawthorne and Melville. Much as *Edgar Huntly* translates European gothicism into terms of the American wilderness, *Wieland* uses an exotic Old World religion to help define in the New World wilderness the intellectual themes that, we have already suggested, mark Brown as an American author. The shadowy Albigensian background of the senior Wieland—which manifests itself in the next generation as the "calvinistic inspiration" (25) of Theodore—is meant to expose and explain the tragic errors to which a blind leap of faith may lead. Resonant with, perhaps even inspired by, the particular situation of the American Puritans, *Wieland* was written neither to approve of nor to condemn them.

Whatever their "calvinistic inspiration," the two Wielands are what the eighteenth century called "enthusiasts," a kind of fanatic the Reverend Charles Chauncy described and cautioned against in a sermon written during that violent spasm of revivalist emotion in America known as "The Great Awakening": "He mistakes the working of his own passions for divine communications, and fancies himself immediately inspired by the SPIRIT of GOD, when all the while, he is under no other influence than that of an over-heated imagination."[14] Men like Chauncy feared that error lay behind the upheaval of religious affections, egocentric error that could lead to such disasters as the Yates murders, which, like the Awakening, were in part fostered by the conditions of wilderness life. What might begin as belief in a divine commission to "deliver [God's] message to the world" (6), Chauncy observes, may evolve into unmitigated horror:

> Sometimes [enthusiasm] appears in their imaginary peculiar intimacy with heaven. They are, in their own opinion, the special favourites of God . . . and receive immediate, extraordinary communications from him. The tho'ts, which suddenly rise up in their minds, they take for suggestions of the SPIRIT; their very fancies are divine illuminations; nor are they strongly inclin'd to any thing, but 'tis an impulse from GOD, a plain revelation of his will.
>
> And what extravagances, in this temper of mind, are they not capable of, and under specious pretext too of paying obediences to the authority of GOD? Many have fancied themselves acting by immediate warrant from heaven, while they have been committing the most undoubted wickedness. (4)

In just this manner did the seeds of the senior Wieland's enthusiasm bear deadly fruit in the son.

As thoroughly as Chauncy's description anticipates the Wielands, it is of course impossible simply to infer that Brown had read the sermon, which, after all, had appeared more than a half-century before *Wieland*, and in Boston, a city Brown may never even have visited. More important is what "Enthusiasm Described and Cautioned Against" suggests about the nature of faith in America. It shows us how the religious theme in *Wieland* reaches beyond Calvinism as such and toward broader questions about the assumptions on which men habitually construct "truth." While this is not so peculiarly American a theme as Puritan Calvinism, such phenomena as the Yates atrocity show that it is no less a function of culture and physical environment.

Chauncy's sermon is related thematically to a document we do know that Brown used in the composition of *Wieland*. Chauncy recommends Scripture and reason as antidotes to the egocentricism of enthusiasm, yet he observes that "in nothing does the *enthusiasm* of these persons discover itself more, than in the disregard they express to the Dictates of *reason*." Both James Yates and Theodore Wieland are contemptuous of the reasonings of their captors. In Chauncy's terms, "They are above the force of argument" (5). Enthusiasm is actually beyond the power of reason, for " 'tis properly a disease, a sort of madness," the result of "bad temperament of the blood and spirits" (3). Here the minister anticipates a treatise to which Brown refers in a footnote to *Wieland* (179). Erasmus Darwin, Brown points out, described Theodore Wieland's disorder in his *Zoönomia; or The Laws of Organic Life*, which was published in a complete American edition the year before Brown wrote his novel. Darwin defines "Mania mutabilis" as a state of delusion wrought by some "physical defect"—thought to be hereditary—in the nervous system or sensory organs. Instances of the mania Darwin recounts include a woman who hallucinates the presence of an angel, another who hears a voice commanding "Repent, or you will be damned," and others of like nature.[15] Somewhat ironically, perhaps, Darwin illustrates his "scientific" description of Mania mutabilis with a number of religious examples, whereas the clergyman Charles Chauncy defines this malady of the religious affections scientifically. Larzer Ziff was right to note elements of something like the Calvinist notion of innate depravity in *Wieland*, but Chauncy's "medical" definition of enthusiasm comes even closer to precisely what we find in the novel. The roots of enthusiasm are not to be explained theologically, but physiologically, as a "disease, a sort of madness: And there are few; perhaps none at all, but are subject to it" (Chauncy, 3).

In a similar vein, at the conclusion of the misadventures of *Edgar Huntly*, Brown has Huntly's friend Sarsefield declare: "Consciousness itself is the malady, the pest, of which he only is cured who ceases to think." In this strictly intellectual sense, depravity is a fact of human existence. In the world of Brown's novels, to think is to invite error, and to act upon thought is to invite calamity. As Edgar Huntly himself concludes: "Disastrous and humiliating is the state of man! By his own hands is constructed the mass of misery and error in which his steps are forever involved. . . . How little cognizance have men over the actions and motives of each other! How total is our blindness with regard to our own performances!" (267). And Clara Wieland cries out from the pages that recount her brother's life of holy error: "What is man, that knowledge is so sparingly conferred upon him!" (102).

While Brown's absorption in intellectual themes suggests that he was no simple product of a Calvinist heritage, the fact remains that his themes do at least smack of such a background. Ziff suggests, in effect, that Brown's use of depravity, predestination, even the hellfire spontaneous combustion attending the senior Wieland's demise, is reason enough to enroll the novelist with such Calvinist-influenced writers as Hawthorne and Melville in an important tradition of the national literature. But William L. Hedges, in a 1974 article, raises a well-founded objection to this view. He concedes that "concepts such as innocence, puritanism and the Protestant ethic might be adequate to discussions of Brown if liberally enough construed," but when "the construction is too strict . . . we risk forgetting that Charles Brockden Brown the Quaker and Young Goodman Brown the New England puritan are not identical." When we stop to consider that Brown grew up not in Puritan Boston but Quaker Philadelphia, that his parents were indeed Quakers, and that his only formal education was the six years he spent at the Friends' Latin School, we are inclined to second Hedges's objection that Larzer Ziff "approaches . . . an . . . untenable extreme in arguing that in [*Wieland*] Brown reverts to something like a Calvinist doctrine of 'inherited depravity' and a 'confused acceptance of supernatural causation.' "[16] But, turning back to the novel itself, we *do* see in Theodore Wieland something very like inherited depravity. And rather than a display of William Penn's gentle doctrine of the Inner Light we are treated to the Day-of-Doom spontaneous combustion of Theodore's zealot father.

How do we reconcile the biographical fact of Brown's Quaker background with the aesthetic fact of his most famous novel, the darkness of whose themes suggests the Calvinist heritage of a Hawthorne or Melville? To begin with, we can no more call Brown simply a Quaker than we can call him simply a Calvinist. True, his parents were Quakers; but of their six children, four, including Charles, married non-Quakers (Warfel, 19–20). Moreover, an exchange between Brown's closest friends, Smith and Dunlap, reveals that the novelist's marriage to Elizabeth Linn, the daughter of a Presbyterian minister, was not his first romance "outside the Meeting." On March 29, 1798, Elihu Hubbard Smith showed William Dunlap a letter in which Brown described himself "as assiduously writing Novels & in love" (Dunlap, *Diary*, 236). By April 24 Smith was calling a

Miss Susan A. Potts Brown's "Mistress" (Smith, 439–40), while Dunlap, a few days later, was content to identify her as "CBB's wished for" (Dunlap, *Diary*, 252). But at the end of September Dunlap tersely recorded that Brown had related to him "the manner in which his mother breaks off his connection with Miss Potts" (Dunlap, *Diary*, 343). It is most likely that Mrs. Brown's objection was made on religious grounds: Susan Potts was not a Quaker (Clark, 195).

No hard evidence exists that Brown harbored ill will toward either his mother or Quakerism; however, interestingly enough, in *Arthur Mervyn* (Part 1, published the year after *l'affaire Potts*) Brown puts the young title character through a romantic experience analogous to his own. Arthur, who is not a Quaker, falls in love with a Quaker farmer's daughter but dejectedly puts off proposing to her because he knows her father will object to the marriage on religious grounds. Brown, conveniently, kills off the father and has Arthur acknowledge that the old man's death has removed the only obstacle to marriage. Even if we take the episode from *Arthur Mervyn* as evidence of Brown's covert rebellion against the religion that may have cost him his Miss Potts, we must still conclude that his attitude toward Quakerism was ambivalent rather than wholly antagonistic. For he is careful to paint the old Quaker of the novel as a kindly, mild, and generous man. Perhaps the extent and longevity of such ambivalence toward the religion of his parents is most fully suggested by a document he wrote the year before his death. In *An Address to the Congress of the United States, on the Utility and Justice of Restrictions upon Foreign Commerce*, an 1809 pamphlet directed against Jefferson's embargo, Brown counseled that the President's action was not only ineffectual, but immoral, an act of war, greed, and vengeance. "There are [some] who will pass me by as a visionary," Brown wrote:

> And some, observing the city where I thus make my appearance [Philadelphia], may think my pacific doctrine, my system of rational forbearance and forgiveness carried to a pitch of *Quaker* extravagance. The truth is, I am no better than an outcast of that unwarlike sect, but cannot rid myself of reverence for most of its practical and political maxims.[17]

Cast out from the Meeting—perhaps, indeed, because of his marriage —Brown yet retains a reverence for the Friends, or, at least for their "practical and political maxims."

The novelist's religious ambivalence suggests that, while Charles Brockden Brown indeed was not Young Goodman Brown the Puritan, neither was he, say, John Woolman or William Penn the Quaker. We should, in any case, avoid stereotyping Quakerism as the mild religion of Woolman and Penn; it could, of course, take other forms as well. Though Brown found his bride outside the Meeting, he would not have had to venture that far in order to find a germ he might nurture into the full-blown fanaticism of both the senior and junior Wieland. Available to the novelist in the collection of the Library Company of Philadelphia was William Smith's *History of New-York* (London: 1757; reissued in Philadelphia: 1792), in which Brown would have come across the story of Lewis Morris. Appointed Chief Justice of the New York Supreme Court in 1692 and governor of New Jersey in 1702, Morris nevertheless had been "a little whimsical" in his youth. Bridling under the zealous Quaker tutelage of a certain Hugh Coppathwait, young Morris played a practical joke on him one day: "The pupil taking advantage of [Coppathwait's] enthusiasm, hid himself in a tree, and calling to him, ordered him to preach the gospel among the Mohawks. The credulous quaker took it for a miraculous call, and was upon the point of setting out when the cheat was discovered."[18]

We can do little more, really, than wonder if Brown actually had this comical episode in mind when he wrote of the senior Wieland's call to preach to the Indians or when he had son Theodore heed the "divine" command—which may well have issued from the ventriloquist Carwin—to sacrifice his family. But, considered with the evidence of Brown's ambivalence toward the religion of his parents, the case of Hugh Coppathwait does tell us at least one thing definitely: it is a mistake to label Brockden Brown's religious influences with the stereotyped tags that commentaries have furnished to date.

We turn now to a particular influence upon Brown, about which there has so far been no hard speculation: Robert Proud, author of the first history of Pennsylvania and the schoolmaster of the future novelist. Proud, as master of the Friends' Latin School, was certainly a professed Quaker. Harry R. Warfel describes him as "tall as a tower and commanding in presence, with a prominent Roman nose and bushy brows arching over a large face"—a symbol of "the old patriarchal order." Warfel drew this description from Charles West Thomson's "Notices of the Life and Character of Robert Proud, Author of 'The History of Pennsylvania'" (1826) either directly or through the redaction of it in *The Dictionary of American Biography* (*DAB*). But Warfel added on his own a judgment for which neither Thomson nor the *DAB* gives unambiguous warrant. "Wise, calm, mild, energetic, resourceful, affectionate," Warfel declares, Proud "was the living embodiment of the Quaker philosophy" (Warfel, 22–3).

Charles West Thomson did meet a former student of Proud's who described the schoolmaster as "mild, commanding, and affectionate"; but when Thomson himself, as a boy, caught a glimpse of Proud it was his stern bearing that made the greatest impression.[19] "I well remember the imposing effect, which the curled, gray wig, the half-cocked, patriarchal-looking hat and the long, ivory-headed cane, had on my boyish imagination." Likely that effect was terrifying, especially on a "boyish imagination," which would undoubtedly as well as painfully connect the ivory-headed cane with the profession of schoolmaster. In fact, Proud, "obscure and retiring," emerges from the traces that remain of his life—including the 1797 *History of Pennsylvania*—as a malcontent and misanthrope, desperately forlorn among a nation and people he did not cherish. Thomson wished to record Proud's life precisely because, by 1826, memory of the man had all but vanished.

Born in Yorkshire, England, in 1728, Robert Proud showed such early genius that his parents precipitously steered him into a medical career. But, much as the youthful Brown would himself become disgusted with the profession of law for which he had been trained, so Proud bolted from medicine. This or financial troubles (which were something of a plague upon Proud) may have caused his abrupt departure from England for America in 1759. There were rumors circulating that Proud had actually fled England because of an unhappy love affair—financial embarrassment barred marriage—but Thomson gives these stories no credit; though, it is true, Proud did remain a bachelor lifelong. Whatever his reasons for emigrating, two years after his arrival in Philadelphia he was engaged as a master of the Friends' Latin School, where he presented a figure so stern that he quickly became known as "Dominie Proud." There is no evidence that he discouraged this appellation, though it better suits a Scots Calvinist than an English Quaker.

If the epithet suggests Presbyterian sternness, this bearing actually masked a melancholy as morbid as any found in the diaries of Cotton Mather or Michael Wigglesworth, or, for that matter, in the youthful letters of Brockden Brown himself. Among some verses Proud left in manuscript at his death is "A Plaintive Essay, attempted by R.P. in 6 mo., 1781, after several years of great distress, dejection, and trouble of mind," which Thomson included in an appendix to his biographical sketch of Proud. The schoolmaster addresses God, who, unaccountably, has of late seen fit to forsake his faithful servant:

> But oh! why now this grievous fall,
>> Why am I left forlorn?
> Why am I thus deprived of all,
>> Why was I ever born?

In 1770 Proud had resigned as master at the Latin School to embark upon a financially ruinous decade of foreign trade. The "Plaintive Essay" was written the year after he returned to the school, quite broke, and just a year before Brockden Brown enrolled.

> Oh! why in my declining years,
>> Hast Thou forsaken me!

A commercial failure, Robert Proud never felt at home in America. Furthermore, politically and philosophically conservative, he was a Loyalist Tory during the Revolution, and felt himself doomed to perish:

> Far distant, in a foreign land . . .

Where death and darkness, understood,
    Possess the human mind,
Rebellion, wrath, revenge, and blood,
    The actions of mankind!

The "Plaintive Essay" concludes with a quatrain "Motto":

Our early days are best but quickly gone,
Disease with pain and sorrow soon come on,
Labor and care soon introduce decay,
And death resistless hastens all away.

Such effusions are hardly the work of a "living embodiment of the Quaker philosophy."

At the very least, Proud may well have nurtured in Brown the melancholy that would become a characteristic of the vision embodied in his fiction. Moreover, and more importantly, the schoolmaster may have shaded his somber-hued lessons with tones specifically religious and thereby may have influenced not only the emotional tenor of his pupil's future work but also its themes. The single sentence devoted to Robert Proud in *The Literary History of the United States* mentions the "almost medieval spirit" in which the pedagogue argued "that men were born to obey."[20] Better to have called this spirit Calvinist; for Proud's Toryism was as much the result of religious as of political conviction. These lines from "Vox Naturae, An Elegy," another of the poems printed by Thomson, depict Proud as an exile among a people doomed by their rebellion to everlasting damnation:

Hence eternal reason's voice
I will follow in my choice;
For, as happiness alone
By obedience first was known,
    But was lost
By rebellion, so no more
Shall be known, upon this shore,
That true glory, peace, and joy,
Which did former days employ,
    On this coast.[21]

In a letter to his brother William dated "12 mo. 1st '77," Proud cranks his rhetoric to a pitch just flat of "Sinners in the Hands of an Angry God." Prophesying that America shall surely suffer for its "unnatural Rebellion," he summons up an image of the "over-ruling Hand of Divine Providence, which disposes the Events of Things, and inflicts the Scourge of his wrath on Man-kind, for their Depravity and Revolt from the true Means of their real Interest and Felicity." Revolution is itself the punishment for unnatural rebellion, "the grand Punishment assigned by the Almighty for the wickedness of the human Race, while in the State of Existence."[22]

In the June 1799 issue of his *Monthly Magazine* Brown published a review of Proud's single claim upon posterity, his *History of Pennsylvania* (1797). Judging the author no artist, and the work an exhaustive collection of material rather than a genuine history, Brown nevertheless praised the "humble, honest, and industrious compiler. If his merit were measured by the labour which so large a compilation cost him, it would not be accounted inconsiderable."[23] Nor is it an inconsiderable labor to read the *History*, whose choked syntax recalls the densest passages of Cotton Mather's *Magnalia Christi Americana*.

More significant are the Matherian sentiments Proud entertains in his "Preface Dedicatory," where he conceives history as an interaction of Providence and the perpetual legacy of original sin. Divine Providence ordains government, Proud maintains, but "a constant decay [operates] in human affairs" to undermine it.[24] Through "folly or depravity" men rebel against the felicity of providentially ordained governments. "For the history of all nations abounds with instances of the same nature, operating in all descendants of *Adam* and *Eve*, which we are told, prevailed in these first parents, as representatives, of mankind" (6). Despite the lessons of history, "the interdicted tree, with its *forbidden fruit*, is still as tempting as ever it was" (7). "Ambition is rooted in human nature"—a human nature forever depraved when Adam and Eve first foolishly sought change —and ambition

> demands restraint; it assumes all manner of appearances whatsoever, and is now working wonders, in the world, under the name of *equality* and *the rights of man*;—Hence to mistake innovation for renovation, and a love of change for melioration, connected with such an idea of *self-dependency*, as is inconsistent with the enlargement of civilization, or of the social happiness of mankind, in any great or extensive degree, . . . (14)

So Proud's "sentence" itself decays, syntactically, in the course of another quarter-page.

As we cannot declare with certainty that Proud's evident melancholy fostered Brown's own, so we cannot say for sure that the novelist's "Quakerism" was that of his schoolmaster. We do know some things for certain: Brown's formal education was the work of Robert Proud; Brown respected the schoolmaster's *History*; and the novelist apparently maintained contact with Proud, at least through September 1, 1800, when he addressed a melancholy letter to "R.P." reporting his convalescence from some unspecified emotional wound, possibly the broken engagement with Miss Potts (Dunlap, *Life*, 2: 101). And we know, too, that the ostensibly Quaker novelist produced in *Wieland* a drama of depravity and fatality in which "Inner Light" seems but the product of hallucination and spontaneous combustion.

Without doubt, the best-known episode of *Wieland* or any other Brown novel is that in which the father of Clara and Theodore unaccountably bursts into flame while making his midnight obeisances in his "temple." This instance of "spontaneous combustion" is also the novel's most sensationally "Calvinist" incident—as far as a narrowly popular view of Calvinism is concerned—redolent of the sensibility behind revival sermons, Wigglesworth's *Day of Doom*, and even calling to the mind of the modern reader a famous scene in Melville's *Redburn*.[25]

In addition to considering a scientific explanation for her father's death, Clara Wieland does speculate that his horrible end might have been "the penalty of disobedience"—punishment, apparently, for his vacillation and failure in missionary life—"the stroke of a vindictive and invisible hand." If so, it is the hand of an Angry God, and the senior Wieland's death is "fresh proof that the Divine Ruler interferes in human affairs, meditates an end, selects and commissions his agents, and enforces by unequivocal sanctions, submission to his will" (19). Once again, though, we must avoid narrow interpretations; while popular Calvinist lore may have influenced the origin of the spontaneous combustion scene, it is as a metaphor informing the book's intellectual themes that the episode is more important. As usual, Brown abstracts the literal particulars of his material and raises them to the level of contemplation.

A light emanates from the temple, followed by an explosion. Clara Wieland's uncle runs to his brother's aid and sees "a blazing light . . . between the columns of the temple."

> Within the columns he beheld what he could no better describe, than by saying it resembled a cloud impregnated with light. It had the brightness of flame, but was without upward motion. It did not occupy the whole area, and rose but a few feet above the floor. No part of the building was on fire.

As soon as the uncle enters the temple, the light vanishes, plunging all into darkness (17). The scene is an early climax in the crescendo of the *Wieland* gloom. Yet, in this visually gloomy novel, the scene is also one of only two instances of bright light. The combustion of father Wieland, and son Theodore's description of the "divine" illumination that inspires him to "sacrifice," luridly punctuate the otherwise visually austere novel's pattern of images.

Brown admits light but grudgingly into most of *Wieland*. When seen, it is fleeting, vanishing upon approach, as the temple's illumination dies the instant Clara's uncle passes between the columns. Most often, images of flitting light are associated with the character in whom Brown distills the essence of deception, the enigmatic Francis Carwin, who insinuates himself into the world of the Wielands with little purpose beyond confounding them with his "biloquistic" talents. Years after his father's death, Theodore, on his way to the temple to fetch a letter he has left there, sees "a glimmering between the columns." Naturally, this recalls to him his father's combustion years earlier, but he continues toward the temple until arrested by what is later revealed as Carwin imitating the voice of Theodore's wife Catharine.

Another instance: one night, while Clara sleeps and dreams—like Edgar Huntly—in the wilderness environs of her home, she hears the biloquist's voice. What she dreams is Theodore beckoning her toward a pit into which she surely would have fallen had not "some one" caught her arm, exclaiming "in a voice of eagerness and terror, 'Hold! Hold!'" At this she wakes—like Huntly, into the very wilderness of her dream—and hears the warning again. This time she recognizes the voice as one she had heard earlier, in the closet of her own bedroom, a voice that had threatened to murder her. It warns her of danger now, tells her to flee. Convinced that her life is in peril, Clara is also aware of the hazards of flight through a woods that is as dangerous and dark as any dream-image of it, a place where one "could not take a step without hazard of falling to the bottom of the precipice." The darkness is unrelieved until, pondering whether to stay or leave,

> I perceived a ray flit across the gloom and disappear. Another succeeded, which was stronger, and remained for a passing moment. It glittered on the shrubs that were scattered at the entrance, and gleam continued to succeed gleam for a few seconds, till they, finally, gave place to unintermitted darkness.

As it had for her brother, such a flitting gleam recalls the horror of her father's death. The girl is paralyzed by fear until she beholds the "new and stronger illumination" of a "lanthorn" carried by Henry Pleyel, the most rational (and pedestrian) figure in Brown's novel (62–4).

And, a final example. Chapter 15 closes with Clara entering the deathly silent parlor of her brother's house, "in which a light was just expiring in the socket" (142). Leaving the apparently deserted house, she walks toward her own, and, at the beginning of Chapter 16, is startled to see a light in her chamber window. "As I eyed it, it suddenly became mutable, and after flitting to and fro, for a short time, it vanished" (145). The next sound she hears is, again, Carwin's piercing "hold! hold!" She gets a glimpse of his face—its eyes emitting sparks—finds a fragment of his writing, and, lastly, discovers the corpse of Catharine Wieland (142–51).

The association of Carwin with these images is not casual. His function in the novel is to counterfeit knowledge; the "illuminations" Carwin furnishes are as evanescent as lights that appear one moment, only to vanish the next. Since images of illumination are common in everyday speech as metaphors for discovery, revelation, and knowledge ("I see the light," for example), it is easy to overlook their apparently casual occurrence throughout *Wieland*. We might not think much about Clara's observation that, although Carwin quickly became an intimate of her tight little family and social circle, he "left us wholly in the dark, concerning that about which we were most inquisitive" (71–2). Nor would we be particularly apt to remark Clara's desire to reflect "some light . . . on the actual situation of" Carwin (127). Common as such figures of speech are, Brown takes pains to make his reader conscious of the link between the physical darkness of his story and the figuratively dark state of human knowledge. One evening, shortly after Carwin's biloquism first manifests itself as Catharine Wieland's warning voice, Clara remarks to her brother: " 'How almost palpable is this dark; yet a ray from above would dispel it.' 'Ay,' said Wieland, with fervor, 'not only the physical, but moral night would be dispelled' " (36).

Would that all humankind enjoyed the privilege of Abraham: a ray from above, a revelation of absolute truth. " 'But why,' " Clara asks Theodore, " 'must the Divine Will address its precepts to the eye?' He smiled significantly. 'True,' said he, 'the understanding has other avenues' " (36). Perhaps, then, we should say that the evanescence of light in *Wieland* figures as something even more than metaphor. For, as this conversation suggests, light is literally the means of "seeing," of acquiring knowledge: the chief means by which "the Divine Will addresses its precepts" to humankind. Locke, as Brown well knew, held that knowledge was the product of the senses. Yet, like Carwin's counterfeited voices of revelation, which address the understanding through another of its sensory "avenues," the light of *Wieland* is deceptive, vanishing as quickly as it appears: "What is man, that knowledge is so sparingly conferred upon him!"

Ironically, the second explosion of light in the otherwise flickering visual scheme of *Wieland*, the "illumination" that bursts only upon the deranged mind of Theodore, is, of all the lights that flicker through the book, by far the steadiest and most certain. All of his life, Wieland tells judge and jury, has been spent "searching for the revelation of [God's] will." Hitherto the search has failed: "I turned on every side where glimmerings of light could be discovered." Although never "wholly uninformed," his "knowledge has always stopped short of certainty." But that night of the murders, entering the dark house of Clara, revelation was total and blindingly brilliant. "I had no light. . . . The darkness required some caution in descending the stair. I stretched my hand to seize the balustrade by which I might regulate my steps. How shall I describe the lustre, which, at that moment, burst upon my vision!" Dazzled, blinded, chilled by a nameless fear, Theodore closes his eyes; but still this "irradiation did not retire or lessen. It seemed as if some powerful effulgence covered me like a mantle."

Opening his eyes, he finds all about him "luminous and glowing. It was the element of heaven that flowed around. Nothing but a fiery stream was at first visible; but, anon, a shrill voice from behind called upon me to attend," and the sacrifice was demanded (165-8). This most intense "illumination," a product of Mania mutabilis, lacks the physical substance of the father's spectacular combustion—or, for that matter, lacks the substance of any of *Wieland's* other and dimmer lights. Its unflickering brilliance fueled exclusively by Theodore's imagination, the truth of its revelation is but the certainty of solipsism.

As the senior Wieland's spontaneous combustion is significant on the level of image and beyond its more specific resemblance to Calvinist pyrotechnics, so the drama of light and dark, of which the combustion is a spectacular part, extends beyond the immediate story of *Wieland*. By linking the two literally brightest moments of his novel to the darkness of error rather than to the illumination of truth, Brown inverts the very metaphor that informed an "Age of Enlightenment."[26]

It was an age for which Joel Barlow spoke in 1787, when he brought before the public his *Vision of Columbus*. Barlow depicted America as the political, moral, and religious utopia for which Christ himself had died. In images of light and flame Barlow welds reason to religious revelation on the free soil of the United States:

In no blest land has fair Religion shone,
And fix'd so firm her everlasting throne.
Where, o'er the realms those spacious temples shine,
Frequent and full the throng'd assemblies join;
There fired with virtue's animating flame,
The sacred task unnumber'd sages claim;
The task, for angels great; in early youth,
To lead whole nations in the walks of truth,
Shed the bright beams of knowledge on the mind,
For social compact harmonize mankind,
To life, to happiness, to joys above,
The soften'd soul with ardent zeal move;
For this the voice of Heaven in early years,
Tuned the glad songs of the life-inspiring seers,
For this consenting seraphs leave the skies,
The God compassionates, the Saviour dies.[27]

In *Wieland*, Barlow's shining religion and shining temples, worshippers fired with virtue's flame, become the fuel for spontaneous combustion; and the voice of heaven becomes that of Francis Carwin, biloquist. Not that Brown necessarily had Barlow in mind when he wrote his dark book, but he knew the poem, praised it in a review, and had been, in his youth, almost certainly influenced by it. But the popular *Vision of Columbus*, like its later reworking as the *Columbiad* (1807), and like

Philip Freneau and Hugh Henry Brackenridge's *Poem, on the Rising Glory of America* (1772), did draw upon conventional images emblematic of a national optimism.[28] We shall, in the next chapter, examine in some detail Brown's relation to Barlow's *Vision* and the vision it embodied. For the present, though, we might observe that the novelist's praise for the poem suggests an impulse to share in its optimism; but, speaking in the voice most his own—the voice of fiction—Brown intoned Barlow's pious images reversed, as it were, in a kind of Black Mass.

Barlow's vision is of a rational America, and his images of illumination reflect the dominance of reason. In *Wieland*, light suggests revelation rather than reason, and, at that, false revelation. Nevertheless, the temple, in which the first spectacular "illumination" takes place, is an architectural *hommage* to an age of reason. As such, it might be seen as a simple moral icon, caging behind its neoclassical columns the flames of enthusiasm. Furthermore, as if to suggest that reason endures while passion burns itself to ash, the temple survives the conflagration to be appropriated by Wieland's children and their friend Henry Pleyel for classical study and harpsichord music, rational amusements that seem better suited than religious worship to the structure's twelve Tuscan columns and undulating dome.

Converted by Theodore and the others of his circle ostensibly to serve the cause of Enlightenment reason, the structure actually continues—even under Pleyel and the Wieland progeny—as a *temple*. It is sacred to Marcus Tullius Cicero, whose bust, commissioned by Theodore from an "Italian adventurer," presides on a pedestal opposite the harpsichord (23–4). For the "chief object of [Theodore's] veneration was Cicero."

> He was never tired of conning and rehearsing his productions. To understand them was not sufficient. He was anxious to discover the gestures and cadences with which they ought to be delivered. He was very scrupulous in selecting a true scheme of pronunciation for the Latin tongue, and in adapting it to the words of his darling writer. His favorite occupation consisted in embellishing his rhetoric with all the properties of gesticulation and utterance.

Theodore worships Cicero almost as his father had worshipped his dark Albigensian God. Theodore collected all the editions and commentaries he could find, employing "months of severe study in exploring and comparing them" in order to settle and restore "the purity of the text" (24).

The rationality suggested by the architecture of the temple notwithstanding, Theodore's veneration is not for Cicero the archapostle of Roman reason, but for Cicero the orator, persuader of men and instigator of their actions. If Theodore's enthusiasm betrays an excess of zeal, it is not without some basis in the conventional critical opinion of Brown's day. The Scots rhetorician Hugh Blair, whose *Lectures on Rhetoric and Belles Lettres* was almost a household book in America, expressed great admiration for

Cicero, pointing out, however, that his chief and almost too artful appeal is to the emotions, and that in purely intellectual argument he is inferior to the Greek Demosthenes.[29]

Theodore's weakness for the Roman orator both foreshadows and reveals his susceptibility to the voices of Carwin. Clara herself attests to Carwin's powers as an orator. When she first saw Carwin he appeared to her rustic, ungainly, malproportioned, unprepossessing, and unremarkable. Then he spoke—asked for a simple cup of water. Clara instantly became obsessed with his image and voice. Theodore's voice and Pleyel's "were musical and energetic," but Carwin's surpassed even theirs. "It was wholly new."

> I cannot pretend to communicate the impression that was made upon me by [Carwin's] accents, or to depict the degree in which force and sweetness were blended in them. They were articulated with a distinctness that was unexampled in my experience. But this was not all. The voice was not only mellifluent and clear, but the emphasis was so just, and the modulation so impassioned, that it seemed as if an heart of stone could not fail of being moved by it. It imparted to me an emotion altogether involuntary and incontroulable [sic]. (52)

In moving "especially the softer passions," Hugh Blair observed, Cicero "is very successful. No man knew the power and force of words better than Cicero." As Carwin's verbal emphasis was always just, so the structure of Cicero's sentences "is curious and exact to the highest degree." Full, flowing, never abrupt, "Ciceronian eloquence"—whether that of Cicero or Carwin—is almost too "dazzling by its beauties," its rhetoric at times "showy rather than solid" (2: 204–6).

One day, while "bandying quotations and syllogisms," Theodore and Pleyel fall to friendly argument over the merits of Cicero's oration for Cluentius. Pleyel, genial contestor of Cicero's divinity, holds that the orator had embraced a bad or doubtful cause, and criticizes the logic of his argument. Although there is nothing in the *Defense of Aulus Cluentius Habitus* that bears directly upon *Wieland*, Brown's citation of this oration is not without significance. Among the more dramatic of Cicero's speeches, its narrative and "plot" are surely the most complex, involving charges and countercharges, and the guilty accusers' baroque obfuscations of the truth. The novelist who would soon prove himself capable of the gnarled second part of *Arthur Mervyn*, and who was already manifesting a fondness for sub-subplot in the relatively direct *Wieland* (follow, for example, the alive-dead-alive-dead fate of Pleyel's shadowy European fiancée, Theresa de Stolberg), was understandably attracted by Cicero's command of a complex narrative. Hugh Blair himself had singled out the *Pro Cluentio* for careful analysis and praised Cicero (though he cited another speech) for his "very remarkable" talent of narration (2: 281–98, 394–6). Clara

Wieland's appraisal of Carwin's early discourses on mysterious voices from invisible sources might well have expressed her brother's (or even Blair's) admiration for the Cicero of the *Pro Cluentio*:

> [Carwin's] narratives were constructed with so much skill, and rehearsed with so much energy, that all the effects of a dramatic exhibition were frequently produced by them. Those that were most coherent and most minute, and, of consequence, least entitled to credit [!?], were yet rendered probable by the exquisite art of this rhetorician. For every difficulty that was suggested, a ready and plausible solution was furnished. (74)

Thus Carwin is curiously identified with Cicero—and (we may reasonably infer) like the Cicero of *Pro Cluentio*, he is also identified with the novelist, whose business it is to furnish plausible solutions for every difficulty suggested.

Brown, who at an early stage of composition bestowed upon Wieland his own first name, also shared something of Theodore's regard for Cicero. While the orator was Theodore's "darling author," Brown's own favorites were Shakespeare and Milton, as well as Cicero, whose Latin Robert Proud had taught the boy, sometime between his tenth and sixteenth years, "to cherish" (Warfel, 9 and 225). Much later the novelist would make Cicero the hero of a forty-eight-page tale incongruously bound in the third slim volume, second edition, of *Edgar Huntly*. "The Death of Cicero, a Fragment" tells the story of the orator's last days as he is pursued by agents of the Triumvirate, which, declaring him an enemy of Rome, have ordered his execution. At first glance the "fragment" appears to be a straightforward celebration of Cicero's stoic valor. The orator, weary of the ignominy of flight, resigns himself to death despite the expostulations of his companion Tiro, who argues that to die at the hands of the Triumvirate is more ignominious. Over Tiro's objections, confronted at last by his enemies, Cicero orders his retainers to put up their swords. One Papilius Laenas, whom Cicero had once defended in court, executes the sentence of the Triumvirate.

Though it picks up the story of Cicero's flight *in medias res*, "The Death of Cicero" is essentially a complete tale; so we might question why Brown chose to call it "A Fragment." Perhaps it was intended as part of a projected fictional treatment of Cicero's life. More likely, Brown was acknowledging the emotionally unsettling and dramatically unsatisfying ambivalence of the piece's denouement, which leaves the tale at loose ends. Tiro, telling the story of Cicero's death in a letter addressed to Atticus, concludes his narration entirely of two minds about the orator's "heroic" resignation. He should have seen escape as his duty, Tiro asserts, only to end by suggesting that perhaps Cicero had been right to choose a dignified death after all. The pattern of ambivalence in "The Death of Cicero" is a familiar one in Brown's writing. Brown would announce to his brother the aim of creating in Arthur Mervyn a model of moral rectitude; the result was a figure as ambiguous as Melville's Pierre. Brown set out to celebrate the heroic moral conviction of his favorite Roman author, only in the end to question the basis of Cicero's heroism. We are left with the unspoken possibility that Cicero's stoicism is akin to the Wieland fanaticism.

It is therefore no surprise that Brown implies an identification of Carwin with Cicero. To be sure, Brown nowhere equates the two, but the identification, pivoting on Theodore Wieland's weakness for rhetoric, suggests that Cicero's powers make him a potential Carwin—and, for that matter, Carwin's powers (had he developed commensurate moral principles) make him a potential Cicero. Further to compound an already complex system of identification, Brown, as a creator of narrative, implicitly associates himself with Carwin/Cicero, and, as a seeker of certitude, with Theodore ("Charles") Wieland. Nothing in Brockden Brown's writings illustrates more strikingly the "double mental existence" the novelist explained to John Bernard. Brown projects himself into *Wieland* as both the deceiver and the deceived. What is more, the "deceiver" in him is the novelist, a Carwin/Cicero, yes, but also the Christoph Martin Wieland/Theodore Wieland seeker of certitude. The novel, for Brown a means of discovering truth, is also a rhetorical exercise in which the novelist, like the Cicero of *Pro Cluentio*—and like Carwin—is obliged merely to furnish a "ready and plausible solution" for every difficulty suggested. Perhaps it was a growing awareness of an irreconcilable tension between "seeker" and "deceiver" that led Brown to abandon fiction, to relinquish "romance" in favor of "history." For history (he explained in his 1800 *Monthly Magazine* article, "The Difference between History and Romance") catalogs surfaces only, while romance is always speculative.[30] And in speculation Brown always found space for the disturbing doubleness of his mental existence.

In *Wieland* he was unwilling to relinquish either half of the doubleness, though both must have distressed him. He passes no absolute judgment against Carwin, except obliquely in the epigraph to the novel:

> From Virtue's blissful paths away
> The double-tongued are sure to stray;
> Good is a forth-right journey still,
> And mazy paths but lead to ill.

But even this apparently "forth-right" condemnation of doubleness and duplicity has its twists. Those "mazy paths" recall the "pleasant paths" in the "metaphysic wilderness" of "Devotion: An Epistle." While the young poet of 1794 had recognized a duty to "beat with indefatigable heels, / Th' highway" of reason, the mazy paths of darker speculation simultaneously attracted and disturbed him.

There are some more obvious means by which Brockden Brown seeks to extenuate the guilt of Carwin. The biloquist is himself pictured as a victim. The fragmentary "Memoirs of Carwin the Biloquist," begun immediately after the completion of *Wieland*,[31] detail the protagonist's naïve association with the sinister and powerful Ludloe. Carwin is pictured also as the victim of an ignorant and brutal father. Finally, Brown leaves the extent of Carwin's involvement in the Wieland murders so much in doubt that the subject has become a matter of critical controversy.[32]

The potential Carwin in Cicero, the classical orator whose greatest appeal is ultimately to the passions, recalls the flames at the heart of the temple. It is not enough merely to oppose enthusiasm with reason: the always speculative, ever ambivalent Brown shows himself wary of an enthusiasm to be found at the heart of reason itself. It is likely, as Larzer Ziff argues, that Brown is critical of the early Republic's facile rationality, but not only because it was impotent to deal with an irrational element at the core of human nature. The young Republic of the United States was, to use Howard Mumford Jones's phrase, founded on "Roman virtue," which permeates architecture no less than government.[33] Cicero, the embodiment of Roman virtue, emerges ambiguously, as Brown depicts him, both through his identification with Carwin and through his actions in "The Death of Cicero" fragment. Like Hawthorne after him, Brown was critical of those who serve a principle of "reason" reared irrationally as a homemade god. Both male Wielands, like Roger Chillingworth, or Rappaccini, or Aylmer, or Ethan Brand, serve gods they themselves have created and to whom they sacrifice their love and heart's desire, relinquishing at last nature itself.

Brown's uneasy examination of the classical background behind his nation's culture does not stop with his ambivalent criticism of Cicero. "My brother's skill," Clara observes, "in Greek and Roman learning was exceeded by that of few." Where he had earlier concerned himself with the textual problems of Cicero's works, after the first two manifestations of Carwin's voice Theodore begins "collecting and investigating the facts which relate to that mysterious personage, the Daemon of Socrates" (48).

Socrates, as Plato represents him to us, refers to his Daemon a number of times, describing it most succinctly in the "Apology":

> You have often heard me speak of an oracle or sign which comes to me, and is the divinity which Meletus ridicules in his indictment. This sign I have had ever since I was a child. The sign is a voice which comes to me and always forbids me to do something which I am going to do, but never commands me to do anything.[34]

Little wonder that Theodore had taken sudden interest in the subject. When Carwin's mysterious voice made its debut it was to warn Wieland, who was walking to the temple, to stop: "There is danger in your path" (33). The second manifestation of the voice, heard by Wieland and Pleyel, interrupted their debate about the merits of Pleyel's plan to visit his betrothed in Europe. Pleyel, endeavoring to convince Wieland to accompany him abroad, was just suggesting that Catharine, as a good wife, would abide by Theodore's decision, when "a negative was clearly and distinctly uttered from another quarter" before Wieland could answer. This voice goes on to "warn" against making a useless journey: for Pleyel's fiancée (it says) is dead (44).

The resemblance to the Daemon of Socrates, which warns rather than commands, is unmistakable. As Edgar Huntly reacts to the horrifying newness of the pit by making of it a horrible but more familiar dungeon, or as Theodore's father recoiled from the wilderness by building the Palladian temple, so Wieland launches upon a study of a classical parallel for the mysterious voice, as if to bring it within the range of what is not only familiar, but venerable. The Daemon of Socrates, one modern writer reports, has been the subject of numerous commentaries and has given rise to any number of interpretations, both ancient and modern.

> Apuleis treated it as a private god. The Fathers of the Church were completely divided about it. Some, like Tertullian, St. Cyprian and Lactantius held it came from Satan; others, like Justin Martyr, Clement of Alexandria, Eusebius and St. Augustine thought of it as some kind of angel. Today certain people think it may have been a type of hallucination that occurs in epilepsy. Still others have seen nothing more in it than Socrates recognizing the voice of conscience.[35]

Brown's linking Carwin with the Daemon, a figure subject to ambiguous interpretation, reflects the complexity of the novelist's own identification with the biloquist. Indeed, in at least one way, Carwin seems to be associated with the clearly benevolent voice of warning. Seven of the nine confirmed instances of biloquism in the novel are warnings: to Theodore, not to approach the temple (32ff.); to Theodore and Pleyel, not to go to Europe (41ff.); again to Theodore and Pleyel, to aid Clara, who had fainted after hearing "murderers" in her closet (59); to Clara, preventing her dream-fall into a dream-pit, and warning her to avoid a certain secluded wilderness nook (63ff.); and again to Clara, forestalling her discovery of Carwin behind her closet door (85). Lastly, Carwin saves Clara from death by uttering his favorite monosyllabic injunction—"Hold! Hold!"—as her brother is about to execute upon her, as he had upon wife, children, and ward, the sentence of God (299).

But neither does Brown let us see Carwin as a genius of pure benevolence. The first two instances of biloquism proceed not so much from malice, as from Carwin's perverse and diabolically unconscious curiosity. The third is the product of this same curiosity, Carwin having created the closet dialogue between two "murderers" (he says) simply to test Clara's courage. When Clara panics, running out of her house, collapsing in a dead faint at her brother's threshold, Carwin, alarmed himself at the effect of little more than a deadpan practical joke, cries: "Awake! arise! hasten to succour one that is dying at your door!'' (59). A more deliberate motive is behind Carwin's wilderness warning to Clara: he wishes to secure the privacy of an amorous retreat—he is intimately occupied with Judith, Clara's chambermaid. Also self-serving is his warning Clara not to open her closet door; he is inside, reading a personal memoir left Clara by her father.

The motive for his final biloquistic performance would seem the least suspect. That he exhibits enough presence of mind to exercise his powers to prevent Clara's murder redeems Carwin from, at least, absolute villainy. Yet this instance of Carwin's benevolence is supremely ironic, since it was necessitated by his previous mischief. Even if Carwin is not directly guilty of the Wieland atrocities, his biloquistic stunts in large measure set the stage for Theodore's madness. Carwin's last injunction—his final "Hold! Hold!''—merely denies madness its consummation. To compound the irony, in a gesture typical of Brown's "do-gooders,'' Carwin is not content to stop with the utterance of his "favorite monosyllable,'' but continues, addressing Theodore: "Man of errors! cease to cherish thy delusion: not heaven or hell, but thy senses have misled thee to commit these acts. Shake off thy phrenzy, and ascend into rational and human. Be lunatic no longer'' (230). Where the "delusion,'' called the "delicious idea'' by Erasmus Darwin in *Zoönomia*, "produces pleasurable sensations, as in personal vanity or religious enthusiasm[,] it is almost a pity to snatch [the maniac] from [his] fool's paradise, and reduce [him] again to the common lot of humanity.''[36] So reduced, "transformed at once in the *man of sorrows*'' by Carwin's final "benevolence,'' Theodore plunges Clara's penknife into his own neck (230–1).

Isaiah prophesied that, despised and rejected, the Messiah would be "a man of sorrows'' (53:3). This is the ironic measure of divinity Brown at last allows Wieland: identification with Christ as the man of sorrows, but incarnated in the "Man of errors.'' And though we would despise and reject that man, he, surely, bears "our griefs and carrie[s] our sorrows'' (Isaiah, 53:3–4); for, as Christ was sent among us as our sorrowful advocate, so Wieland, the man of errors, is even more our representative. Charles Chauncy defined enthusiasm as a "disease'' endemic perhaps to all men. "Consciousness itself,'' Sarsefield declares in *Edgar Huntly*, "is the malady.'' And so Clara's lament—"What is man, that knowledge is so sparingly conferred upon him!''—sadly inverts the Paul of Hebrews 2:6–7. "What is man,'' the Apostle rejoices, "that thou art mindful of him?'' Man—"a little lower than the angels'' and crowned with glory and honor!

Carwin is not evil, but the moral basis for his motives is in no way commensurate with his powers. His talents enable him to approach Cicero in forensic skill and the Daemon of Socrates in authority, but Carwin lacks the moral principles by which he might regulate his powers. The association of Carwin with Cicero and the Daemon ameliorates his character at the same time as it underscores its weaknesses, answering to the needs of Brown's ambivalent identification with the biloquist. The association seems also a response to the broader ambivalence of Brown's relation to some of his nation's adopted cultural values. Not only does the identification of Carwin with Cicero and the Daemon fail to vindicate Carwin unequivocally, it also fails to elevate the classical figures by contrast. Their association with the biloquist diminishes their status as cultural models.

In modern English the distinction between *daemon* and *demon* is not always clear. Defining *demon*, the *Oxford English Dictionary* shows how *daemon*, for Socrates a "*divinum quiddam* . . . a certain divine principle or agency, an inward monitor or oracle," evolved pejoratively through the interpretations of Socrates' accusers and the Christian Fathers into what we understand by the modern English word *demon*. The blurred distinction between *daemon* and *demon* suggests the ambivalence with which the idea of any inspirational voice or spirit has traditionally been regarded. In the case of *Wieland*, Brown frequently associates Carwin with demons in the sense of the word given by Samuel Johnson in his *Dictionary*, as a "spirit; generally an evil spirit; a devil."

But, curiously, whereas Johnson spells the word *demon*, Brown persists in *daemon*, as if to preserve through orthography the idea of a *divinum quiddam* even as he calls Carwin a devil. Pleyel, Clara, Theodore, and even the elusive Ludloe identify the biloquist as—to use Brown's spelling—a *daemon*. Ludloe (who has tenaciously as any "demon" fastened himself upon Carwin) says that the biloquist is "in league with some infernal spirit" (130). The reasonable Pleyel sees the "daemons" with whom Carwin is leagued as nothing more substantial than metaphors of man's darker side. "As to an alliance with evil geniuses," he explains to Clara, "the power and the malice of daemons have been a thousand times exemplified in human beings. There are no devils but those which are begotten upon selfishness, and reared by cunning" (132). But Clara, despite her rational education, entertains more literal notions of Carwin's daemons: "Where is the proof, said I, that daemons may not be subjected to the controul of men?" (180). Brought before the bar of justice, Theodore denies that he acted under the "influence of daemons" (176), meaning, presumably, evil spirits or devils.

Yet it is Theodore who finally and positively defines Carwin as a "daemon," not a "demon," but something of a *divinum quiddam*. Theodore had made good a third escape from his dungeon for the purpose of "sacrificing" Clara. But Carwin's stammering and ambiguous confession forestalls him. Enraged beyond revenge after Carwin's "incoherent confessions," Wieland contemptuously orders the biloquist from the room. Apparently disabused of his errors now, Theodore is about to spare Clara—but, suddenly: "A new soul appeared to actuate his frame, and his eyes to beam with preternatural lustre."

> Clara! [he exclaims] I must not leave thee in doubt. I know not what brought about thy interview with the being whom thou callest Carwin. For a time, I was guilty of thy error, and deduced

from his incoherent confessions that I had been made the victim
of human malice. He left us at my bidding [actually, Wieland had
threatened him], and I put up a prayer that my doubts should be
removed. Thy eyes were shut, and thy ears sealed to the vision that
answered my prayer.

I was indeed deceived. The form thou hast seen was the incarnation of a daemon. The visage and voice which urged me to the
sacrifice of my family, were his. Now he personates a human
form: then he was invironed with the lustre of heaven.

"Clara," Wieland concludes, "thy death must come" (225).

Theodore claims to have seen and heard a "daemon" when he
murdered his family, not a devil or an evil spirit, but a being "invironed
with the lustre of heaven." Now the hapless Wieland recognizes Carwin as
the "incarnation" of that "daemon," personating "a human form"; for
Carwin's "visage and voice" (Wieland says) urged the sacrifice of his family. In this, his penultimate moment upon earth, Theodore comes to regard
Carwin much as Socrates had regarded his own Daemon. Of course, Brown
does not mean to call Socrates and the classical tradition of rational inquiry
evil; but the novelist's spirit could not rest in a Socratic symposium anymore than it could in a Ciceronian temple. Some imp of the perverse seems
always to knock down whatever figure Brown's imagination suggests, no
matter how exemplary. Abraham, Cicero, Socrates—in *Wieland* all wob-
ble on their pedestals.

The philosopher whose rational method triumphed over the mysticism
of Anaximides, Parmenides, Heraclitus, and Empedocles, also allowed for
the influence of the irrational. One modern student of Socrates finds the
source of the philosopher's originality in the remarkable union of "a
critical mind, a gift for analysis, a taste for free investigation and doubt,
and a wonderful practical sense, with a sincere religious faith, deep burning enthusiasm and a tendency to ecstacy, or at least toward the possibility
of it."[37] For Brown such a happy synthesis was not possible. Carwin, as
Brown's version of the Socratic Daemon, does indeed have an affinity for
the rational mind—but as a cat for the mouse. Carwin's stunts can operate
successfully only upon the rational individual who has quite reasonably
come to depend upon the truth of what his senses tell him.

Conceived in the American halcyon of John Locke's epistemology,
Brown's Carwin must have appeared as an extraordinarily dangerous
figure. Though the biloquist deals in illusion, the voices are real enough in
their appeal to the senses; and in an epistemology where ideas are ultimately the products of sensation, Carwin is able to create and interpose his
private universe of mysterious voices between mind and nature itself.
Pleyel, the reasonable Lockean, is merely duped by Carwin's counterfeit of
Clara's seduction. Although the result is upsetting, even emotionally painful, for both Clara and Pleyel, it is hardly tragic. But when Carwin works
his tricks upon an individual in whom both the rationalist and the

enthusiast contend, then the biloquist finds he has "rashly set in motion a machine, over whose progress I had no controul, and which experience [shows as] infinite in power" (215–6). The tragedy, however, does not proceed from any grand malice. Why, for example, did Carwin counterfeit a terrifying dialogue between "two" murderers in Clara's closet? Because "some daemon of mischief seized me" (201).

As a youth, doubtless prompted by the same "daemon," Carwin delighted in making people think his spaniel talked. The dog "asserted the dignity of his species and capacity of intellectual improvement. The company [that had gathered in amazement to hear the animal] separated lost in wonder, but perfectly convinced by the evidence that had been produced" ("Memoirs of Carwin the Biloquist," 260). This harmlessly impish parlor trick is actually of a piece both with the "murderous dialogue" counterfeited for Clara and with a divine command to murder that Carwin may have counterfeited for Wieland. Ludloe, the youthful biloquist's mysterious mentor, explains how men

> believed in the existence and energy of invisible powers, and in the duty of discovering and conforming to their will. This will was supposed to be sometimes made known to them through the medium of their senses. A voice coming from a quarter where no attendant form could be seen would, in most cases, be ascribed to supernal agency, and a command imposed on them, in this manner, would be obeyed with religious scrupulousness. Thus men might be imperiously directed in the disposal of their industry, their property, and even of their lives. Men, actuated by a mistaken sense of duty, might, under his influence, be led to the commission of the most flagitious, as well as the most heroic acts. ("Carwin," 263–4)

The spaniel's name was "Daemon."

Ludloe, a hyperambitious member of the Illuminati, insinuates a motive for the exercise of talents such as Carwin's: "If it were [a man's] desire to accumulate wealth, or institute a new sect, he should need no other instrument" (264). Such motives are not always admirable, but they are reasonable, and are therefore by no means Carwin's. Spurred only by a "daemon of mischief," Carwin's *primum mobile* is, in fact, a *mobile* without motive, to use Edgar Allan Poe's definition of his own version of the daemon of mischief, "a motive not *motivirt*":

> Through its promptings we act without comprehensible object; or, if this shall be understood as a contradiction in terms, we may so far modify the proposition to say, that through its promptings we act, for the reason that we should *not*. In theory, no reason can

be more unreasonable; but, in fact, there is none more strong. With certain minds, under certain conditions, it becomes absolutely irresistable.

Poe called this the "Imp of the Perverse." "Beyond or behind this, there is no intelligible principle" (Poe, 6:150).

"It is a radical, a primitive impulse," Poe's narrator says of the Perverse, "—elementary" (6:147). Certainly, Carwin obsessed Brown's imagination as thoroughly as Wieland, but while Theodore's motives are as clear as Abraham's, Carwin's are so elementary as to defy analysis. Just the same, Brown, having divided his identity between Wieland and Carwin, was at pains to explain the biloquist. His name had figured in the list of titles Brown included with his outline of *Wieland*, clearly legible though canceled by a stroke of the pen (a subtitle following it is more thoroughly obliterated and illegible: *possibly* it reads "the road of crime"). Hard upon the completion of *Wieland*, the novelist began "The Memoirs of Carwin the Biloquist," breaking it off after he had written enough to fill some sixty printed pages.

Both before and after the composition of the novel, then, Carwin had enjoyed a shaky existence independent of *Wieland*. This is as it should have been, for Carwin's fictional origin is significantly different from that of the Wieland children. Clara and Theodore were first-generation Americans, highly conscious of their European ancestry and steeped in the neoclassical culture of eighteenth-century Europe. Carwin is more truly a native American. Unlike the Wielands, whose rural home in southeastern Pennsylvania lay but a few miles from what was America's most cosmopolitan metropolis, Carwin was raised on a farm in a "western district of Pennsylvania." His father was a hostile stranger to knowledge outside the farm, his ideas never ranging "beyond the sphere of his vision," and young Carwin's insatiable—even Faustian—"thirst of knowledge" was met by the stern farmer with scorn and "stripes" (247).

One evening, in his fourteenth year, the boy was sent to bring his father's cows in from a distant meadow. He had been "menaced with severe chastisement" if, as was the youth's inquisitive custom, he lingered beyond a strict time limit. He reached the meadow only to discover that the cows had broken the fence and run off. "It was my first duty to carry home the earliest tidings of this accident, but the first suggestion [of an unappeasable curiosity] was to examine the cause and manner of this escape." Soon absorbed in speculative reverie, young Carwin grows heedless of the passing time until "some accident" calls to mind the painful consequences of delay. He resolves not to return home by the "beaten path," but by a wilderness shortcut that would take him through a landscape anticipating *Edgar Huntly*, a "sublime" scene of precipitous cliffs and swirling water. Presently "entangled in a maze" of "abrupt points" and "gloomy hollows"—thoroughly "bewildered," as Edgar Huntly was to say of himself—Carwin discovers a glen through which passage would be shorter and safer than the path he had first proposed to follow. But even this is steep and narrow, so overshadowed by a great cliff that all is plunged into midnight, though the sun has just set. Fearful of "goblins and spectres," Carwin tries to distract himself "by hallowing as loud as organs of unusual compass and vigour would enable me." He calls to the errant cows "in the shrill tones of a Mohock savage"—perhaps he had heard such cries in western Pennsylvania—and the rocks of the wilderness landscape reverberate, though their echo is at first indistinct.

But at one particularly treacherous turn, after a short pause, he calls out again. "In a few seconds a voice, as I then imagined, uttered the same cry from the point of a rock some hundred feet behind me." Carwin casts "a fearful glance behind . . . The speaker, however, was concealed from my view." Again giving voice to the "Mohock" cry, the boy is treated to a "new occasion for wonder." His "ditty" is repeated, a perfect imitation, after a few seconds, but from "a different corner"—the imitator, as before, invisible.

When the quick-witted boy realizes that he has discovered "an echo of an extraordinary kind" he is delighted and, forgetting the prospect of his father's punishment, amuses himself for an hour in talking to the cliffs. He returns frequently to what he now calls his "vocal glen" until he hits upon the idea of producing the echo without aid of the cliffs. "From speculation I proceeded to experiment." And in the wilderness of America, Carwin's biloquism—a talent (he admits) "too liable to perversion for a good man to desire to possess"—is in the most literal sense born (248–53).

Like Edgar Huntly, then, Carwin discovers in the wilderness a hitherto unknown elementary—radical and primitive—aspect of himself. The conditions of the wilderness, of the New World, provoke such discoveries, and the story of *Wieland*, however fleshed out by German, Roman, Greek, and biblical sources, is, as John Neal said of Brown himself, American to the backbone.

Born in and of the wilderness, Carwin's biloquism is the child of confusion's own landscape. As usual, the landscape of the novel is abstract; but if Brown intellectualized the details of the scene into mere emblems, he could not dismiss the intellectual and emotional fact embodied in those emblems. Clara repeatedly presents her situation through metaphors drawn from the landscape. At the beginning of her narrative she pictures herself placed upon a "dreadful eminence" (6) by a train of events unparalleled in the experience of any other human being. Later she sees herself set upon the "brink of danger" (189) and upon the "brink of fate" (22). The revelation of her brother's atrocity threatens to push Clara to the "brink of the same abyss" into which Theodore has already fallen (180). Pleyel, fearful and jealous of what he takes to be her clandestine affair with Carwin, tells Clara how he felt compelled to interfere: "Should I see you rushing to the verge of a dizzy precipice, and not stretch forth a hand to pull you back?" (129). But it is just such a verge that invites Clara as she is about to write of her brother's suicide. Why recall such a horrible scene? Why even continue to live? "Why not terminate at once this series of horrors?—hurry to the verge of the precipice, and cast myself for ever beyond remembrance and beyond hope?" (228). Despite a paucity of picturesque landscape, the wilderness, of which Carwin is product and personification, permeates *Wieland*.

Such figures of speech as those in *Wieland* would be melodramatically banal in the civil scenes of Europe's great cities. Uttered in the American wilderness, they take on crucial significance as evidence of an interpenetration of mind and landscape, an absorption in the spirit of the place. The wilderness was for Brown the territory of the mind's most obscure recesses. Huntly sleepwalks and dreams there, fully awakening into what seems yet another dream. Clara falls asleep in a remote wilderness spot only to dream of the wilderness, a dream within a seeming dream. Given the almost casual equation Brown formulated between mind and landscape, it is not surprising that, along with images of light and dark, the wilderness provides a source of figures through which Brown defines his novel's moral and epistemological themes.

The very epigraph resolves the moral content of *Wieland* into the opposing figures of "Virtue's blissful paths" and the "mazy paths" of deceit. This figure is repeated throughout the novel, from its opening page—where Clara disdains "supplication to the Deity," declaring that the "power that governs the course of human affairs has chosen his path"—through a description of the "austerer and more arduous path" of study Wieland pursued (23). It is continued through Carwin's assurance to Clara that she is under the protection of a divine power so that her "path will be without pits to swallow, or snares to entangle" her (92); and through Pleyel's assertion that Carwin has chosen to conduct his life along an "obscure path" (126). Numerous additional examples might be cited, and frequently these figures of speech are counterpointed to the occasional glimpses Brown affords of the actual paths, narrow and obscure, that run through a sketchily rendered Pennsylvania wilderness. On several occasions the figurative and the physical are not merely counterpointed, but actually dissolve into one another. "There is danger in your path," Carwin warns Theodore, who is at that moment walking the literal, physical path to the temple (33, 46). Although Theodore does turn from the temple and walk back down the path, he of course continues along a metaphorical path to the catastrophe that his father's temple represents.

Long "has been the march," young Brown wrote in his 1794 "Devotion: An Epistle," "And weary, through the thorny tracts that lead / To nothing in the metaphysic wilderness." This might well serve to describe the intellectual journey the novelist took in *Wieland* four years after writing the poem. In a sense, *Wieland*, a book of the metaphysic wilderness, does lead to "nothing"—at least to the frustration of knowledge and revelation. Like the story of Abraham and Isaac, *Wieland* is an epistemological fable; but the biblical episode affirms man's capacity for attaining absolute truth, whereas Brown's novel denies the human capacity for attaining any truth absolutely. In *Edgar Huntly* the wilderness functions both as metaphor and as place, while in *Wieland*—as in Poe's "The Pit and the Pendulum"—the wilderness is realized almost exclusively as metaphor. Because the physical facts of *Edgar Huntly's* wilderness force the sleepwalker to call upon "natural" instincts beyond (or beneath) his civilized reason, Huntly finds within himself an untapped reserve of strength and cunning. Although the wilderness defines the limit of knowledge born in the lightsome chamber of civilized existence, it also reveals a truth outside that chamber. In *Wieland*, however, the wilderness is not present as a *place* of revelation, but only as a *metaphor* of limitation. Essentially, the novel's characters remain lost along figurative paths, tottering on the emotional verge of this or that intellectual abyss.

The discovery of limits, of the "nothing" at the end of thorny tracts, is itself a crucial truth, though. The abrupt and anticlimactic ending of *Wieland*—in which Pleyel, time, and Europe have quite healed Clara's emotional wounds—precludes any divine revelation of the sort Theodore craved. Ironic revelation there is, however, couched in figures of paths, abysses, precipices, darkness, and light. It is the novel's unremitting and unresolved ambiguity, a paradoxical revelation of the absolute limit of revelation.

One of the topics we shall take up in the next chapter is Brown's failure to realize his youthful plan of writing an epic on Christopher Columbus. We may anticipate that discussion here by observing that, in one important sense, Brown did not completely fail. In his four major novels he continued the Navigator's exploration of America, not as a geographical entity, but as a phenomenon of mind. By adding a New World to the geographical and intellectual cosmogony of Europe, Columbus forced the Old World to define its limits. J. H. Elliott, in *The Old World and the New*, quotes Etienne Pasquier, a Parisian lawyer of the early 1560s:

> "It is a striking fact that our classical authors had no knowledge of all this America, which we call New Lands." With these words [Pasquier] caught something of the importance of America for the Europe of his day. Here was a totally new phenomenon, quite outside the range of Europe's accumulated experience and of its normal expectation.[38]

The writings of Columbus himself reveal both the newness of the "New Lands" and the inadequacy of Europe's limited experience fully to comprehend it. Howard Mumford Jones criticizes the letter Columbus wrote to describe the New World as "vague," nonspecific, with little "beyond the repetition of a few simple formulas" common to conventional Renaissance evocations of nature. Later writers and compilers of voyages, particularly Peter Martyr in the early sixteenth century, "translated reports of Columbus, Vespucci, and others" even more deliberately into Renaissance terms, drawing desperately upon classical authors for inadequate formulaic imagery. To be sure, the United States of Brown's century was not Columbus's Europe. But the wilderness, upon whose frontier Brown and his countrymen lived, was yet New Land, and Brown, like Columbus three hundred years before him, struggled to comprehend it, to encompass it within the narrow bounds of his experience. Howard Mumford Jones said, "The nightingale, by the by, which does not exist in the New World, haunted Columbus: twice on his outward voyage, when the weather was especially fine, he noted in his journal that nothing was wanting for perfection but the song of the nightingale."[39]

Nor do European dungeons exist in America, until Edgar Huntly projects one into the Pennsylvania landscape. Or if the wilderness lacks the temples of ancient Rome, men like Thomas Jefferson and the senior Wieland readily supply Palladian equivalents. As late as 1835 Washington Irving would suggest that the American prairies "only want here and there a village spire, the battlements of a castle, or the turrets of an old family mansion"—as foreign to the New World as a nightingale—"rising from among the trees, to rival the most ornamented scenery of Europe."[40] Brown, like Columbus and like Irving, participates in Europe's dialogue with America, the dialogue that is (according to J. H. Elliott) the history of the Old World and the New. On the one hand, there is "the attempt of Europe to impose its own image, its own aspirations, and its own values on a newly discovered world"; but on the other hand, "a growing awareness of the character, the opportunities and the challenges represented by the New World of America helped to shape and transform an Old World which was itself striving to shape and transform the New" (Elliott, 7).

In the case of a writer like Thoreau, who tells us that the "frontier" exists wherever a man "fronts" a "fact," we can be certain of a conscious awareness of America as an epistemological metaphor. It would be asking too much to expect that degree of self-consciousness from Brown. Although it is difficult to believe him unaware of his own obsession with epistemological themes, it is just as difficult to believe that Brown was fully cognizant of the role America played in working them out. The epistemological metaphors of *Wieland* seem more the inevitable emanations of the spirit of the American place than the carefully wrought products of conscious design. Just the same, at least one of Brown's fellow Americans exhibited an acute awareness of his country as a phenomenon crucial in the world's intellectual cosmogony. Jeremy Belknap, biographer, historian, and novelist, was also a minister. Called upon by the Massachusetts Historical Society in 1792 to deliver a commemorative discourse upon Columbus's discovery of America, Belknap began with a text from Scriptures: "Many shall run to and fro and knowledge shall be increased" (Daniel 12:4).

For, Belknap said, Columbus's voyages "opened to the Europeans a new world; which gave a new turn to their thoughts." The Navigator's heroism consisted in his fulfillment of Daniel's prophecy. Columbus was a divinely inspired but thoroughly empirical scientist: "not a closet projector, but an enterprising adventurer [who,] having established his theory on principles . . . was determined to exert himself to the utmost to demonstrate its truth by experiment." America was the place of empirical truth; Europe, the closed land of abstract dogmatic belief. "Ignorance and error were canonized" by Europeans, such as St. Augustine, who "doubted the diurnal motion of the earth, or the existence of antipodes." The philosophers of the Old World judged—prejudged—the "torrid and frigid zones" uninhabitable: "It is now known by experience, that the human constitution is capable, by proper management, of enduring all the vicissitudes of heat and cold, of moisture and dryness, to which any accessible part of the earth is subject; and that its health may be preserved in all climates and situations."[41] With dead aim, a battered and exhausted Edgar Huntly hurled an Indian tomahawk between the eyes of a panther. Huntly observed: "No one knows the powers that are latent in his constitution"—until they are discovered "by experience."

How commonplace Belknap's notions of America and Columbus were is impossible to determine exactly. Certainly, American audiences were capable of enjoying the likes of the British playwright Thomas Morton's *Columbus*, little more than the thinnest of excuses to find an exotic setting for the thinnest of love stories, and without the slightest intellectual pretensions.[42] But Belknap's more thoughtful interpretation did circulate well beyond the Massachusetts Historical Society when, two years after the commemorative address was delivered, he included an altered version of the piece in his encyclopedic *American Biography*, a work reviewed in Brown's *Monthly Magazine*.[43] A more significant indication of the currency of Belknap's views is their affinity with Joel Barlow's genial and popular vision of America. At bottom, Barlow's utopian vision rests upon the New World's epistemological status. Both Belknap and Barlow argue that the American "experiment," in revealing a new world of God's creation, brought man to a greater knowledge of God himself, so that America serves the Old World as, in effect, the book of the Lord. The ramifications of this revelation are, of course, not only intellectual but social and political.[44]

For Barlow, America was the land of light; but through the dark pages of *Wieland* light is a fugitive thing. The brightest and steadiest, which bursts only upon the mind of Theodore, is the least real. As the novel perverts the idea of Abrahamic revelation, so it inverts the values represented in Barlow's metaphors of enlightenment. The enduring revelation of the New World is not of light, but of darkness, the limit of knowledge. Joel Barlow summons up Hesper, the genius of the Western world, to guide Columbus through his vision. Brown substitutes a flesh-and-blood native of western Pennsylvania. Carwin's double tongue proclaims the relativity of man's knowledge, even as the discovery of a New World some three hundred years before Brown wrote *Wieland* revealed the relative nature of truths long held sacred by the Old. At the end of *Wieland*,

Brown's "genius" returns to his place of origin, retiring to a farmer's life in the wilderness of western Pennsylvania in order to elude Ludloe.

Clara Wieland, however, abandons America for Europe. We leave her in the penultimate chapter longing for death; her entire family, after all, has died, and died horribly. But, summarily, in the final chapter—"written three years after the foregoing and dated at Montpellier"—she flatly declares: "Such is man. Time will obliterate the deepest impressions" (234). Clara confesses that, three years earlier, with the catastrophe fresh in her mind, she was "enamoured of death." Indeed, she fully expected to die, "yet here am I, a thousand leagues from my native soil, in full possession of life and of health, and not destitute of happiness" (234). What is more, she has married that avatar of neoclassical enlightenment, Henry Pleyel! A conventional comic token of the restoration of cosmic order, the marriage ends the tragedy on a note of comedy.[45]

Clara's removal to Europe is not merely a "happy ending" thrown as a sop to a smiling American public. It is a purgation, and more for Brockden Brown than Clara Wieland. After she finished her narrative of the Wieland family tragedy Clara betook herself to bed, "in the full belief that my career in this world was on the point of finishing." She apparently languished for several days until, one night, "after some hours of restlessness and pain, I sunk into deep sleep." She dreamed:

> My fancy became suddenly distempered, and my brain was turned into a theatre of uproar and confusion. It would not be easy to describe the wild and phantastical incongruities that pestered me. My uncle, Wieland, Pleyel and Carwin were successively and momently discerned amidst the storm. Sometimes I was swallowed up by whirlpools, or caught up in the air by half-seen and gigantic forms, and thrown upon pointed rocks, or cast among the billows. Sometimes gleams of light were shot into a dark abyss, on the verge of which I was standing, and enabled me to discover, for a moment, its enormous depth and hideous precipices. Anon, I was transported to some ridge of Aetna, and made a terrified spectator of its fiery torrents and its pillars of smoke. (236)

At first this seems another of Brown's wilderness dreams, replete with images of abyss, verge, and precipice. There is even the dissolution of the boundary between dream and waking reality that is also a feature of Huntly's wilderness experience and Clara's earlier dream in the woods: "I was conscious," Clara reports, "even during my dream of my real situation" (236). However, here the wilderness images have undergone a subtle but crucial transformation. There are not only abysses and precipices in this dream, but the whirlpool, rocks, and billows of an ocean and, more significantly, a smoke-belching Mount Aetna. The wilderness has become European, a Dantesque landscape with the addition of classical overtones in Aetna and its *pillars* of smoke. Just as Edgar Huntly preferred the more familiar horror of a European dungeon to the entirely new terror of an American wilderness, so Clara's dreaming mind molds the images of the American wilderness into European, even classical, shape. The horror is vivid; but it has been fashioned into a form familiar to the experience of the Old World.

The dream that purges Clara's mind, and Brown's book, of New World images is a dream of combustion. And for good reason: due to a servant's carelessness in disposing of some live embers, Clara's bedroom is actually aflame as she dreams, and she narrowly escapes a fate that recalls her father's. But escape she does, and more: "This incident, disastrous as it may first seem, had, in reality, a beneficial effect on my feelings. I was, in some degree, roused from the stupor which had seized my faculties. The monotonous and gloomy series of my thoughts was broken." Not only does the fire cauterize Clara's emotional wounds, it sends her packing off to Europe: "My habitation was levelled with the ground, and I was obliged to seek a new one" (237). The "new" habitation, however, is "the shore of the ancient world," where, although the memory of catastrophe does not leave her, "the melancholy which it generated, and the tears with which it filled my eyes, were not unprofitable." This catharsis, an *affective* forgetfulness, is due largely to the influence of the European "spectacle of living manners and the monuments of past ages" which Clara contemplates "with ardour." The "ancient world" reinstates in Clara's heart "its ancient tranquillity" (237).

The empiricism of John Locke took especial root in America most likely because the demands of New World experience were themselves so eminently empirical. The further revelation of *Wieland*, itself rooted in the Lockean soil of America, is the inadequacy of human perception and understanding to interpret the reality the New World so immediately represents. Clara's removal to an ancient world of ancient tranquillity was doubtless an emotional and intellectual necessity for Brown. Reversing the utopian stereotype, he pictures a Europe in which forgetfulness approaches innocence, and an America made guilty by its discovery of the frontier of knowledge itself. The novelist allowed his unconscious and speculative "literary" self full expression in *Wieland*, pushing his characters through a territory of paradoxical revelation. But Charles Brockden Brown could not live wholly in the revealed gloom of this American "literary mood." Having used her to probe the New World's primeval darkness, he returns Clara to the civilized sunshine of Europe. Her name, after all, means "light."

IV

Great Plans: A Foreword to *Ormond* and *Arthur Mervyn*

Joel Barlow's *Vision of Columbus*, an epic poem in nine books, which numbered among its cast of characters Cortez and Pizarro in addition to the hero of its title, appeared in 1787. That same year the sixteen-year-old Charles Brockden Brown concluded his studies with Robert Proud at the Latin School prior to embarking upon a reluctant legal apprenticeship. He also "sketched the plan of three distinct epic poems, one on the discovery of America, another on Pizarro's expedition against Peru, and a third on Cortez's expedition to America." Although young Brown was "much engrossed" in his epic plans "and for a long time . . . thought life was only desirable to accomplish them" (Allen, 51 and 53), nothing of these sketches survives, and probably as much had ever come of them.

Yet the themes Barlow worked were never wholly to loose their grip upon Brown. Some six years after he had abandoned fiction to devote himself entirely to magazine editing, Brown read the galleys of *The Columbiad* (1807), Barlow's extensive reworking of the *Vision of Columbus*. He published in his *American Register* a review of the poem while it was still at press—an extraordinary thing for Brown to have done, since his magazine did not usually "undertake to give an account of unpublished works." But *The Columbiad*, Brown claimed, was an extraordinary work, spreading before the reader a panorama of events "unequalled by any . . . that had ever before employed the epic muse . . . no subject within the compass of human actions can be more important or more affecting to a mind susceptible of great [i]deas." For, Barlow

> has attempted to unfold, in an ample manner, the past and the future of man upon earth, with the moral causes of his frequent relapses from truth and reason. The mind is then taught to dwell with pleasure on the immense improvements that must follow from the removal of those causes.[1]

Brown thought Barlow's epic most important for the utopian drama it unfolded, of which America's discovery was but the opening act. The poem shows how the voyage of Columbus signaled the beginning of an end to "slavish bonds of monkish lore"—intellectual, religious, and political tyranny. Whereas Europe had been settled and "civilized" by men who lusted after power and riches, the settlement and civilization of America called forth "nobler honours":

> Sublimer views and deeds of happier fame;
> A new creation waits the western shore,
> And reason triumphs o'er the pride of power.[2]

Barlow's American epic hero was truly a utopian hero, in whom benevolent reason triumphs over self-serving passion.

Though the youthful Brown had imitated Barlow and the mature Brown had praised him, the novel-writing Brown, with an apparently unconscious diabolism, stood Barlow on his head. The *Vision*'s light and enlightenment are manifest in *Wieland* as darkness and error; and with the fairly ineffectual exception of Henry Pleyel, none of the characters in *Wieland* is fully sane, let alone rational. What is more, while America was crucial to Barlow's idea of utopian reason, it is instrumental in the fanatical unreason of the Wielands. The senior Wieland is called to the New World wilderness by the extremity of religious affections; that wilderness defeats him, breaks him, and he retires to the privacy of the "temple" that becomes the scene of his fiery death. Theodore Wieland, who first hears at the temple a voice that will presently command the sacrifice of his family, destroys all that he loves, going about the massacre like a crazed caricature of a wild Indian, or like James Yates, "white" resident of Tomhannock, New York. Clara, unbalanced and finally suicidal in America, regains sanity only in the "ancient tranquillity" of Europe. Carwin, however, retires to the wilderness of Pennsylvania, the very territory that brought to birth and nurtured his fatal "biloquism." The embodiment of the nonrational and perverse, Carwin dwells deep in the New World.

For Brown, the idea of America and the epic utopianism of a Joel Barlow were incompatible. Nevertheless, Brown entertained a notion of the writer as, essentially, a utopianist. We might recall his comments to John Bernard: "in my literary moods," Brown declared, "I am aiming at making the world something better than I find it; in my social ones I am content to take it as it is."[3] And, in October 1796, Brown did read to his close friend Elihu Hubbard Smith "some notes toward his *great plan*, drawn from reading [William] Coxe's 'Russian Discoveries'" (*An Account of the Russian Discoveries between Asia and America* [London: Printed by J. Nichols for T. Cadell, 1780]) (Smith, 239). The project intrigued Smith sufficiently for him later to take special note of an article in the *Monthly Review* for August 1796 because it suggested a further model for Brown's "great plan." Smith comments on an anonymous review of the French traveler François le Vaillant's *Second Voyage in the Interior of Africa*, finding the reviewer "judicious" in his choice of extracts, the most interesting of which was one "relative to the 'Houzuana.'" "In this race of man [Smith comments] are found the very qualities—I mean physical qualities—which are most desirable: Activity, force, insensibility to changes of temperature, agility, temperance, acute vision. Here is a nation for the purposes of Ch. B. Brown.''[4]

In addition to these "physical qualities," Brown would have found other aspects of the "Hoozuanas" (as le Vaillant spells it) attractive for a utopian race. Their "custom of working for their comrades," le Vaillant observes in the extract, "announces a sociable character, and benevolent dispositions. In fact, they are not only good husbands and fathers, but excellent associates" (*Monthly Review* 20:530). Promising material for the would-be utopianist; yet, by December 14, 1796, Smith despaired of Brown's progress:

> A visit from Ch. B. Brown—who read me several passages from his Journal. I wish he would turn his Aloas & Astoias, his Buttiscoes and Carlovingas, to some account. He starts an idea; pursues it a little way; new ones spring up; he runs a short distance after each; meantime the original one is likely to escape entirely. (Smith, 272)

Little of what Brown read to Smith survives. Nothing of Astoias, Buttiscoes, or Carlovingas, and only two vague fragments concerning the "Alloas" or "Alloans." Bennett summarizes the subject of the fragments: "Brown's plan was grand indeed. He appears to have intended a novel about how a Greek people, the Alloans, gained dominion over China and Japan and then by their enlightened administration sought to realize a better, perhaps even a utopian society."[5] Even more fragmentary and vague are the manuscripts loosely related to a Schuylkill estate called Ellendale. These, along with a fragment published in Paul Allen's *Life* of Brown, touch on various utopian matters. Their composition probably spans 1793 to 1796 (Bennett, 163–80).

A more sharply focused glimpse of utopia is found in the posthumously published sequel to Brown's first book. *Alcuin*, a dialogue focusing for the most part on the rights of women, contains a brief narration of an imaginary journey to an "Isle" Alcuin calls a "paradise of women." Alcuin tells his friend Mrs. Carter how a guide showed him a society in which women are regarded as wholly the equals of men. In the paradise of women all unnecessary distinctions between the sexes—in dress, in intellectual matters, and in division of labor—have been abolished. The glimpse of this utopia is shadowy and brief, coming to an abrupt end when Alcuin becomes embarrassed about discussing with Mrs. Carter the nature of "sexual intercourse" in a society that has done away with the institution of marriage; but Brown was at work on this material in 1797, just a year after he announced his "great plan" to Smith.[6]

Harry Warfel, in his biography of Brown, suggests that two other posthumously published works, the "Sketches of a History of the Carrils and

Ormes" and the "Sketches of a History of Carsol," also were part of the "great plan."[7] It is true that these pieces are extended historical accounts of imaginary societies; but, as Warner Berthoff observes, their social and political vision is "distinctly anti-Utopian." Berthoff continues: "Tradition, cultural uniformity, despotism, an established church: these are the political values stressed in the 'Sketches.' "[8] Brown did become increasingly conservative, exchanging his youthful Godwinianism for a prematurely middle-aged Federalism; and internal evidence—references in the "Sketches" to the years 1805, 1807, and 1810—also suggests that the pieces were composed late in Brown's career. Warfel's claim, that the "Sketches" are part of Brown's "great plan," implies an early date of composition. While internal evidence and the conservatism of the "Sketches" argue against early composition, a formal similarity to Coxe's *Russian Discoveries*, the work Smith had cited as a model for the "great plan," does suggest that the "Sketches" may have occupied Brown, in some way, from an early date.[9] Although there is no similarity between the content of Coxe's work—which treats of the Russians' dealings with the primitive peoples of Kamchatka, the Aleutians, and Siberia—and the distinctly European material of Brown's "Sketches," there is a striking similarity in tone, form, and in the kinds of subjects discussed. Both Coxe and Brown present flat chronicle accounts of discovery and conquest, followed by minute inventories of government and demographic data. Neither attempts to characterize individuals, but both devote attention to describing dress, ornaments of religious and civil office, and buildings.

The buildings in the "Sketches" bear a powerful but inconclusive resemblance to some thirty architectural drawings Brown left in manuscript. One is tempted to identify these plans and elevations of gothic cathedrals, towers, doorways, quasi-romanesque, quasi-grecian and Palladian public buildings, colonnades, and entrances as illustrations for the "Sketches"; yet nowhere do the dimensions given in the "Sketches"—and they are given with tedious precision—exactly match those of the drawings. The drawings are on deposit at the Humanities Research Center of the University of Texas at Austin along with other Brown manuscripts, a group of which is cataloged simply as "mathematical calculations." That the drawings and the so-called calculations are grouped together and are on paper of similar size and texture suggests that the two are closely related. Indeed, some of the "calculations" appear to be dimensions, as for architectural plans. Here is the top quarter of a typical page of manuscript:

[illegible]	/Mental. Instruction by	Meditation. Solitude. Silence. devotion. [illegible]
Astetica [*sic*]	[illegible]	Study. Reding [*sic*] / Writing
		Converse. with artists [?] /
		Rehearsals. Musical. /. (l. 35. by 60.)
		Oratorical. /.
	120 / 8 / 960 / 1020	Mimetics— (l. 112 by W. 60)—1 / (33. — 24)—2 / (18. 18)—4 } 7

It is impossible wholly to decipher the cryptic scribblings that make up these "mathematical calculations," but it does appear that Brown was toying with designs for a school or college, the very architecture of which was intended to reflect his system of pedagogy and his conception of the division of knowledge. Once again there is no precise correspondence to be found between the dimensions in the "calculations" and those in the drawings. But at least two of the drawings seem to be directly associated with education. One is a grid, perhaps a floorplan, perhaps a plan for a campus. Some of the grid squares are further divided and shaded, bearing such legends as "Mim" (mimetics?), "Ag" (agriculture?), "Art," "Math," and "Archit" (architecture?). Another of the drawings, a gothically pointed tower beside what appears to be one with a neoclassical dome, bears the following inscriptions: "sophos," and below this, "main diss. properties," and below this, "music, a profession. in esteem. harmonics. Vocal music. a part of education universally." Perhaps the drawings and the "calculations" are part of a youthful utopian scheme. As early as the beginning of the 1790s, Brown looked to education as the practical means of achieving utopian perfection. Young Brown said as much in an address he delivered at the first meeting of the Belles Lettres Society, an organization (Paul Allen tells us) that originated as a "substitute" for an answer to an inquiry Brown had made of one "Emilius" (John Davidson) concerning "the relations, dependencies, and connections of the several parts of knowledge."[10]

The drawings and "calculations" are undated, but they are collected with some of the Ellendale material dated 1793, July–August—and also a thirty-two page fragment of a novel called *Don Manuel*, a poem probably written by Brown, an obituary for Brown, some legal documents, and a number of letters. The ambitious utopianism of the drawings and calculations, and their association with the dated Ellendale fragments, suggest that they are of the same vintage as the founding of the Belles Lettres Society and the "great plan." However, the resemblance that the drawings bear to the historical "Sketches" tends to suggest a later date of composition. In fact, architectural drawing may have occupied a broad span of Brown's life. At least such activity was sufficiently characteristic of the man to merit prominent mention in the eulogy with which William Dunlap closes the narrative portion of the *Life of Charles Brockden Brown*:

> Though attached to the seclusion of the closet, though he would for hours be absorbed in architectural studies, measuring proportions with his compasses, and drawing plans for Grecian temples or Gothic cathedrals, monasteries or castles, though addicted to every kind of abstraction, and attached by habit to reverie, he would break off with the utmost ease from these favourite occupations of his mind, and enter into conversation on any topic with a fluency and copiousness which approached to the truest eloquence. (Dunlap, *Life*, 2:89–90)

Drawing, not novel writing, is what Dunlap chooses to number among his friend's favorite occupations.

Whether the architectural drawings should be associated with the early utopian manuscript fragments, or with the dystopian vision of the (most likely) late historical "Sketches," or with both, they prompt two more general speculations. They are an admixture of gothic cathedrals and neoclassical "temples" (as well as more secular Palladian designs). In a few cases, gothic arches are found together with Palladian or neoclassical domes on the same structure, or side by side on the same sheet of paper, as if Brown had intended these juxtapositions as icons of his cultural ambivalence. Certainly his interest, if not his allegiance, is divided in these renderings between gothic design, with its mysterious, superstitious, barbarous connotations, and the blithe rationality of the enlightened eighteenth century as it is embodied in a neoclassical architecture based upon Vitruvius and Palladio. That the neoclassical drawings outnumber the gothic will surprise those who see the novelist as a mere gothicist. As early as 1794, in "Devotion: An Epistle," the autobiographical poem we looked at earlier, Brown's utopian vision was dominated by "Roman grandeurs" —specifically those of Roman architecture:

> The dome that, rear'd aloft, repos'd in air
> Sublime as Heaven's high arch, in tranquil state,
> Majestic as a slumbering deity;
> Or, springing upward, seemed averse to yield
> Obedience to the power that check'd his flight
> Audacious, and confin'd his foot to earth. (Clark, 324)

Several lines earlier in the poem Brown stiffly acknowledges a conventional affinity with nature; but the actual nature of the American landscape evokes nothing like the rapture excited by the imagined prospect of classical Rome. In fact, the young writer found the scenery along his native Schuylkill downright loathsome—at least in and of itself. "In Fancy's fairy land," he begins, "my steps have long / Been wont to stray, where Schuylkill pours her tide." This fairyland is not the domain of river Schuylkill; rather, it is the property of "fancy" set quite against external reality:

> In Fancy's fairy land, my steps have long
> Been wont to stray, where Schuylkill pours her tide
> Twixt unaspiring banks, lowbrow'd, and rich
> In naught but waving rushes, sight deform'd
> And indelectable; o'er downs that stretch
> On either hand, for many a weary mile,
> By many an ox and many a ranging steed
> Depastur'd, scenes that sober thought abhors;
> Scenes unakin to beauty, health estrang'd,

"But," the poet continues, "deck'd with orient charms, when Fancy wav'd / Her wand" (322). Imagination tears the veil of vulgar reality from the landscape, revealing "scenes dear only to poetic eyes." These "orient charms" are not the voluptuous trappings of the Far East, but of an "east" that represents a more ordered time and direction, the east of classical Roman grandeur. Brown's Alcuin, who appeared about four years after "Devotion" was written, found while traveling through the "paradise of women" that he "could trace in their buildings the knowledge of Greek and Roman models" (Allen, 75-6). Brown had been more specific in the 1794 poem, the autobiographical speaker of which is subject to rapture before the imaginary image of a Roman dome. And this "rapture rose"

> To dizzy heights: the eye too narrow . . .
> To grasp the vast design, the brain too small
> To harbor the gigantic thought that grows
> At every glance . . .

It is a "dream / Of ecstasy," a "beatific dream," the "Child of Vitruvian, and Paladian [sic] art" (Clark, 324).

Although Brown's enthusiasm for neoclassical architecture is extreme, it is not unusual in a cultivated man of late eighteenth-century America. Andrea Palladio had looked back from his sixteenth-century Venice to classical antiquity—and to architects like Marcus Vitruvius Pollio, who flourished in Rome shortly after the birth of Christ—in order to " 'free' his country from the Gothic in a return to 'correct' classical proportions and a proper understanding of the orders." The influence of his architecture was worldwide, reaching not only beyond Venice, but well beyond the Renaissance. "The Palladian style reigned supreme in Colonial America. Free to develop in an architectural void, it remained the accepted style of building for a hundred years until the Greek and Gothic revivals of the 1830s and the Victorian revolt which followed."[11] Palladian neoclassicism is part of the Founding Fathers' vision of what Howard Mumford Jones calls "Roman Virtue." From Jefferson's plans for the University of Virginia, for the capitols of Virginia and of the nation, as well as Monticello, to the 1893 World Columbian Exposition in Chicago, classical Roman architecture has traditionally embodied the Roman values of American government and culture.[12]

Because Brown's drawings reflect the "official" culture of the early Republic, we might call them typically American. Yet this conventional vision, enthusiastic though it is, fails to acknowledge the possibility of realizing new values in a New World. Rather, it sees America as a void simply to be filled by the revived artifacts of the Old World's golden age. This is curious in the case of Brown because we have already seen how he took enthusiastic notice of Barlow's specifically American utopia. What is more, Brown himself seems to have recognized—albeit casually—the single most significant feature of America that would make it a fertile field for the planting of a utopia: "space, in which [a people] will become happier in themselves, and more beneficial to the whole." This is the keystone of the argument for New World colonization Brown anonymously published as the work of that "French Counsellor of State" in the audacious *Address* on the Spanish cession of Louisiana. Limitless land, the councilor declares, distributed among the needy of an overcrowded France will accomplish the utopian miracle of establishing *"equality* without detriment to order."[13]

That Brown in some measure recognized the utopian potential of America, yet failed to realize his great plans in this setting, actually attests to the power that the New World exercised over his literary imagination. Utopias, as the imagery of Barlow's poetry demonstrates, are bright places, places of enlightenment. Though Brown had formulated for John Bernard the utopian function of the writer, he also told Bernard that his literary imagination was an abode of darkness and that the impulse to write was for him asocial and volitionless. Brown's dark vision of the New World, which suited and excited the darkness of his literary moods, was incompatible with the bright rationality of utopian thought. Not that "dark" was the simple equivalent of evil for Brown: he confessed to Bernard that his dark moods, insofar as they excited his literary imagination, were pleasurable. Indeed, we might interpret his utopian remark to Bernard—the desire to make the world something better than he found it—as thoroughly though unconsciously self-indulgent, meaning that writing creates a private "world," a territory of fulfilled fantasy, superior to the public domain of society. Edgar Huntly leaves the conscious and self-conscious lightsome chamber of civilized existence for the darkness of a cave and wilderness in which new powers and sensations come to birth. We have seen, though, that Brown's ambivalence—a moral, intellectual, and cultural allegiance divided between Old and New Worlds—worked both pain and pleasure upon Huntly. Imagining himself the victim of some invisible and omnipotent tyrant, Huntly, recounting his imprisonment in the cave, declares: "The author of my distress, and the means he had taken to decoy me hither, were incomprehensible" (156). Of course, Brown and his character intended *author* to signify one "who gives rise to or causes an action, event, circumstances, or condition of things" (*OED*), a meaning of the word more current in Brown's time than in ours. Yet, Brown *is* the author of Huntly and of his distress as well as his triumph. If Huntly serves as the fantasy fulfillment of Brockden Brown's desire for contact with the red man's wilderness, he serves also as the projection of a white conscience that must suffer in that wilderness.

Edgar Huntly's distress is but one of many expressions of Brown's own anguish, which was at its most acute where the matter of his vocation was concerned. As his conversation with John Bernard suggests, Brown was torn between an essentially self-indulgent, even antisocial, impulse to write and a consciousness of the writer's social responsibility. In his social mood, however, Brown was insufficiently excited to write; and, in his private literary mood, he was incapable of the kind of "public" writing necessary for the creation of utopias.

Brown attempted to dramatize the plight of the would-be utopianist writer in America by means of a fragmentary narrative concerning a Signior Adini.[14] An Italian member of the Illuminati (a secret society that, as we shall see, greatly intrigued Brown), Adini dreamed of a South American utopia. He came to the newly independent United States in 1784, settling the next year near Ellendale, the estate of a retired Scots-American physician named Mr. Ellen. It was here that the narrator, then aged eleven, met and became fascinated by Adini and the beautiful ten-year-old girl Adela, who is—apparently—his daughter. Aloof, but neither haughty nor impolite, private but not secretive (his door is always unlocked), Adini conducts his life with a spartan austerity relieved only by his absorbing affection for Adela. Though he "could in no light be regarded as an object of suspicion" (360–1), he in fact becomes the object of intense curiosity, and neither Mr. Ellen nor his wife is content to leave him alone. Mr. Ellen, after gentle but unrelenting effort, manages to persuade Adini to visit and chat with him.

> It may seem improper . . . to urge a proposal which is confessedly disagreeable, but I own I cannot relinquish this without extreme reluctance. Let us try what we can do. Strange if your happiness allows no increase or your misery no alleviaton from intercourse with those whose intentions are pure, and their hearts affectionate. (366)

"A reluctant consent was at length extorted. It evidently gave [Adini] acute uneasiness" (367). But this hardly matters to Mr. Ellen. In a manner typical of Brockden Brown's well-meaning characters, Mr. Ellen determines to help Adini regardless of what pain his help may inflict.

In the course of their first reluctant conversation, Adini mentions that he would like to instruct the Ellen children in handwriting, an innocuous offer that leads Adini to a disquisition on the inadequacies of language. "If words could flow with the celerity of thoughts, it would be well. If writing could keep pace or even outstrip the rapidity of speech, it would be well" (368–9). He goes on to discuss the merits of shorthand, and then to criticize the "chance-framed" alphabet of standard longhand.

> Characters are prolix, confused and tedious. Nothing easier than to make them simple, concise and regular. The purposes of daily life, philosophy and reason, demand a reformation. To simplify and expedite the mode of communicating thoughts, is no inconsiderable step to the goal of happiness and wisdom. The condition in this respect of that nook called Europe is mournful in one view, hatefully stupid and ludicrously forlorn in another. The whole mass, indeed, wants a thorough shifting.

The innocent subject of alphabet reform culminates in the partial exposure of Adini's utopian dreams: "He paused a moment; then vehemently exclaimed: would I were a ruler in Socratic land, the change should come quickly" (369). The outburst is immediately followed by a fit of silent, impenetrable musing.

Mr. Ellen and Adini have a few more conversations touching upon utopia, but the Italian persists in making nothing more than tantalizingly obscure allusions to "Socratic land." Mr. Ellen does not know whether to take these as "metaphors" or as references to an actual place, and although he is aching with curiosity and puzzlement, it remains for Mrs. Ellen to push the inquiry further. She rationalizes a pernicious nosiness readily:

> Surely, the curiosity is laudable. How can he suppose us indifferent? Have we not given him sufficient proofs that we feel considerable interest in his happiness? [R]emember that the knowledge we seek is with a view not merely to our own gratification, but likewise to his benefit. It will enable us to conduct ourselves, as to avoid giving him offence. Surely this motive is commendable. It must be an irresistable apology for any freedom. (376)

Armed now, however superfluously, with her husband's blessing, Mrs. Ellen sidles up to Adini and begins to pry, justifying her curiosity by explaining that she and her husband must know the secret of his burden precisely so that they can avoid the offensive topic in future conversation. Adini reacts with a pained but subdued irritablity, and Mrs. Ellen plunges ahead. When Adini mutters a final resolution of silence, she turns to outright mockery of his precious "Socratic land." Marking her cruel smile, Adini moans: "Is the world leagued to overwhelm me with insult and scorn? . . . Daemon of wrath . . . get thee behind me" (378-9). Despite this unwonted anger in a man hitherto so serene, Mrs. Ellen persists, justifying her cause by explaining how "it is plain that [Adini's] intellects have received some injury. It must be our business to discover it, and if it be curable, to administer the cure" (379).

Like Brockden Brown in his literary mood, Adini is a private man, a dreamer; yet, also like Brown, he desires to share his dreams with the world—a mocking, scorning world that would pry into his great plans without bothering to understand them. Tormented by Mrs. Ellen's insensitive curiosity on the one hand, Adini is met with Mr. Ellen's literal-minded incomprehension on the other. Mr. and Mrs. Ellen reveal that the narrator, up to this point called simply Raff, is the ward of a Mr. Malcombe, who named the boy after Sir Thomas More's utopian traveler, Raphael Hythloday. At hearing this, Adini mentions that he has also traveled through "Eutopia," a remark Mr. Ellen finds impossible to fathom. "Did he mean any thing more than to declare in his figurative way, that he had read the book?" Or was Adini serious—had he found such a place? Or—perhaps most likely—was Adini insane? (382–3). When Adini and Mr. Ellen fall to a discussion about unexplored islands in the Pacific, Adini asks why Mr. Ellen does not travel. "We Scots[,] my dear sir," Ellen answers, "must travel to live, not live to travel." He explains that he has seen much of India, but only in the practical capacity of military surgeon, which "engrossed that attention which I would willingly have bestowed upon the Hindoos." To which Adini replies:

> "Your curiosity never wandered farther than the Hindoos? Did the question never occur, what might their conquerors be?"
> This was uttered with apparent hesitation, which [Mr. Ellen[15]] ascribed to a disinclination to give offence, supposing his friend alluded to the English whose maxims of Indian warfare were sufficiently censurable. (387)

And here the "Adini" fragment abruptly ends. Surely, Brown intended to write much more; but the irony against Mr. Ellen is sharper for the piece's having been broken off here. Likely, Adini's allusion is to some utopian race that might conquer even the spiritually formidable Hindus. Persisting to the last in the most pedestrian interpretation of Adini's remarks, Mr. Ellen quite misses the Italian's point.

It is no accident that Mr. Ellen is an American of Scots birth. Not only does his origin provide a plausible reason for his background as a surgeon in British India, but it also serves to identify him with a people renowned for their solid, if dull, common sense. We shall encounter briefly in *Ormond* Constantia Dudley's second suitor, one Mr. Balfour, wealthy, shrewd, sensible, boring, and, like Ellen, a Scot. More significantly, however, the identification of Scotland with common sense was neither peculiar to Brockden Brown nor the result of a simple (though durable) national stereotype. As William Charvat demonstrates in his *Origins of American Critical Thought: 1810–1835*, the philosophy of "common sense" that dominated American intellectual life at the beginning of the nineteenth century was imported from Scotland. Although Charvat notes possible connections between Scots commonsense philosophy and American Transcendentalism (by virtue of the former's doctrine of intuition), it was as a system of natural realism that the philosophy made itself most immediately felt in the early part of the century. Intellectual historian I. Woodbridge Riley drew upon Samuel Miller, an early American exponent of Scots common sense, for a statement of its principles, chief among which is the notion that "the mind perceives not merely the ideas or images of external objects but the external objects themselves . . . and that [external objects] possess the qualities we witness [in them], not by a train of reasoning, by formal reflection or by association of ideas, but by a direct and necessary connection between the presence of such objects and our consequent perceptions." The Scots philosophy is directly opposed to the idealism of Berkeley and Hume, turning from these to a faith in "the common sense of mankind as a tribunal paramount to all subtleties of philosophy."[16]

Likely, then, Brown was consciously pointing to a limitation of the reigning American philosophy when he brought Mr. Ellen's hard Scots head to bump against Adini, an enigma who dwells neither in the commonsense realm of physical sensation nor in the wholly ideal sphere of metaphor. His allusions to "Socratic land" locate him in the twilight between these two realms, in a territory that calls to mind Brown's own mental residence on the frontier. There can be little doubt, in any case, that Brown was familiar with the Scots philosophy, just as he must have been thoroughly versed in the Scots rhetoric of Hugh Blair and others, which was itself firmly rooted in notions of common sense. Not only was the Scots philosophy in the American air, or on the American bookshelf, but, more specifically, Brown was personally acquainted with at least one of its leading exponents. From Brockden Brown, Samuel Miller himself solicited advice about, and probably a contribution to, his *Brief Retrospect of the Eighteenth Century* (1803).[17]

Tormented by Mrs. Ellen's prying and her husband's obtuse common sense, Signior Adini is, ironically, a sojourner in the United States, which "at the conclusion of a revolutionary war, might appear to his fancy like the abode of liberty and virtue, and obviously present itself as a suitable asylum" (362). The word "asylum" appears again a few pages later, where we are told that, after a conversation with Mr. Ellen touching upon painful utopian subjects, Adini "retired into the asylum of his own thoughts" (373). Even in America—perhaps Brown is suggesting *especially* in this country—the only real "asylum" is found in the privacy of one's own imagination.

The tension between the private impulse to write and the public ambition to share that writing in the form of a great plan for the improvement of society was active in Brown from the beginning of his publishing career. The young author's second published writing (after a verse epitaph intended to honor Benjamin Franklin), "The Rhapsodist," appeared in four installments from August to November 1789 in a periodical called, of all things, *The Universal Asylum, and Columbian Magazine*. Probably based quite loosely on the blameless hermit of Jean Jacques Rousseau's *Rêveries du promeneur solitaire* (1782), Brown's rhapsodist is a solitary whose "strong and vivid fancy . . . inspires . . . being, instinct, and reason into every object, real or imagined, and the air, the water and the woods, wherever [the rhapsodist] directs his steps, are thronged with innumerable inhabitants."[18] His life, "literally a dream," is lived almost wholly in the fancy (7) and requires the isolation of the wilderness, where the rhapsodist can live in unmediated proximity to nature (8–13). He "who affects the manners of a recluse, and demeans himself in the midst of a populous city, like the lonely inhabitant of a desert, will often incur the censure of inveterate folly." Like Adini, the rhapsodist pays "obedience, tho' grudgingly, to the laws of society" lest he expose himself to the scorn and mockery of a hostile world (12). The rhapsodist looks upon the publication of his thoughts as a kind of social enslavement. "Every person who commits his writings to the press," he declares, "has by that means voluntarily parted with his ancient liberty and becomes the general vassal" (3). A rhapsodist who publishes himself is really a contradiction in terms, for his language is a dialogue of the self, "artless and unpremeditated" (5). Indeed, the rhapsodist's language, "unintelligible to any but" himself (13), is dangerously close to raving and must be tempered, compromised, before it is made public.

At the very least an inhibiting force in "The Rhapsodist," society figures more menacingly in a series of pieces Brown wrote nine years later. "The Man at Home" appeared in *The Weekly Magazine* from February through April of 1798. Here the protagonist is not a rhapsodist, but simply a man who has led an innocent life of hard work. He "laboured not for riches, but security," and once this was obtained, much like Adini, he dropped out of society, living alone in quiet retirement. One day an old friend—really more an acquaintance than friend—asks him to endorse some "notes, which his own credit would not enable him to negotiate." After deliberating about committing himself to "an act which could not be retrieved," Brown's protagonist signs the papers.

> It was nothing but writing my name in the space of an inch. The employment scarcely demanded a moment. The act, habit had rendered almost spontaneous and mechanical. It was done, and what was the consequence?

His friend proves incapable of making good on the notes and a warrant is issued for the arrest of "the man at home."[19] There is a tinge here of the justified paranoia Franz Kafka would articulate for our own century. In civilized society, an action as seemingly insignificant as it is kind can result in the ruin of an innocent life. Like Kafka, though, Brown does not simply and unambiguously fault society. Certainly the man at home is innocent, but rhapsodism may not be. There is a nagging sense that the judgment of the majority is right, that rhapsodism borders on insanity. Like the Wieland of Brown's outline for the novel, the solitary rhapsodist builds a system of his own, a system that includes daemons, genii, and guardian angels ("The Rhapsodist," 7–8). Heeding similarly invisible beings, Theodore Wieland murders his family—in fiction—as James Yates—in fact—had murdered his.

If tensions embodied in "Adini," "The Rhapsodist," and "The Man at Home" spurred Brown on to more complex treatment of them in his novels, the failure to resolve his problems in extended fiction may have moved Brown to abandon storytelling altogether. "Adini" adumbrated a program, a utopian mission for the writer. Much as the senior Wieland struggled and failed to carry out his own missionary project, though, Brockden Brown found himself unable to accomplish his. We have already noted that Adini's first allusion to "Socratic land" follows a diatribe against the "prolix, confused and tedious" alphabet of the Old World. The diatribe began innocently enough when Adini volunteered to tutor Mr. Ellen's children in penmanship, suggesting further that he be allowed to teach them shorthand. Not merely an aid for the writer, Adini's shorthand was meant to begin a utopian epoch: "To simplify and expedite the mode of communicating thoughts, is no inconsiderable step to the goal of happiness and wisdom" (368). Among Brown's own manuscript jottings, conceivably drawn up during the same period as "Adini," is a leaf headed "Rejang Alphabet," which David Lee Clark identifies as a "partly worked out" system of shorthand, "an original alphabet" the novelist was developing (Clark, 17 and 41). About thirty wedge-shaped characters are written over a quarter of the manuscript leaf. Beside many of them Brown has written their standard alphabet equivalents, which in some cases are not single letters but common clusters, such as *ng* and *nd*. This alphabet *is* unusual, but not original with Brown. For the Rejang are a people indigenous to the southwestern corner of Sumatra, and Brown almost certainly copied their alphabet from specimens reproduced in William Marsden's 1783 *History of Sumatra*.[20]

Still, David Lee Clark's error, his mistaking the alphabet for Brown's own creation, is suggestive. Simple, streamlined, and—to judge from the instances in which a single character stands for a cluster—economical, the Rejang alphabet might well make an efficient system of shorthand notation and might even serve as the basis for the kind of utopian alphabet Signior Adini imagined. We know that Brown consulted accounts of various actual societies as models for his own abortive "great plans." Coxe's *Russian Discoveries* and le Vaillant's *Travels* seem to have figured somewhere in his early musings; perhaps likewise in Marsden's presentation of the Rejang alphabet he saw the basis of a utopian system of writing. In as much as the Rejang alphabet manuscript seems to be of a piece with other manuscript leaves containing utopian material, and given Signior Adini's allusion to a project of utopian writing, we may guess that Brown saw in the glyphs from far-off Sumatra the promise of means by which an author might employ himself fully in the work of the world. Founded upon the Rejang model, a utopian alphabet would be at once the product of private rhapsody and yet a directly public means of making a mark on civilization. By offering to the world a practical artifact, the utopianist-writer-rhapsodist might live and work without guilt or compromise in the commonsense culture rising in the early Republic.

But "Adini" is a fragment and "Rejang," if it means much of anything at all, is the merest gesture toward a scheme. Brown's precarious notion of himself as a writer could not be resolved simply by inventing—or copying—a utopian alphabet. Instead, in his published fiction, Brown attempted two expressions of his utopianism, developing two characters in whom he tried to reconcile the values embodied in the private impulse to write and those entailed by the public role of the writer. In the character of

Ormond, Brown presented a utopianist whose greatest plans were utterly self-serving, self-indulgent, violent, and violently sexual. A figure of the Old World, Ormond yet embodies many of the values associated with Edgar Huntly's New World wilderness.

Far milder, and by design unsophisticated, is the American hero Arthur Mervyn. The month before the first part of *Arthur Mervyn* was issued, Brown wrote to his brother that the title character was intended as "a hero whose virtue, in order to be productive of benefit to others, and felicity to himself, stands in no need of riches."[21] Like so many figures in early American fiction, Mervyn was meant to serve as a paragon of virtue, whose example might leave the world something better than it had been found. As he appears in the finished novel, Arthur Mervyn seems to have been modeled upon the example of Benjamin Franklin, who successfully reconciled altruistic with self-serving ends in a kind of public-private utopian self. Franklin proves to be a dangerous model, though; for Brown cannot maintain in Mervyn Benjamin's delicate balance between self and society. While young Arthur is never as wicked as Ormond, disturbing ambiguities of virtue appear in the first volume of the novel, and by the second, published a year and a half later, it becomes all the more apparent that the exemplary lad's "virtue" is quite inextricably joined to riches and considerably shadier things. The civilized savagery of Ormond's great plans and the crooked, if not twisted, Franklinianism of Arthur Mervyn are the subjects of the next two chapters.

V

Utopian Romance

Absent from the review pages of the magazines he edited are the names and works of Charles Brockden Brown's fellow novelists. William Hill Brown, Hannah Foster, Susanna Rowson, Royall Tyler (whose travel-romance *The Algerine Captive* [1797] was read by William Dunlap and Elihu Hubbard Smith), and Hugh Henry Brackenridge are nowhere mentioned. Only Jeremy Belknap's *The Foresters*, published at Boston in 1792 and bearing the intriguing subtitle "An American Tale," finds its way into the *Monthly Magazine*, where it is amply and favorably reviewed; though, as a satiric allegory of the American Revolution, *The Foresters* is more an ingenious exercise in political *belles lettres* than it is a novel.[1] Brown's general public statements on fiction are at best unenthusiastic and at worst disparaging.[2] We do know, however, that he read Samuel Richardson's *Clarissa*, William Godwin's *Caleb Williams*, of course, and *Hermsprong*, Robert Bage's response to Godwin's novel.[3] Moreover, the yellow fever scenes in *Ormond* and *Arthur Mervyn* suggest a familiarity with Defoe's *Journal of the Plague Year*, and, for that matter, the treatment of Philadelphia as the stage for deceit, swindling, and even counterfeiting calls to mind the London of *Moll Flanders*. *Arthur Mervyn*, its plots rising one upon the other like so many hydra heads, suggests (in light of Brown's knowledge of French) an affinity with Denis Diderot's *Jacques le fataliste et son maître*, a novel to which both Elihu Hubbard Smith and William Dunlap make reference.[4] *Wieland*, we have seen, indicates a familiarity with some German fiction. And, of course, Brown must have known something of the English gothicists, though he never mentions any gothic works by name, and alludes to the genre in his preface to *Edgar Huntly* only to revile it.

Despite Brown's public aloofness from the productions of his contemporaries, the novelist's works do betray a kinship with them, and none so much or so significantly as *Ormond*. Like many productions of early American novelists, *Ormond* is a tale of seduction, and what it most obviously shares with such popular books as William Hill Brown's *The Power of Sympathy* (1789), Susanna Rowson's *Charlotte Temple: A Tale of Truth* (1794), and Hannah Foster's *The Coquette; or, The History of Eliza*

Wharton (1797) is a debt to Samuel Richardson's master of seduction, the diabolical Lovelace. Leslie Fiedler, in *Love and Death in the American Novel*, argues that the popularity of the early American seduction novel was due to its essential duplicity. Though William Hill Brown, Rowson, and Foster each took pains to protest that the seducers they depicted were characters in a cautionary tale, their actual appeal was erotic and illicit. Fiedler argues that the special attraction of the early American seduction figures was defined by national character. Embodying the dark, sophisticated, worldly, "phallic" quality—as Fiedler calls it—of the European Lovelace, the seducers of our early fiction make the American male seem insipid and sexlessly immature by comparison.[5]

It should be observed that, of the three best-known early American seduction novels, none fits Fiedler's paradigm flawlessly. The victimized heroine of *Charlotte Temple* is seduced by a dashing British officer named Montraville (aided by Charlotte's French teacher, who, according to Fiedler, "projects all the American fear of Latin perfidy"); but Charlotte is also a European—albeit on her way to America at the time of her sea-going defloration. In *The Power of Sympathy* and *The Coquette*, the seducer is not ostensibly European at all. Yet, in all three novels, the seduction figure is in fact drawn according to the Lovelace model. This is true of *Ormond* as well, which, if anything, fills out Fiedler's paradigm more amply than any other early novel does. The title character could not have been made more "European." Ormond was a soldier almost from the cradle, having served with Potemkin and Romanzov, and having "executed secret and diplomatic functions at Constantinople and Berlin," where he "met with schemers and reasoners who aimed at the new-modelling of the world [through] subversion of all that has hitherto been conceived elementary and fundamental." Nor could he be more "phallic." At eighteen, while serving in the Russian army, he "made prey of a Tartar girl," and when one Sarsefield, a comrade-at-arms, tried to wrest her from him, Ormond neatly dispatched him in a sword fight. Bearing "his prize unmolested away, and having exercised brutality of one kind upon the helpless victim, [he] stabbed her through the heart, as an offering to the *manes* of *Sarsefield*." As if this were not "expiation" enough, Ormond rushed alone against a troop of Turks, bringing away "five heads, suspended, by their gory locks, to his horse's mane." For this exploit he was commissioned an officer of Cossacks (252 and 263–4). And it is this man who threatens not Charlotte the English (though naïve) girl, but Constantia Dudley, the full-blooded daughter of Columbia.

Ormond was issued in twelve editions during the nineteenth century, while *Charlotte Temple*, even though it does not fit Leslie Fiedler's explanation of the seduction novel's popularity as well as *Ormond*, ran through more than two hundred by 1905.[6] Fiedler attributes what he calls the popular failure of *Ormond* to the introduction of a markedly homoerotic relationship between Constantia Dudley, the heroine of the novel, and Sophia Westwyn Courtland, the narrator. The critic correctly points to the contrast between the coolness with which Sophia discusses Courtland, the man she marries, and the rhapsody attending her reunion with Constantia after long absence. Indeed, Sophia leaves her new husband in England in order to search for Constantia in America. Fiedler argues that Brown, caught up in America's passion for the Richardsonian tale of seduction, was also too much the original artist wholly to pander to public demand. "Only by bypassing normal heterosexual love as a subject could such [original] writers [as Brown] preserve themselves from sentimentality and falsehood" yet still hope to please their public (Fiedler, 89).

This important insight needs more precise definition. As Fiedler suggests, Brown is not interested in homosexuality as such, but in preserving the form of the popular sexually oriented novel while altering its content to suit the demands of his originality. It is the same originality that influences Brown's treatment of the wilderness, which appears in *Edgar Huntly* and *Wieland* much as sex and seduction do in *Ormond*: as metaphor. We shall see that Constantia is passionately attracted to Sophia and indifferent to at least two eligible male suitors; but we shall see as well that she does conceive a dangerous passion for a third, Ormond. Brown takes little interest in this network of relationships for the sake of sexual intrigue; far more important is how Constantia's divided and confused sexual alliances represent her—and her author's—moral and intellectual allegiances. This does not mean that *Ormond* is a self-conscious allegory, but the habit of abstraction that abridges Brown's wilderness also raises the erotic content of *Ormond* to a level of contemplation. The novelist is so passionate about the life of the mind that, in *Ormond*, he expresses it through a drama of sex and seduction inspired by the intellectually slim popular fiction of his American contemporaries.

For a novel that includes harrowing scenes of a yellow fever epidemic, an attempted seduction and rape, ancillary stories of actual rape, revolution and European intrigue, and two murders, *Ormond* is oddly static. This quality, detrimental to the fiction as fiction, is a symptom of Brown's overweening intellectualism. The ostensible intellectual subject of the novel, the utopian topic of education, does threaten a formidable tedium. In this novel, the mild feminism of which recalls *Alcuin*, we witness the effects of a traditional male education upon Constantia Dudley. Trained by her father in "the school of Newton and Hartley," thoroughly grounded in mathematics, physics, metaphysics, anatomy, and history (33), Constantia is contrasted to the alluring but ill-fated and feckless mistress of Ormond, Helena Cleves, who has been educated in the effete manner of an eighteenth-century young lady. The treatment of Constantia's education goes beyond this simple contrast, however, as Brown suggests that an undue concentration on matters of mind is responsible for a certain lack of emotion and femininity in Constantia. For all her intellectual shortcomings, Helena, after all, possesses definite charm, warmth, and sincerity of emotion. While Constantia does stand in considerable contrast to Helena, Helena's absolute opposite is Ormond's sister, the amazonian Martinette de Beauvais. A ruthless European revolutionist like her brother, Martinette had been subjected to an education perilously similar to that of Constantia, void of emotion and religious sentiment. We see, then, that Helena and Martinette represent extreme results of extremes in education, between which Constantia must learn to balance.

Like the heroines of Samuel Richardson, Constantia is introspective, a lover of seclusion (32), among whose chief pleasures is the writing of letters (27). Unlike Pamela, she apparently has little of the sex-tease about her. Her icily rational reaction to an early suitor befits her education. "Her scruples," Sophia, as the novel's narrator, comments approvingly, "did not relate to the temper, or person, or understanding of her lover, but to his age, to the imperfections of their acquaintance, and to the want of that permanence of character which can flow only from the progress of time and knowledge" (22). When word of Mr. Dudley's financial ruin at the hands of his apprentice Thomas Craig reaches the young suitor, he embarks "on a voyage which he had long projected, but which had been hitherto delayed by a superior regard to the interests of his passion." Attributing the loss of interest to the knowledge of Constantia's sudden poverty, Sophia labels it a "desertion" (22). Truth there may be in this judgment, but, faced with Constantia's measured indifference, how else should the young man have been expected to respond? Nevertheless, Sophia remarks of Constantia that "the lady had not foreseen the event" (22). Intelligent and introspective as she is, Constantia is also quite divorced from her emotions, something dramatically demonstrated in her response to the horrors of a yellow fever epidemic.

With great difficulty, Constantia manages to scrape together enough money to pay the rent on the miserable quarters she shares with her father. Although payment of the sum would leave them destitute, Constantia conceives it her "duty" (a word that is virtually a leitmotiv for the girl) not to wait for the landlord to call but to carry the money to his house, even though it is in the neighborhood hardest hit by the fever. At the same time, however, she decides that "to bereave herself and her father of bare subsistence was surely no dictate of duty." No sense of the very real horror in which Philadelphia in general, and the Dudleys in particular, are immersed enters into Constantia's abstract deliberations. She perceives the situation as a problem of conflicting duties—principles—complicated by the guilt she feels over breaking a promise to the landlord. While Constantia's adherence to the ostensibly reasonable dictates of "duty" is certainly unreasonable enough, Brown introduces another element of irrationality into her decision to venture into the fever-stricken neighborhood. Like Carwin, she is subject to an insatiable curiosity. Wondering whether the landlord will demand the money, knowing that if he does the Dudleys will starve, Constantia does not suffer the pains of terror and despair, but the "torments of suspense" (39). Despite her father's pleading, the girl thrusts herself "into" what Dudley calls the "fangs" of the disease, an image befitting the terror of the epidemic, which is heightened by the disparity between Brown's graphic rendering of the yellow fever scenes and Constantia's numbed response to them.

> Near the entrance [to the landlord's house], in the street, stood a cart. The horse attached to it, in his form and furniture and attitude, was an emblem of torpor and decay. His gaunt sides, motionless limbs, his gummy and dead eyes, and his head hanging to the ground, were in unison with the craziness of the vehicle to which he belonged, and the paltry and bedusted harness which covered him. No attendant nor any human face was visible. The stillness, though at an hour customarily busy, was uninterrupted except by the sound of wheels moving at an almost indistinguishable distance. (41)

The horse and cart belong to municipal undertakers, who presently are seen carrying a coffin out of the landlord's dwelling. Constantia, shaken by the sight, trembles and steps back. This genuine and immediate reaction is short-lived, however. Brown has Sophia tell us that Constantia's mind was "a stranger to pusillanimity," that she thought her own death "an evil to be ardently deprecated" only because it would leave her father, already blind and broken, utterly without support. Still, despite her "complacency for death and speculative resignation to the fate that governs the world, disquiet and alarm pervaded her bosom on this occasion."

> The deplorable state to which her father would be reduced by her death was seen and lamented; but her tremulous sensations flowed not from this source. They were, in some sort, inexplicable and mechanical. In spite of recollection and reflection, they bewildered and harrassed her, and subsided only of their own accord. (42)

The flatly impersonal phrases which frame Constantia's reaction to the scene before her contrast absurdly with Brown's uncharacteristically concrete depiction of the death cart and the all-but-dead horse that draws it. Virtually destitute in the midst of a plague, Constantia should have little cause for puzzlement over the source of her "tremulous sensations," yet she lives at such a remove from her emotions that they have taken on an autonomous existence, "inexplicable and mechanical."

Brown has Sophia attribute the girl's unwonted intellectual paralysis to the inadequacy of the education her father had given her. She had learned about the Greek and Egyptian plagues, but practical matters, such as the nature of the disease and the danger of contagion, were "subjects foreign to her education" (42). Yet, with the yellow fever episode, Brown has already taken the subject of his novel beyond a narrow interest in education. Elicited by the extremity of the epidemic, the sensations and impressions to which Constantia is subject are wholly new, taking her, beyond any volition, out of her familiar self. Like Edgar Huntly, who unconsciously advances across a Pennsylvania frontier, Constantia finds herself "bewildered." Her education is inadequate to the plague just as Edgar Huntly's lightsome chamber is inadequate to the wilderness. The point is not so much that Constantia's particular education fails, but that any civilized and abstractly acquired knowledge is bound to fail at the "frontier" of concrete extremity. Moreover, the "frontier," by calling up powers and sensations buried under civilized life, reveals the limits of self-knowledge. *Sky-Walk*, an early unpublished (now lost) novel by Brown, perhaps an "Urtext" of *Edgar Huntly*, was subtitled "The Man Unknown to Himself."[7] This precisely describes Edgar Huntly as well as the Wielands and, changing the gender of noun and pronoun, Constantia Dudley.

Constantia's problems proceed from Brown's own self-bewilderment. He had lived through four major yellow fever epidemics himself, two in Philadelphia—in 1793 (the historical basis for the epidemic scenes in *Ormond* and *Arthur Mervyn*) and in 1797—and two in the city of New York—in 1796 and also during the summer of 1798, which was surely the most harrowing experience for Brown, who not only lost a close friend when Elihu Hubbard Smith succumbed on September 21, but who had fallen dangerously ill himself.[8] The strength of the impression left upon Brown by the yellow fever may be remarked in the vividness of the plague scenes in *Ormond* and *Arthur Mervyn*. Here was one subject that would not wholly yield to a passion for abstraction. The epidemics actually worked to galvanize feeling and idea. Sophia's portrait of the undertaker's wagon horse is graphic—gaunt sides, motionless limbs, dusty harness, and, most striking, the "gummy and dead eyes"—but Brown also has Sophia call the horse and wagon "an emblem of torpor and decay," as if to mitigate immediate reality with allegory. Yet the final effect is one of synthesis through which the horse remains sharply present to the senses, not as an emblem, but as a highly wrought synecdoche of "torpor and decay."

More suggestive evidence of the degree to which Brown identified Constantia's experience of the yellow fever with his own is found in Paul Allen's biography of the novelist. "Taking the extremest boundary of duty as his starting point," Allen observes, young Brockden Brown "followed the principle down through all its bearings until he brought it home to himself." As an example of this, Allen cites the 1798 New York epidemic, during which Brown insisted upon remaining in the stricken city despite the entreaties and arguments of his brother. Charles protested that it was his "duty" to attend his friends, who, were he to fall ill, would in turn conceive it their duty to attend him. "If such duties were reciprocal," Allen summarizes Brown's argument, "and they undoubtedly were, could he without performing his part, without running his share of the danger,

demand that assistance which he had refused to impart[?]'' (Allen, 60).
The logic is as cold as Constantia's, almost comic in its cavalier indifference
to the horrible realities of the epidemic. "It might be urged indeed,"
Brown's argument continues,

> that the inhabitants were flying from the city, and the danger
> hourly increasing. From hence he would infer the necessity of his
> longer residence, for indubitably the greater the number which
> fled from the city the more difficult must it be to procure atten-
> dants for those who remain. (Allen, 60)

To the obvious counterargument that, by remaining in the city, he might
fall ill himself and become a burden rather than a help, Brown blandly
replied: "this was a hazard incident to the nature of man, and for which he
was in no shape responsible." Were he somehow assured of immunity
from the disease, he would still hold it a duty to remain, though there
would be no "merit" in "such an action." "Where no danger existed,
what fortitude was required? Danger made this act of his a double duty;
and in fact, if there had been no such hazard, no question of this kind
could have occurred" (Allen, 60–1).

Though Brown's modern biographer, Harry R. Warfel, calls this
behavior "lofty," Paul Allen thought it an example of the extravagance to
which the writer's "romantic turn," operating through "nicety of argument," could carry him. Warner Berthoff, in his unpublished Ph.D.
dissertation on the novelist, interprets the *romantic* turn more literally.
Suggesting that Brown's affair with Susan A. Potts had reached a critical
stage during the months of the epidemic, Berthoff speculates that the
young man was anxious to remain near her in New York.[9] Virtually no explicit connection exists between the fever and seduction plots in *Ormond*,
and Brown seems to have been aware of structural flaws in the novel
generally. In a prefatory epistle addressed to a fictitious personage named
"I. E. Rosenberg," Sophia apologizes that her "narrative will have little of
that merit which flows from unity of design" (3). But Berthoff's speculation about Miss Potts does provide a biographical link between sex and the
epidemic: like the wilderness, both admit of dramatic extremity. The
"frontier" existed in many forms for Brockden Brown, and fiction served
to take him there, often in spite of conscious design.

Constantia Dudley's most enduring passion through the course of the
novel is her love for Sophia Courtland; but the first homoerotic episode is
occasioned by a gloomy tale told about Martinette de Beauvais. She is in-
troduced early in the book under the name of Ursula Monrose[10] when Constantia's neighbor, Sarah Baxter, tells the girl what Mr. Baxter saw at the
Monrose house. It was Ursula dragging—so it seemed to Sarah's
husband—"a corpse, livid and contagious" to an improvised grave.

Astoundingly, Constantia does not respond to this macabre aspect of the story at all, but instead falls in love with Ursula-Martinette sight unseen. She remarks a close parallel with her own situation; like herself, Ursula is "immersed in poverty, friendless, burdened with the maintainance and nurture of [a] father" (72). Ursula Monrose would prove worthy of her love," Constantia decides, but despairs of ever meeting her (72). A short time later, Constantia reluctantly takes her blind father's beloved lute to a music shop, hoping to sell it in order to raise rent money. At the shop she sees a young woman whose "person and face" instantly arrest her attention. Unbeknownst to Constantia, it is Ursula (or Martinette) who buys the lute—which eventually becomes the means by which Constantia and Martinette are brought together. When the Dudleys' fortunes take a turn for the better, Constantia decides to recover the instrument, though she has no idea where to find it. While out for a stroll one day, however, she hears it, and commissions the music shop owner to purchase it for her. He delivers the instrument to Constantia, telling her that the lady refused to take any money for it. At this point, Constantia is once again assailed by pangs of "duty." With financial recovery, Dudley, aided by Ormond's physician, had also recovered his sight; this makes Constantia decide that the lute, consoling to her father in his impoverished blindness, would now be more necessary to the happiness of the "unknown lady." She has the shopkeeper return it.

This episode is not just another instance of Brown's overfondness for unnecessary subplot; nor is it only another opportunity for Constantia to exhibit her commitment to the principle of duty, though Brown may have intended it as such. As Berthoff suggests that Brown's protestations of duty masked his real desire to remain with Miss Potts, so, perhaps, Constantia returns the lute in the hope that it will bring about a meeting with the young woman who has so moved her. Whatever Brown's and Constantia's conscious intentions, this does, in fact, occur. Martinette calls upon Constantia, who becomes "daily more enamored" (189) of her as she relates revolutionary adventures, military exploits, and political intrigues worthy of Ormond himself, who, indeed, proves to be Martinette's brother. They share a polyglot and exotic European background: Martinette was born in "a garden at Aleppo" of a Cyprian mother and a "sclavonian" father from Ragusa (Dubrovnik).

As if to underscore the homosexual element of Constantia's character, Sophia, just a few pages after her friend first encounters Martinette at the music shop, tells us how Constantia spurned the attentions of one Mr. Balfour. This worthy Scot rescued the girl from two would-be rapists, after which he began to pay court. A "strict adherance to the maxims of trade" had made the middle-aged man wealthy, and though the figure he cut was not "elegant," neither was it "ungainly," though his face "betrayed few marks of intelligence" (80–3). The prospect of marriage with him launches Constantia into feminist speculations (83–5) reminiscent of *Alcuin*. Of course, of itself, the girl's refusal to marry the solid but dull Balfour does not indicate homosexuality. Still, it does recall her indifference to the young man who had courted her earlier in the story, and it provides a passionless heterosexual backdrop for the markedly more intense Martinette episode.

Martinette de Beauvais is herself something of a substitute for Sophia Westwyn Courtland. Sarah Baxter's tale of Ursula-Martinette serves first to recall Sophia to Constantia's mind (72) and, later, when the girl contemplates intimate friendship with Martinette, she is reminded even more forcefully of Sophia, "a being like herself, who had grown up with her from childhood, who had been entwined with her earliest affections, but from whom she had been severed from the period at which her father's misfortunes commenced." Ignorant of Sophia's fate and whereabouts, Constantia is filled with "excruciating" sadness that "formed a kind of paroxysm, which, like some febrile affections, approached and retired without warning, and against the most vehement struggles" (187). We see how correct Fiedler was in pointing out the erotic vocabulary of the relationship between Sophia and Constantia. Sophia speaks of her "love" for Constantia, and her "caresses" (224–5). When the two women are reunited, the rational Constantia, so distant with two male suitors, swoons upon first sight of Sophia. The women spend three days in a "state of dizziness and intoxication," their appetite for sleep and food lost as they are confounded "amidst the impetuosities of a master passion. . . . O precious inebriation of the heart! O pre-eminent love!" (250–1).

At their blissful reunion only one thing disturbs Sophia about Constantia: "The name of Ormond was, of course, frequently repeated by my friend. . . . I could not but harbor aversion to a scheme which should tend to sever me from Constantia, or to give me a competitor in her affections. Besides this," Sophia adds, "the properties of Ormond were of too mysterious nature to make him worthy of acceptance" (251). Sophia tells us that "Constantia's unacquaintance with the doctrines of that school in which Ormond was probably instructed, led her to regard the conduct of the man with more curiosity and wonder than fear" (263). The American girl "had lived at a distance from scenes where principles are hourly put to the test of experiment; where all extremes of fortitude and pusillanimity are accustomed to meet; where recluse virtue and speculative heroism give place, as if by magic, to the last excesses of debauchery and wickedness; where pillage and murder are engrafted on systems of all-embracing and self-oblivious benevolence, and the good of mankind is professed to be pursued with bonds of association and covenants of secrecy" (252). Sophia knows of Ormond's association with European "schemers and reasoners who aimed at new-modelling the world, and the subversion of all that has hitherto been conceived elementary and fundamental in the constitution of man and government" (252). An early American reader of *Ormond* would immediately recognize this as an allusion to the Illuminati, a utopian "secret society" that had a brief and fitful, though highly publicized, existence in Europe. Elaborate rumors of Illuminati activity in the United

States caused a disproportionate panic among many Americans at the end of the eighteenth century.[11]

The Order of the Illuminati was founded on May 1, 1776, the result of a malcontented law professor's conflict with the Jesuit administrators of his institution. When the Jesuits of the University of Ingolstadt in Bavaria tried to discredit Adam Weishaupt, protesting the payment of his salary and spreading word that he was a dangerous freethinker, he responded by founding a secret society. Inspired by his early wanderings through French utopian philosophical books, by fuzzy notions of the Eleusian mysteries, the secret cult of the Pythagoreans, and the contemporary Freemasons, Weishaupt intended to gather about him an undercover army of intellectuals who would "new-model" the world. They would set up "schools of wisdom" to teach in seclusion and mystery able and susceptible youths about the errors of priestcraft, to the end of perfecting the "morals and the felicity of the race." More egotist than visionary, inept and unprepossessing, Weishaupt started with five members. After four years, membership had increased only to sixty, until a wealthy and influential North German diplomat, Baron Adolf Friedrich Knigge, joined and, in effect, took over. Under the Baron's leadership, the Order grew to some two or three thousand by 1784, including students, merchants, doctors, pharmacists, lawyers, judges, professors, civil authorities, pastors—and priests. Dukes and princes joined, as did Herder, Goethe, Pestalozzi, and others.

At its very zenith, in 1784, internal conflict and outside pressure began to plague the Order. In June, Carl Theodore, Duke of Upper and Lower Bavaria, moved against the Illuminati, demanding that military personnel, civil and government officials, professors, students, and clerics resign from the Order under pain of dismissal or even deportation. Badly crippled, the Illuminati were not silenced: a war of pamphlets ensued, through which the "secret" society became a public sensation culminating in October of 1786 when Bavarian government police raided the house of one Xavier Zwack. Here the officials found a cache of papers relating the most intimate workings of the Order. Published, the documents raised an outcry against a secret organization that had been plotting the overthrow of religion and government. By 1787 the Order of the Illuminati had been broken, after scarcely more than a decade of existence.

The Illuminati, never really a significant political or ideological force, nonetheless left a considerable legend in the wake of its passing. As it does today, the idea of conspiratorial networks captured the public imagination. When the French Revolution erupted in 1789, many were ready to see it as the work of the Illuminati. It was not until 1798 that the theory took hold in America, when the Reverend Jedidiah Morse preached to his congregation in the New North Church, Boston, on May 9, that the Illuminati, already responsible for a European Reign of Terror, had infiltrated the United States.[12] The sermon, immediately and widely publicized, not only created public alarm but prompted a number of statesmen, including President Adams and George Washington, to voice concern over the possible presence of such conspirators on American shores. New Englanders in particular may have recalled the agitation some four years earlier over liberal clubs—known as "Democratic Societies"—in their part of the country. Denounced in 1794 by Washington himself, these organizations seemed now to fit into an overall pattern of conspiracy. And evidence mounted. The May 14, 1798, *Connecticut Courant*, but five days after Morse preached his sermon, published the contents of three anonymous letters thrown into John Adams's house, announcing a plot to burn Philadelphia. In 1799, Morse claimed to have in his possession "an official, authenticated list of names, ages, places of nativity, professions &c. of the officers and members of a Society of *Illuminati* . . . consisting of *one hundred* members, instituted in Virginia, by the *Grand Orient* of FRANCE." A similar society, Morse added, was also operating in New York.[13]

On September 14, 1798, William Dunlap wrote in his diary: "Afternoon read C B Browns [*sic*] beginning for the life of Carwin—as far as he has gone he has done well: he has taken up the schemes of the Illuminati" (338-9). With the nation in the first throes of an Illuminati scare—a condition that would endure in varying degrees of intensity through the remaining two years of the century—it is almost certain that Brown was familiar with, or at least knew about, the May 9 sermon of Jedidiah Morse.[14] However, as early as April 11, 1798—almost a full month before Morse's sermon—Dunlap records visiting the book shop of Thomas Dobson, where he paused to "look into 'Proofs of a Conspiracy, &c,'" which Dunlap tentatively judged "at least a curious book." Perhaps he had even found it curious enough to mention to his friend Brown, with whom he took tea after stopping at the bookstore (*Diary*, 241). Dunlap does not record actually reading John Robison's *Proofs of a Conspiracy against All the Religions and Governments of Europe, Carried on in the Secret Meetings of Free Masons, Illuminati, and Reading Societies* until August 3 (finishing it on the tenth), when the reaction to Morse's sermon must have been well under way (*Diary*, 321 and 324). Not only might we guess that the clamor following the sermon piqued Dunlap's curiosity, but it seems reasonable to infer that Dunlap's novelist friend also read the book after Morse's sermon had been made known and before writing part of "The Memoirs of Carwin the Biloquist" early in September. In any case, Jedidiah Morse himself knew Robison's *Proofs*, basing many of his anti-Illuminist pronouncements upon it. The reverend also reported that, just three weeks after the Scotsman's book reached Philadelphia and New York in April 1798, it was issued in an American reprinting (Stauffer, 233). By the end of the year, British and American printings of the work totaled seven.[15]

Brown's sketch of Ludloe, the diabolical mentor of young Francis Carwin in "The Memoirs of Carwin the Biloquist," does owe a good deal to Robison. Not only do Robison and Brown share a broad depiction of the sinister utopian schemes of the Illuminati, but also details of the Order's operations. Ludloe swears Carwin to absolute secrecy, an oath that means swift and certain death if broken—just as Robison had reported of Illuminati practice. Robison described how a Novice of the Order was expected to probe mind and soul, withholding no secret from his Master; "The Memoirs of Carwin" depicts a similar process of introspection and confession.

"Nothing was so frequently discoursed of [among the Illuminati]," Robison remarks, "as the propriety of employing, for a good purpose, the means which the wicked employed for evil purposes; and it was taught, that the preponderancy of good in the ultimate result consecrated every mean [sic] employed; and that wisdom and virtue consisted in properly determining this balance."[16] This moral paradox is also central to Brown's delineation of Ludloe and Ormond as Illuminists. It was a question, though, that had concerned Brown at least two years before he could have read Robison. One day in October of 1796 he had a dispute with Elihu Hubbard Smith and two other members of the New York Friendly Club over what Smith called "the old subject of Truth." The youthful physician wrote in his diary:

[William H.] Woolsey, [William] Johnson, & I, maintain that *on all occasions* truth is to be spoken: i.e. that nothing will justify a falsehood; or that utility can never be promoted thereby. Brown & Dunlap pretend that tho' our position is, *generally*, true, yet there [are] occasions when it will be our duty to speak falsely, since by so doing we shall promote the general good. Long discussion —grounds of argument gone over several times—no conclusion. (Smith, 239 [October 29, 1796])

Two years before he wrote "Carwin," then, Brown's regard for principle was flexible enough to permit his entertaining the moral subordination of means to end; but when it came actually to working this question out in the character and schemes of Ludloe, Brown faltered, abandoning the "Carwin" fragment with "no conclusion." Because they share so much with Ludloe, Ormond and his story may be taken as an attempt to follow up and conclude the intellectual implications of the Ludloe tale.

Both Ludloe and Ormond are Illuminists, professing similar goals of human perfection and expressing identical sentiments about the nature of sexual love ("Carwin," 291; *Ormond*, 160). Both exercise a diabolical influence over similar protégés. Francis Carwin and Thomas Craig—Mr. Dudley's disreputable apprentice—are habitual and highly skilled deceivers. Ludloe would exploit Carwin's biloquistic talents as the dubious means of achieving utopian ends. Ormond also exploits Craig, convincing him to murder Constantia's father, a deed Ormond calls an act of benevolence. In a telling stroke of black satire, Brown has Ormond eagerly admit to Constantia that he had caused the murder of her father. The murder, he explains, proceeded from the same "benevolence" that had prompted Ormond to send Dudley to a physician capable of restoring the old man's sight. "I gave him sight and took away his life, from motives equally wise." Having conceived a passion for Constantia, Ormond assisted Dudley in his need, hoping to win the girl's love and the old man's consent to marriage. When Dudley persisted in his opposition to marriage, Ormond reasoned that his life had become an "obstacle" to the happiness both of himself (Ormond) and Constantia.

> For killing him, therefore, I may claim your gratitude. His death was a due and disinterested offering on the altar of your felicity and mine.
> My deed was not injurious to him. At his age, death, whose coming at some period is inevitable, could not be distant. To make it unforeseen and brief, and void of pain, to preclude the torments of a lingering malady, a slow and visible descent to the grave, was the dictate of benevolence. (280–1)

As *Wieland* is, in part, the vision of Joel Barlow inverted, so the title character in *Ormond* represents an inversion of utopian benevolence. As Theodore Wieland sought revelation and found only tragic error, so Ormond, in working "benevolence," brings evil. The character of Ormond is a measure of the tensions that developed in Brown's thought between 1796 and 1799. The opinion Brown held in the 1796 dispute with Smith and the others, that in some cases a lie is benevolent, argues a solid confidence in the rectitude of human nature and the soundness of human judgment. It is the position of one who could in good conscience subscribe to the method of the Illuminati Robison described, the use of "wicked" means to accomplish good ends. By refusing to equate wisdom and virtue with absolute external principles, Brown early on expressed faith in the individual's ability to determine the just balance between means and ends. In this confidence Paul Allen judged him too much the "ardently romantic" philanthropist: "Whatever of defect was discernible in existing systems, he imputed to the wrong cause, which was to some inherent ineffectiveness in the system itself, and not the depravity of our common nature, so capable of perverting the best systems to the worst of purposes" (Allen, 70).

By the last year of the eighteenth century, however, when he wrote *Ormond*, the novelist, with full volition or not, was calling into question the human capacity for intellectual and moral judgment. Organized benevolence had become the high-minded but ruthless and unbalanced Illuminati; the benign utopianist had become Ormond, who hints at plans of setting a "newborn empire" in an "*austral* continent, or in the heart of desert America" (252). It is the very conspiracy Brown's countrymen most feared.

It would be convenient simply to conclude that "The Memoirs of Carwin the Biloquist'' and, even more, *Ormond* betoken a rejection of youthful radicalism. Carwin, in fact, does dismiss his own utopian notions as mere "visions of youth" ("Carwin," 278). But Brown failed to divorce himself so neatly from Ormond and the values he represents. Ormond's resemblance to the novelist is marked. A utopianist like Brown, he is also a "secret witness," spying on the Dudleys and on Constantia and Sophia so that he knows "everything." Having overheard Sophia counsel Constantia to avoid him, Ormond declares that "not a tittle has escaped me" (256). In this secret omniscience he approaches the vocation of novelist, observing, indeed, "every thing with the accuracy of an artist" (125); for Ormond "blended in his person the functions of poet and actor" (116). Like Carwin, with whom Brown—as a creator of fiction—seems also to have identified himself, Ormond discovered in early youth "a remarkable faculty in imitating the voice and gestures of others" (115). Like Carwin, he is as persuasive as Cicero: "Listening to his discourse, no one's claim to sincerity appeared less questionable" than Ormond's (114-5).

Speculations about what such characters as Carwin and Ormond meant emotionally and intellectually to Brown are not idle. We are not talking about a merely personal identification of the author with his creations; rather, Brown identified his characters with certain objective values and positions. Projecting onto them various intellectual and moral qualities, he was able to experiment with his own. In the character of Ormond he combined aspects of utopianism and art, taking these to a moral extreme in order to probe the nature of his own vocation. What he found could not have reassured him.

Absolute candor, "sincerity," is Ormond's chief "boast" to Constantia when the two first meet. He claims an "aversion to duplicity," an aversion born of personal experience. "One transaction had occurred in his life, in which the consequences of being misled by false appearances were of the utmost moment to his honor and safety." Not only did the "usual mode of solving his doubts" seem inadequate in this case, but the "eagerness" of a Carwin-like "curiosity" tempted Ormond to employ "his talents at imitation" (115). In the pursuit of absolute truth, Ormond becomes a creator of fiction. Fiction, for Brown the route to revelation, is perilously close to deceit. Deceit figures in *Wieland* as "concealment," the unpardonable sin that preys upon the cardinal human weakness: "limited perceptions [that] debar us from a thorough knowledge of any actions and motives but our own" (*Ormond*, 262). (We must add that here Sophia is too sanguine in her judgment. We have seen time and again in Brown's novels that human perceptions are so limited that they *especially* debar characters from a thorough knowledge of their own actions.) Deceit attains in Brown's fiction a little of the awful grandeur it assumes in Milton:

For neither Man not Angel can discern
Hypocrisy, the only evil that walks

Invisible, except to God alone.
(*Paradise Lost*, bk. 3, ll. 682–4)

"All that duty enjoins," Sophia admonishes, "is to design and to execute nothing which may not be approved by a divine and omniscient Observer" (262). As if the truth-seeking novelist had not created dilemma enough, by having Sophia substitute the periphrasis "omniscient Observer" for the simpler "God," Brown associates Ormond—the all-knowing secret witness—with God, though his nature, like that of Milton's Satan, is deceit. Worse, the omniscient observer is the novelist himself, whose fictional truths, while God-like, are reared upon Satanic deceptions.

Of course the expression of these identifications and projections is exaggerated, Brown having taken it to what Paul Allen called the "extremest boundary." Yet the tensions present in *Ormond* do accurately foreshadow the author's final abandonment of fiction. In October 1803, when Brown undertook the *Literary Magazine and American Register*, he apologized to his readers for ever having written novels:

> I have written much, but take much blame to myself for something which I have written, and take no praise for any thing. I should enjoy a larger share of my own respect, at the present moment, if nothing had ever flowed from my pen, the production of which could be traced to me.

He followed this with a pledge to embrace in his new magazine the cause of religion, so important in "an age like this, when the foundations of religion and morality have been so badly attacked."[17] The juxtaposition of his renunciation of novel writing and his espousal of religion in an unbelieving age is especially poignant, suggesting that Brown stopped producing novels for reasons more serious than an overly punctilious sense of propriety. For Brown, novels end in doubt, negation of belief, loss of faith. Writing them, he is drawn through a "metaphysic wilderness" opening onto a terrifying "nothing." To Ormond, the "universe was . . . a series of events connected by an undesigning and inscrutable necessity, and an assemblage of forms to which no beginning or end can be conceived" (180). An unkind critic might quote this as a comment on the structure of a Charles Brockden Brown novel. A more sympathetic one would identify it as the ultimate tendency of Brown's vision. If the universe is absurd, truth is mutable, definable only by what one person can make another believe. This nihilistic cosmogony allows Ormond to act without moral compunction. It also helps make him insane. Little more than a year after *Ormond* appeared, Brown quit writing novels.[18]

If in *Ormond*, as in *Wieland*, Brown identified himself with a dangerous deceiver, he also followed the *Wieland* precedent in identifying himself with the seeker of truth as well. Like Theodore Wieland, Constantia Dudley is driven by a "thirst of knowledge" (29), laudable enough in itself, but, taken to an extreme, potentially fatal. Unlike Wieland's, Constantia's thirst does not proceed from a religious desire for revelation. It is a passion in its own right, an innate curiosity that recalls Carwin, whom Brown described with the same phrase he applied to Constantia. Like the girl, the biloquist had "a thirst for knowledge" ("Carwin," 247). In all cases—for Wieland and Constantia, as well as for Ormond and Carwin—the obsessive search for knowledge leads through dangerous deception to a revelation of the ultimate impossibility of attaining absolute truth. In *Wieland*, Brown projected this quest in figures of a metaphysic wilderness leading to nothing. We shall see that the wilderness does play a significant, if subtle, role in *Ormond*, and images of paths and "bewilderment" are plentiful. These, however, are subordinated to another epistemological metaphor, drawn not from the American landscape, but from the American novel. It is the popular motif of seduction.

In the course of the novel, Constantia exhibits three principal passions: for Sophia, for Martinette, and for Ormond. Two young men, both of whom seek marriage, Constantia rejects. Obviously, the common denominator of her emotional life is not simply sexual. Constantia is drawn to two women and one man and is indifferent to two other men. What Martinette, Sophia, and Ormond do have in common is knowledge. Martinette embodies an exciting and mysterious intimacy with European revolution and intrigue. Sophia, whose very name means "knowledge,"[19] was raised in America with Constantia but has also lived in Europe and, like Martinette, has experienced the titillation of amoral revolution. Ormond combines European knowledge with the dark, illicit, and violent sexual appeal Leslie Fiedler identified as the hallmark of the popular seduction figure. The youth who woos Constantia near the beginning of the novel is nothing more than a callow young American; and Balfour, who courts the girl after rescuing her from would-be rapists, is only a commonsense Scot.

It is Constantia's curiosity, her thirst for knowledge, more than her sexual drive, that draws her to Ormond. Yet this curiosity is so basic to the girl's being that it assumes sexual magnitude. Just as her curiosity had pulled her into the dangers of a yellow fever epidemic, it beckons her to a man she knows to be dangerous. And, as Sophia observes, "what knowledge [Ormond] imparted, instead of appeasing, only tended to inflame, her curiosity" (177). Sophia is careful to point out just how her friend's rational education shaped her curiosity so as to put the girl in "imminent" peril from Ormond (179). Constantia "was unacquainted with religion. . . . She formed her estimate of good and evil on nothing but terrestrial and visible consequences" (179). Ormond's customary prey is precisely this combination of philosophies so popular in Brown's America: common sense and Lockeanism, a faith in a universe fully knowable through sensation. Like Carwin, he possesses the talent, motivated by a nihilistic sense of universal absurdity, necessary for manipulating sensation and perception.

In order for Ormond's deceit to succeed, his victim must have faith both in the rational order of the universe and in Ormond himself. Perhaps as a function of Brown's mutual identification with Ormond and Constantia, as representatives of the intellectual poles within himself, the seduction becomes a mutual relation. Thinking only to seduce Constantia, Ormond falls in love with her—though, again, his passion does not emerge through Brown's narrative as strictly romantic or sexual. If Constantia is drawn to the mysterious Ormond by her thirst for knowledge and is made vulnerable by her exclusive reliance on the truth of the "terrestrial and visible," Ormond is attracted to the girl by her "simplicity" (98). He is drawn inexorably to, and would be powerless without, Constantia's simple faith in what she sees and hears. Ormond actually goes so far as to confront her with this fact when he pleads with her for "understanding." She replies that Ormond can have no need of her understanding, since he understands himself so thoroughly, never scrupling to say what he thinks. "Your designs," she says, "are no sooner conceived than they are expressed. All you know, all you wish, and all you propose, are known to others as soon as to yourself. No scruples of decorum, no foresight of consequences, are obstacles in your way." Yes, Ormond ruefully agrees, "all obstacles are trampled under foot but one . . . incredulity in him who hears" (255). As Constantia is nearly ruined by her belief in Ormond, he is in fact driven mad by her "incredulity," the final lack of belief Constantia betrays in heeding Sophia's advice to leave him.

Sophia convinces her friend to leave Ormond and Philadelphia, journey to New York, and, thence, set sail with herself for the safety of England. Despite Sophia's anxiety, though, Constantia "conceived it necessary to spend a few days at her house in Jersey" before coming to New York. It had been built by Dudley in his prosperous days, "in a manner strictly classical." Set in the woods, built on the classical model, it recalls the temple of the senior Wieland. Because the house and its lovely garden had been "modelled by the genius of her father," Constantia finds herself exposed to "unforeseen" sensations that threaten to persuade her to remain on her "natal soil" rather than leave with Sophia. Though the father's role in *Wieland* echoes rather sinisterly here, Constantia's sense of filial duty, her reluctance to leave the house in the hands of unfeeling strangers, is understandable and even laudable. But Brown takes pains to insinuate an ambiguity of motive by furnishing the history of the house. After Dudley's financial collapse, it was sold to a man who, eventually, signed it over to Ormond, who had Helena Cleves set up housekeeping. We might justly wonder now about the true cause of Constantia's "unforeseen" sensations, as she lingers in Ormond's house so recently occupied by his mistress.

Like Clara Wieland—and Richardson's Pamela—Constantia is given to writing letters, "shutting herself in a kind of closet on the second floor, illuminated by a spacious window, through which a landscape of uncommon amplitude and beauty was presented to the view." She was about to write, when "her eyes rested a moment on the variegated hues which poured out upon the western sky and upon the scene of intermingled waters, copses, and fields." This is an abstract landscape, typical of Brown, but a landscape just the same, and the only view of something at least close to a wilderness we are given in this novel of the city. A horseman appears from the west, something in his "figure and movements" reminding Constantia of Ormond. "She started from her seat with some degree of palpitation. Whence this arose, whether from fear or from joy, or from intermixed emotions, it would not be easy to ascertain" (269).

When the European seducer comes to rape the American girl, he rides from the west. Up to this point, Ormond and his efforts at seduction have followed the pattern described by Fiedler: a sophisticated European attempts the honor of a naïve American girl. But just as the failed seduction is about to come to violent consummation, something in Brown prompts him to translate the scene into terms of the wilderness. He goes so far as to have the European approach his fatal work from the direction of America itself. As he approaches, the scene darkens, anticipating the primeval blackness of the cave in *Edgar Huntly*. The "light hastily disappeared, and darkness, rendered, by a cloudy atmosphere, uncommonly intense, succeeded" (271).

Ormond begins his assault by ghoulishly depositing the corpse of Thomas Craig at Constantia's chamber door. Then, in an exchange we have already glanced at, he rapidly but coolly tells the girl how he had used Craig, Dudley's own apprentice, to murder the old man. We have already mentioned Ormond's justification of the act, a murder committed from motives of pure "benevolence" (280). "I am not tired of well-doing," the mad utopianist continues. "Having ceased to labor for an unattainable good"—meaning the hand of Constantia Dudley—"I have come hither to possess myself of all that I now crave, and by the same deed to afford you an illustrious opportunity to signalize your wisdom and your fortitude" (282). He deems the rape an act of benevolence, much as Theodore Wieland had murdered his family in the name of God.

Ironically, Ormond really *is* about to afford the girl an opportunity to "signalize" wisdom and fortitude. Like Clara Wieland confronted by the mad Theodore, Constantia seizes a penknife, threatening to kill herself to save her honor. "Poor Constance," Ormond contemptuously replies, "so! thou preferest thy imaginary honor to life! . . . Living or dead, the prize that I have in view shall be mine" (284). We know that, at eighteen, Ormond raped and then murdered a Tartar girl. Now he proposes to "have" Constantia alive or dead. The man has graduated from the merely brutal to a cultural taboo on the order of Edgar Huntly's approach to cannibalism. But if extremity drives Huntly to the brink of cannibalistic suicide, extremity also rescues him. As he is about to bury a tomahawk in his own heart, a panther materializes from the wilderness and, without time for deliberation, Huntly hurls the weapon at the animal. "No one knows the powers that are latent in his constitution," Huntly reflects. "Called forth by imminent dangers, our efforts frequently exceed our most sanguine belief." So Constantia turns the penknife upon Ormond. "My deed was scarcely the fruit of intention," she later reports.

> It was suggested by a momentary frenzy. I saw no other means of escaping from vileness and pollution. I was menaced with an evil worse than death. I forbore till my strength was almost subdued: the lapse of another moment would have placed me beyond hope. (291)

"I had acted without foresight," wrote Edgar Huntly, "and yet no wisdom could have prescribed more salutary measures. The panther was slain . . . from . . . involuntary impulse." Constantia, likewise, is all disbelief: "My stroke was desperate and random. It answered its purpose too well" (291).

That Brown set the violent climax of *Ormond* in a landscape and among motifs suggesting the wilderness indicates once again the role that the New World played in his imagination. Though a sinister and sophisticated European, with beliefs that originated in a utopian Illuminist movement founded upon fanatical devotion to reason, Ormond nurtures ideas and performs actions that partake of a darkness well beyond the frontiers of reason. Not only does the wilderness provide an appropriately "gothic" stage upon which Ormond's fanatical rationality and inverted benevolence play out a grotesque fifth act, it also serves as a territory beyond reason and volition, much as it had in *Edgar Huntly*. Constantia's self-defense slaying of Ormond was "suggested by a momentary frenzy," the stroke "desperate and random," an instinctual response elicited from the cool disciple of Locke, Hartley, and Hume. Ormond is almost equally unconscious of his final actions, going about the rape as Theodore Wieland had committed murder, executing some necessary but impersonal decree. "I shall be grieved for the fatal issue of my experiment," Ormond tells Constantia. "I shall mourn over thy martyrdom to the most opprobrious and contemptible of all errors"—by which he means the notion that a maiden's "honor" is more valuable than her life—"but," he continues, "that thou shouldst undergo this trial is decreed" (284).

More intriguing is the hint that Ormond's "wilderness" deed represents an unconscious wish for Constantia to accomplish his suicide. In an earlier scene, in which Ormond had pleaded with the girl to ignore the advice of Sophia and to marry him, he besought Constantia's understanding. "Look at me," he demanded:

> Can you read my thoughts? Can your discernment reach the bounds of my knowledge and the bottom of my purposes? Catch you not a view of the monsters that are starting to birth *here*? (and

he put his left hand to his forehead). But you cannot. Should I
paint them to you verbally, you would call me jester or deceiver.
What pity that you have not instruments for piercing into
thoughts! (254)

It is only later, and with a penknife for an "instrument," that Constantia
pierces Ormond, thoughts and all. That Ormond's death-wish was likely
not the product of Brown's own conscious craft points to the significance
this denouement holds for the author's intellectual autobiography. We
have suggested that *Ormond* repeats a pattern present in *Wieland*,
Brown's identification both with a vulnerable seeker after truth and with a
diabolical creator of fictional truths. In this sense, Constantia and Ormond
are glosses upon Brown's conversation with John Bernard about his bifur-
cated self. Ostensibly, Constantia is the dutiful, rational, social aspect of
self, and Ormond, the rapacious, dark aspect, who answers only to the demands of an asocial id. But the two remain neither pure nor separate: Constantia's allegiance to duty is ambiguous, and Ormond, intending to
possess Constantia, becomes her possession. The only resolution Brown can
imagine to this attraction and conflict is violent and unconscious. The disturbing ideas Ormond entertains about the nature of civilization are con-
signed at the last to a wilderness. Constantia, bred in detached and ar-
rogant rationality, counters the threat of Ormond not with the reasoned
products of a pen, but with the instinctual thrust of a pen-knife.

For Brown, *Ormond* was yet another attempt to create a vocation as
writer. He tried to reconcile the demands of his social consciousness with
those of a literary imagination essentially antagonistic to the demands of
civilization. And he attempted to work this task in a fictional frame that
would appeal to his countrymen—and women—the audience of the early
American seduction novel. But *Ormond* demonstrates that such a balance
was not possible for Brockden Brown. More than this, its intellectual con-
flicts, "resolved" only through violence, reveal that the novelist's abandonment of fiction was already imminent in 1799. Ormond, projection of
what Brown sensed as his creative self, is finally a madman, whose radicalism and utopian ideas (crucial to Brown's own early literary endeavors) are
grotesquely twisted and inverted. He is destroyed by Constantia, the
dutiful and rational woman with whom he tries to unite himself—or, more
accurately, the dutiful and rational principle with which Brown tries to
unite an asocial and nonrational force of imagination.

Though *Ormond* failed as a personal document, and failed as a
popular seduction story, it is, like Brown's other works, extremely valuable
as a perception of American civilization during the early years of the Republic. In his description of the seduction novel, Leslie Fiedler identifies
three central stereotypes: the pure and naïve American girl, the inex-
perienced and immature American boy, and the sophisticated, wickedly
sexual European man. The popularity of the seduction novel suggests that
these stereotypes accurately reflected America's perception of itself at the

turn of the nineteenth century. The nation was seen as chaste, callow, dull
in comparison with the stormy lands across the Atlantic. In 1782 or
thereabouts, Benjamin Franklin advised would-be immigrants to America
that this country had "few People so miserable as the Poor of Europe,
[but] also very few that in Europe would be called rich; it is rather a general
happy Mediocrity that prevails."[20] As if in echo, Sophia Westwyn Courtland, who has known both America and Europe, declares

> that the difference between Europe and America lay chiefly in
> this: that, in the former, all things tended to extremes, whereas,
> in the latter, all things tended to the same level. Genius, virtue,
> and happiness, on these shores, were distinguished by a sort of
> mediocrity. Conditions were less unequal, and men were strangers
> to the heights of enjoyment and the depths of misery to which the
> inhabitants of Europe are accustomed. (236)

It is a common enough observation, one which the seduction genre itself
reflects. Yet even as the genre and Sophia both attest to the common view,
the adventures of Constantia, chaste maiden of a chaste Columbia, argue
against it. She courts a man and a woman of radical ideas, she ventures into
the "fangs" of pestilence, and she kills a man.

When Sophia and Constantia first parted, before we take up their
story in *Ormond*, they exchanged miniature portraits of themselves.
Sophia was depicted "with the crescent of Dian," and Constantia with
"the cincture of Venus" (243). Perhaps the emblem of the virginal hunt-
ress suits Sophia, whose language toward Constantia, it is true, borders on
the voluptuous, but whose counsel is most chaste. But that Constantia,
rationally educated, indifferent to at least two suitors, is identified midway
through the novel with Venus is, on the surface, puzzling. It is of course
possible to dismiss the emblems as the hackneyed amenities of a politely
neoclassical age; but the crucial roles that Cicero and the Daemon of
Socrates play in *Wieland* suggest that Brown does not take classical references so casually. Brown, who, in the earlier portions of *Ormond*, paints
—albeit with nervous strokes—Constantia as something of a virginal
Diana, turns abruptly to label his picture Venus. It is as if Brown had begun with the assumptions of the conventional seduction novel, choosing a
heroine born of her country's "happy Mediocrity," more rational and intelligent than the usual girl of early American romance, but just as naïve
and vulnerable. Then the novelist's own daemon took charge—that
literary self which characteristically shapes, even inverts, his intended
vision. Constantia's irrational side emerges, attracted by the spectacle of
yellow fever, by a glamorous European woman, and, most of all, by
Ormond. The chaste Diana of the United States reveals an aspect of Venus,
emotionally and intellectually voluptuous. The nation, which we see for
most of the story in the form of civilized Philadelphia, becomes first a

place of dark plague and, finally, a darker wilderness in which the consequences of passion are played out with fatal results.

Francis Carwin, who dwells wholly in deception, remains in the Pennsylvania wilds that had first taught him to deceive. Edgar Huntly, who
seeks solutions to the mystery of himself, remains in Pennsylvania as well,
forlorn upon a frontier between Old World and New. In *Ormond*, as in
Wieland, Charles Brockden Brown began with the bright assumptions of
the civilized United States, only to conclude with an acknowledgment of
gloomy truths in wilderness America. From these, at the very last, he
turned away. As Clara Wieland had escaped at the end of her American
tragedy to the "ancient tranquility" of the Old World, so Constantia
Dudley, having killed the rapist she herself courted, returns with
Sophia—satisfying but benign combination of sister and lover—to
England. So we shall also see Arthur Mervyn at the end of his story, about
to leave the American land of promise for the Old World, having secured
in the United States the elegant hand of a rich European widow.

VI

The Rise of Arthur Mervyn

To behave "in the midst of a populous city, like the lonely inhabitant of a desert," Brockden Brown's "rhapsodist" declared in 1789, "will often incur the censure of inveterate folly." Having forsaken the wilderness for the city, the rhapsodist is forced to confess himself "little more than a Rhapsodist in theory," because isolation from civilization and the discontents of its many strictures is necessary to blissful egocentrism: "My felicity principally consisted in the liberty I then enjoyed [while living in the wilderness] to follow the dictates of my own inclination, into whatever seeming error, or absurdity, it might chance to lead me." But Brown could no more allow the rhapsodist unalloyed felicity than he could let Edgar Huntly escape to the wilderness without considerable "distress." Isolation, one day, brings a "black moment of despair" upon the rhapsodist, who leaves the "solitary banks of the Ohio" for the "thronged streets of the city."[1]

A decade later, in 1799, Brown created another rhapsodic youth, Arthur Mervyn. Raised on a Chester County farm, he was given to aimless rural ramblings. Mrs. Althorpe, a neighbor of the Mervyn farm, recalls how the boy was a poor hand, performing his chores, when he could be persuaded to undertake them at all, "in a bungling manner, and so as to prove that his thoughts were fixed on any thing except his business." He was a solitary lad who not only disliked manual labor but did not even indulge in sports or other recreation, "never associated with other young people, never mounted an horse but when he could not help it, and never fired a gun or angled for a fish in his life." Some supposed him an idiot, "so very perverse and singular" was his conduct. He was generally to be found "sauntering along the bank of the river, or lolling in the shade of a tree" (233).

Mrs. Althorpe's description is fraught with Brown's guilty doubts about the role of the writer as rhapsodist. Instead of the solitary dreamer pictured in the 1789 sketches, the Mervyns' neighbor describes an inept, lazy, self-indulgent idler. The whole of *Arthur Mervyn*, on its surface, vindicates the young man, clearing him of these charges through an involuted narrative of his entrance into Philadelphia, his progress through its "thronged streets," and his rise as a responsible, respectable, successful citizen of an urban United States. The story at many points runs parallel to those of two other Philadelphians, Benjamin Franklin and Charles Brockden Brown. But it also, at crucial points, veers sharply from these, and, as is characteristic of Brown's other works, superficial intentions and expectations come into ironic, if not conscious, conflict with the actual contents of the finished fiction. Like most serious interpretations of American success—one thinks of Dreiser's novels and Fitzgerald's, as well as of those Jamesian Americans, Christopher Newman and Adam Verver —*Arthur Mervyn* raises some grave questions about the values prized in American culture. Just how much Brown *intended* to criticize is subject to question; for he wrote to his brother James that the character of Arthur was intended as "a hero whose virtue, in order to be productive of benefit to others, and felicity to himself, stands in no need of riches" (Dunlap, *Life*, 2:97). Brown's was an admirable intention, but the rise of Arthur Mervyn, as a Philadelphian and an American, is very much the story of success measured largely by riches.

The fact is that Arthur likes money. He leaves his father's farm when the old man, in his view, desecrates the memory of the recently deceased Mrs. Mervyn by marrying Betty Lawrence, a "rude, ignorant, and licentious" servant girl. Although the greater part of Arthur's outrage does stem from his deep—as we shall presently see, all too deep—affection for his "revered mother," a crucial secondary concern is that Betty will now usurp the patrimony intended for himself (20). Later, during his first night in the city, when Arthur is made the victim of a prank that forces him to hide in a bedroom closet, he overhears the plot of a swindle, and his very first thought is how he might "profit" from his inadvertent detection of the scheme (41). Still later, wandering penniless through the streets of Philadelphia, he finds himself filled with "admiration" and "envy" at the sight of mansions occupied by the wealthy (47). Even more important is the partially materialistic nature of the two major attachments Arthur forms in the course of the story. He sees both the apparently well-connected Thomas Welbeck and the rich divorcée Achsa Fielding as means of establishing himself in society, and Welbeck in particular as a quick and easy way to wealth.

Charles Brockden Brown was not possessed of the special moral vision of his elder Philadelphia colleague, Benjamin Franklin, for whom "riches" and virtue were by no means incompatible. Even as the novel traces a history parallel at many points with that of Franklin, it subverts the traditionally American values Franklin first and most succinctly articulated. To gauge the degree of this subversion we must return to the image of Arthur Mervyn on his father's Chester County farm. He was, quite plainly, a mama's boy, pampered and spoiled. The "idleness" Mrs. Althorpe described went "much against the father's inclination and judgment," but Mrs. Mervyn "excused and countenanced" it (232–3). Admitting that he had been given to stubbornness and fits of temper, Arthur remarks that "a look of tender upbraiding from [mother] was always sufficient to melt me into tears and make me ductile to her will'' (17–8). With nothing but the greatest tenderness for his mother, Arthur expresses utter contempt for his father Sawny. While Mrs. Mervyn was alive, he tells us, Sawny was ''easy'' and ''sober,'' though of ''slender capacity'' (18). He is, not surprisingly, ''a Scotch peasant'' (234). When, after Mrs. Mervyn's death, Sawny takes up with Betty Lawrence (Brown also spells it ''Laurence''), Arthur is outraged to ''think that such an one should take the place of my revered mother'' (20). Betty ''had a gross and perverse taste'' and hated Arthur (he tells us) ''because she was conscious of having injured me [by marrying Sawny], because she knew that I held her in contempt, and because I had detected her in an illicit intercourse with the son of a neighbour'' (21). After his marriage to the girl, Sawny steadily descends into ''depravity.'' He ends his days ''besotted by brutal appetites,'' dying, a dipsomaniac, in a Philadelphia prison. Arthur dismisses his father's death with a businesslike rationality:

> It is useless to keep alive the sad remembrance. He was now beyond the reach of my charity or pity; and since reflection could answer no beneficial end to him, it was my duty to divert my thoughts into different channels, and live henceforth for my own happiness and that of those who were within the sphere of my influence. (393–4)

Sawny Mervyn's death frees the youth for the pursuit of his own happiness and, in the second place, the happiness of others. With the uncanny facility of Constantia Dudley or of Brockden Brown himself, Arthur manages to rationalize self-indulgence as a ''duty.''

As Brown has Arthur portray him, there is little enough to like about Sawny Mervyn; yet he is not the incontrovertibly hateful brute we glimpse in the father of Francis Carwin. Beaten, confined, and thwarted, Carwin would have good reason to greet his father's death as a liberation. But what accounts for such a response in Arthur? ''Every one,'' Mrs. Althorpe reports, ''despised [Arthur] for his idleness and folly . . . but no one feared him, and few were angry with him, till after the detection of his commerce with *Betty*, and his inhuman treatment of his father'' (236). To a post-Freudian reader, even one disinclined to follow Freud, the oedipal situation in which Brown immerses Arthur is so blatant as to be embarrassing. Arthur, who loves his mother but hates his father, is mortally offended when she is replaced by an openly sexual young woman of his own age. For having married the girl, Arthur accuses his father of a depraved appetite. Yet, according to Mrs. Althorpe and, apparently, everyone who knew the Mervyns, Arthur himself was not above ''illicit intercourse'' with his future stepmother. Thus Sawny twice bests Arthur in an oedipal triangle: first, with his natural mother (as must be the case in Freud's picture of the classical ''Oedipus complex'') but then also with Betty. Mrs. Althorpe observes that Arthur ''was studious to palliate the vices of [Betty] as long as he was her only paramour; but after her marriage with his father, the tone was changed. He confessed that she was tidy, notable, industrious; but, then, she was a prostitute'' (236).

One critic has suggested that the oedipal situation in *Arthur Mervyn* is autobiographical, Mrs. Mervyn's indulgence of her son reflecting the relation Charles himself enjoyed with his mother, and Arthur's contempt for Sawny reflecting the novelist's rebellion against his father.[2] Such narrowly autobiographical speculations are only a start. The oedipal material in *Arthur Mervyn* is but one portion of a cluster of antisocial and customarily repressed desires to which Brown gives voice in this and his other novels. Like the self-cannibalism Edgar Huntly contemplates and the necrophiliac rape Ormond threatens, intercourse with one's mother is an extremity of behavior strictly taboo in civilized Christian society. Appropriately, Brown fixes the scene of Arthur's first oedipal drama on the Mervyn farm, removed from the city and close to the wilderness. Betty Lawrence is a ''wild girl from the pine forests of New-Jersey'' (18): a ''Pine Rat'' or ''Piney.'' Highly inbred settlers in New Jersey's wilderness pine barrens, the Pineys were notorious in Brown's day (and even, to a lesser degree, more recently) as wild, anarchical, depraved outcasts from radical religious groups.[3] In young Arthur, then, Brown may well have projected a desire to prolong the irresponsible rhapsodism of youth; he may have also expressed resentment of his father and longing for his mother. But what he particularly or literally wanted is far less important to the interpretation of Brown's fiction than recognizing rhapsodism, cannibalism, necrophilia, and incest as tokens of Brockden Brown's literary imagination, which, most characteristically, was essentially antisocial. Intimations of a buried life he dared not disinter amidst ''thronged streets,'' such extremities became for Brown the proper acts of the American wilderness.

Based on Mrs. Althorpe's testimony, the case against Arthur Mervyn is a convincing one. Certainly, Mervyn's neighbors are ''unanimous'' (232) in their low opinion and dislike of Arthur. What is more, as Mrs. Althorpe points out, the young man ''never denied'' the reports of his affair with Betty. ''When reminded, on one occasion, of the inference which every impartial person would draw from appearances, he acknowledged, with his usual placid effrontery, that the inference was unavoidable'' (236). Of course, this is by no means an admission of guilt. It is, rather, a prima facie instance of ''effrontery,'' the contemptuous playfulness with which Arthur treats his slow-witted neighbors. Brown seems to have intended the question of Arthur's guilt as an ironic epistemological anecdote, deliberately gathering evidence against his hero in order to expose the weaknesses of empirically based knowledge. To Dr. Stevens, whose kindness and skill pull Arthur through a bout of yellow fever, the youth does protest his innocence (302–3 and 345–7). Largely because Stevens is the ostensible narrator of the novel (he is actually only one of many) and a sympathetically drawn character, we accept Arthur's innocence despite the evidence against it.

On its simplest level, the manipulation of our belief needs little explication. The theme is one Brown often worked: appearances and perceptions deceive, so that it often takes the informed intuition of a seasoned man like Stevens to penetrate to the unlikely truth beneath empirical evidence. Still, Brown establishes the ambiguity of his hero's character so thoroughly that his innocence is never proved beyond doubt. We saw in *Wieland* that Brown was unwilling either to condemn or exonerate Carwin absolutely; such was the novelist's ambivalent emotional investment in the character. Similarly, Brown could not introduce into civilized Philadelphia a man who had actually slept with his (step-) mother, anymore than he could have sanctioned those other "wilderness" acts: cannibalism, necrophilia, or even rhapsodism. But, by refusing to establish absolutely Mervyn's guilt or innocence, Brown could allow at least limited expression of the antisocial fantasies of his literary self. These he could not afford to clarify, even to himself, since to do so would mean declaring unambiguous allegiance either to the wilderness or to the city.

Associated not with the uncultivated wilderness, but with the agrarian countryside, is an eighteenth-century vision of a pastoral paradise. Repeatedly in *Arthur Mervyn* the virtues of the country are contrasted to the vices rampant in the moral chaos of the city (see, for example, pp. 10, 21, 123, 154, 170, 311). But while Brown pays lip-service to this "official" Eden, his real concern is with the covert one embodied in the wilderness. Though Arthur lives on a farm, his early life is associated with that farther territory of self-indulgence, where fantasy can be acted upon and taboos enjoyed. In the official version of the American success story, the young man leaves the paradise of his pastoral home in order to build a new one in the city, founded, of course, on Protestant notions of hard work and honest wit. But Arthur Mervyn leaves the country because his father's marriage to Betty Lawrence repels and angers him. With his indulgent mother dead, replaced by a "prostitute" who hates him and who, in fact, may have rejected him for his father, Arthur has lost his covert paradise. Despite the values implicit in the official version of the progress from country to city, it is his private Eden of rhapsodic wilderness indulgence that Arthur seeks to regain in Philadelphia.

We shall see that Arthur, once in the city, does not hesitate to attach himself to a mysterious Mr. Welbeck, who promises the boy a quick and easy way to wealth. And it is true that much of the novel traces the bad consequences of this connection, nearly disastrous for Arthur and wholly ruinous for Welbeck. True, too, that we leave Mervyn at the end of the novel on the verge of an honest medical apprenticeship with the kindly and upright Dr. Stevens. But the real happy ending, which subverts the official moral of the tale, is Arthur's impending marriage to Achsa Fielding, a well-to-do European lady whom the boy loves to call "*mamma*" (397).

Arthur first visits the woman because he has been told that she might help him rescue Welbeck's pregnant mistress, Clemenza Lodi, from the house of ill fame to which her disgrace has condemned her. Arthur fell in love with Clemenza the moment he met her at Welbeck's, though he never confessed his feelings. Although concerned for her welfare, Arthur lost serious romantic interest in Clemenza when he discovered that she was with child; whereupon Eliza Hadwin, daughter of a kindly Quaker farmer, soon replaced her in the young man's affections. After Achsa is persuaded to help poor Clemenza, Arthur continues to call upon his new "mamma" frequently. Their conversation turns from Clemenza to Eliza, whom Arthur wishes Achsa could meet.

> How would that heart overflow with affection and with gratitude towards you. She should be your daughter. No—you are too near-ly of an age for that. A sister: her *elder* sister you should be. *That,* when there is no other relation, includes them all. Fond sisters you would be, and I the fond brother of you both. (398)

A few pages later, he confesses his wish that "would to Heaven, I were tru-ly [Eliza's] father or brother." "Can you seriously wish that?" Achsa replies. "Why no. I believe it would be more rational to wish that the world would suffer me to act the fatherly or brotherly part, without the re-lationship" (404).

But what the "world" demands from an unrelated man and woman is marriage, and Arthur declares to his "mamma" that he no longer feels for the girl a "wedded, or *marriage-wishing* love" (405–6). Achsa asks what kind of woman he *would* marry, and Arthur replies:

> The creature whom I shall worship:—it sounds oddly, but, I verily believe, the sentiment which I shall feel for my wife, will be more a kin to worship than any thing else. I shall never love, but such a creature as I now image to myself, and *such* a creature will deserve, or almost deserve, worship—but this creature, I was go-ing to say, must be the exact counterpart, my good mamma—of *yourself.* (406–7)

Once again, to use Leslie Fiedler's phrase, Brown has contrived to "bypass normal heterosexual love." Arthur prefers an incestuous brother-sister re-lationship with Eliza because it would allow him to love her without hav-ing to accept the responsibility of marriage, which the "world" demands. The attraction to "Mamma" Achsa is even more subversive, perpetuating the egocentrism of childhood and thereby denying any social connections or responsibilities at all.

There is nothing subtle about Arthur's identification of Achsa Fielding with his mother. He poses the rhetorical question: "Was she not the substitute of my lost mamma [?] and, if that were not quite enough, he turns point blank to Achsa herself: "Are you not my lost mamma come back again?" (429–30). He worships Achsa as he had his own mother, and when she agrees to look after Eliza—as a sister or a "new *mamma*"

(411)—Arthur gropes for some way to "manifest" his gratitude. "My senses were bewildered, and I knew not what I did. I intended to kneel, as to my mother or my deity, but, instead of that, I clasped her in my arms, and kissed her lips fervently. I staid not to discover the effects of this insanity, but left the room and the house" (409–10).

"Bewildered," Arthur performs an action practically as "insane" as wilderness cannibalism. He acknowledges desire for the mother he has hitherto regarded as an object of distant worship. When the young man confides to Dr. Stevens that he could marry none but a woman who in every way resembled Achsa Fielding, Stevens asks why Arthur could not marry Achsa herself. "I felt my heart leap.—What a thought is that! Love her I *do* as I love my God; as I love virtue. To love her in another sense, would brand me a lunatic." The very thought throws Arthur's "soul into unconquerable tumults" (431–2). But Stevens persists in his good-humored efforts to convince the boy that proposing to Achsa is well within the realm of the possible. "You have raised up wishes and dreams and doubts," Arthur declares to him, "which possess me in spite of my reason, in spite of a thousand proofs."

> Good God! You say she loves; loves *me*! me, a boy in age; bred in clownish ignorance; scarcely ushered into the world; more than childishly unlearned and raw; a barn-door simpleton; a plow-tail, kitchen-hearth, turnip-hoeing novice! . . . It cannot be. Yet, if it were; if your guesses should—prove—Oaf! madman! To indulge so fatal a chimera! So rash a dream! (434–5)

And what follows his conversation with Dr. Stevens is, in fact, a half-waking dream. Retiring to his chamber, Arthur tries to sleep but is beset by a swarm of distressing images. "I was roused by a divine voice, that said:—'Sleep no more: Mervyn shall sleep no more.'" Whereupon the young man is oppressed by "a nameless sort of terror" (436). Similarly terrified after having murdered the sleeping Duncan, Macbeth confessed to his wife that he had

> heard a voice cry "Sleep no more!
> Macbeth does murder sleep" . . .
> "Glamis hath murdered sleep, and therefore Cawdor
> Shall sleep no more, Macbeth shall sleep no more."
> (Act 2, sc. 2)

Arthur grew up with few books, but these he studied and got "by rote" (25). Among them must have been Shakespeare, a line from whom he quotes early in the narrative (50). The paraphrase from *Macbeth* betrays the intensity of the young man's anxiety, suggesting that his distress approaches that of the guilt-ridden Thane. Of course, the actual association between Arthur's guilt and Macbeth's takes place not in Mervyn's mind, but in Brockden Brown's. It is he who betrays the feelings of guilt attending the creation of an oedipal fantasy. Macbeth kills a king, a father both literally and figuratively, while Arthur, by marrying his "mamma," at last dethrones his own father. For Brown, the actual regicide and the figurative patricide are of equal symbolic magnitude, producing in the figure of Arthur Mervyn a "nameless sort of terror":

> What shall I compare it to? Methinks, that one falling from a tree, overhanging a torrent, plunged into the whirling eddy, and gasping and struggling while he sinks to rise no more, would feel just as I did then. Nay, some such image actually possessed me. Such was one of my reveries, in which suddenly I stretched my hand, and caught the arm of a chair. This act called me back to reason, or rather gave my soul opportunity to roam into a new track equally wild. . . . These were all the tokens of a mind lost to itself; bewildered; unhinged; plunged into a drear insanity. (436)

Arthur's "reverie" frames his oedipal anxiety in images of the wilderness, the territory of extreme pleasure and extreme terror. Achsa figuratively returns Arthur to the wilderness in which his original mother had so lovingly indulged him.

Like Clara Wieland, whose confused sexual feelings toward Theodore are expressed in a wilderness dream, and like Edgar Huntly, whose wilderness experience is a blur of waking reality and dream, Mervyn is presently beset by nightmares. He dreams that he knocks at Achsa's door, which is answered by her erstwhile and profligate husband, who calls Arthur a villain, bids him "avaunt," and, drawing "a shining steel from his bosom," stabs the young man "through the heart." Like Edgar Huntly in the wilderness pit, Arthur is plunged into "darkness and oblivion" before he fully wakes and realizes that he has only been dreaming—sleepwalking, too. "I have little doubt," Arthur reports, "that, in my feverish and troubled sleep, I actually went forth, posted to the house of Mrs. Fielding, rung for admission, and shortly after, returned to my own apartment" (438). As Huntly sleepwalked into the wilderness, so Arthur sleepwalked through Philadelphia to the house of his new "mamma." Nor does the wilderness connection end here. Arthur sets up a rendezvous with Achsa, at which he plans to propose. Before the meeting he wanders off into the countryside, "through embarrassed and obscure paths" (441). "Embarrassed" is common enough in the figurative sense of "obstructed," of course, but it is difficult to overlook an unconscious pun here betraying Arthur's—or, more to the point, Brown's—feelings of shame. In any case, a few lines later, Arthur appears to consummate his sexual longing not with Achsa but with the wild landscape itself: "I rent a passage through the thicket, and struggled upward till I reached the edge of a considerable precipice; I laid me down at my length upon the rock, whose cold and hard surface I pressed with my bared and throbbing breast." He leans over this dangerous and inviting precipice, fixing his eyes on the water below, and weeps (441–2).

In the midst of a populous city, and at the conclusion of an American success story, itself a progress from country to city, Arthur Mervyn realizes his dream of the wilderness. But this is only half of Brown's fantasy. As a substitute "mamma," Achsa does represent the egocentric, asocial aspect of the wilderness; but she is herself a European, who embodies the sophistication and knowledge Constantia sought in Ormond and, to a significant degree, Arthur Mervyn himself sought in the European Welbeck. To a far greater extent than he had in the violent *Ormond*, Brown projects a synthesis of the New World and the Old, accomplished under cover of the respectable ethic of American urban success. Actually, Mervyn's triumph leaps over the civilization of the American city, vaulting from the wilderness beyond Chester County to the civilization of Europe, to which, "in a year or two," the newlyweds plan to "hie" (445).

The American city, as Brown the novelist would have it, marks a paradise lost. With great expectations, Arthur Mervyn early in the narrative enters Philadelphia, the night-time splendor of which calls to the young man's mind a fragment of verse: "in walking through this avenue, I, for a moment, conceived myself transported to the hall 'pendent with many a row of starry lamps and blazing crescents fed by naphtha and asphaltos'" (28). As with the paraphrase of *Macbeth*, it is difficult to decide just how aware the novelist was of the implication of this line. From Milton's *Paradise Lost*, it is part of a description of hell.[4] Many a hellish trial does await Arthur before the end of his story, and the depiction of yellow fever in Philadelphia is Dantesque. If these features of the novel do not sufficiently undermine an optimistic vision of American success, one need only read the lines in *Paradise Lost* that follow the ones Brown quotes. Contrasting the gaudy unreality of hell's allure to the genuine celestial beauty of the heavenly paradise, Milton tells how the "hasty multitude," unmindful of the true beauty they have relinquished, "Admiring enter'd" hell, singing discordant praises of the work and its devilish architect (bk. 1, ll. 730–2). Covertly, perhaps unconsciously, Brown hints that America's errand out of the wilderness—the incipient proliferation of an urban culture based on material success—is a tragically foolish one.

Philadelphia's hellishness is, however, too complexly personal to explain wholly as social criticism. Brown's urban hell is not so much evil as irrational, perverse, and deceptive. Arthur will be tricked many times in Philadelphia. Even before he enters the city proper, the young man is slickered out of his small supply of cash by two unscrupulous innkeepers. The first deception to which he falls victim in the city is a joke, a piece of mischief worthy of Francis Carwin himself. Penniless, dejected, Arthur sits in the common room of a Philadelphia tavern, having inquired in vain after a Mr. Capper, a neighbor of his father's who is supposed to be staying at the tavern. But apparently Capper has returned to the country, and the situation looks grim for the friendless youth. Just then, however, a young man accosts Mervyn, suggesting that he might be able to locate Capper. It is too late to search for him tonight, though, and the young man offers to put Arthur up until morning. He leads Mervyn through what seems a maze of twisting streets—an effect maintained throughout the novel, even though Philadelphia was famous for its broad avenues set in logical grid-iron formations (in *Arthur Mervyn*, even the physical rationality of Brown's native city is transformed into an emblem of confusion). At last they reach a stately mansion, which Arthur and the young man enter; he secures a candle and escorts the newcomer to a third-floor chamber. "This," he says, "is my room. Permit me to welcome you into it." But the candle sputters out at this moment, and, cursing his carelessness, the young man apologizes for having to run downstairs to relight it. Promising to return in a "twinkling," he suggests that Arthur undress in the mean-time and prepare for bed. Instead of doing this, Arthur occupies himself in surveying the room, marveling at its splendor. After some time, he grows anxious about the young man's failure to return, and begins to think him-self the "victim of malicious artifice." Then he hears a sound, like a groan in the darkness, like breathing—yes, it is the breathing of someone asleep.

Mervyn is bewildered. The door is locked, making escape impossible. Perhaps he should simply awaken the sleeper and explain the perfectly in-nocent circumstances of his presence. He glides softly to the bed in order to do this, when the thought occurs to him: "May not the sleeper be a female? . . . My presence might pollute a spotless reputation or furnish fuel to jealousy." The sound of approaching footsteps interrupts his de-liberations, and Arthur summarily locks himself in a closet (31–8).

Later in the story, the rakish fiancé of Susan Hadwin—who is the sister of Eliza, Arthur's own sisterly beloved—admits that he had led Mervyn to the room, intending absolutely no malice, prompted only by some imp of the perverse. The incident is a fitting prelude to the youth's adventures with Thomas Welbeck, who, like Susan's fiancé, or even Francis Carwin, is at bottom an irrational rather than an evil man. More importantly, the closet episode prefigures the random absurdity of the society into which Welbeck is about to usher Mervyn. "My intention was innocent," Arthur protests about the closet predicament, "and I had been betrayed into my present situation, not by my own wickedness but the wickedness of others" (43). Like the protagonist in "The Man at Home," Mervyn discovers that, in the complex society which the city both embodies and represents, one's life is no longer one's own. Unwittingly as well as unwillingly, one's very existence becomes contingent upon the actions of others. One also, un-willingly and unwittingly, comes to affect the lives of others. While in the closet, Arthur overhears first the design of a man (we later learn that he is a merchant named Thetford) to persuade his wife to adopt his mistress's newborn bastard. Next, Arthur is made secret witness to a plot hatched between Thetford and his wife to defraud someone called the Nabob (whom we later discover is Welbeck) of $30,000. This knowledge, of course, comes to Arthur unbidden. As Edgar Huntly had unwillingly learned about his hidden self by falling into the wilderness pit, so Mervyn, immured in a Philadelphia closet, learns of "the most secret transaction" (39), wicked, unlawful, antisocial, in the lives of two strangers. The first step in Arthur's initiation into American society is not taken in the daylight avenues of Philadelphia, but in the dark confines of a bedroom closet.

The closet episode, with its accidental and sudden revelation, heralds a motif of instantaneous transformation at work throughout *Arthur Mervyn*, absurdly undercutting the idea of social initiation as a rational process. In a *Bildungsroman*, such as Goethe's *Wilhelm Meister* or, more to the point, Benjamin Franklin's *Autobiography*, we see the hero grow into his world; but *Arthur Mervyn* is a series of random and coincidental changes and reversals. After escaping from the closet, Arthur wanders to the door of Thomas Welbeck. Thus the youth's introduction to the master of his initiation is the fruit of happenstance orginating in a perverse practical joke.

Welbeck employs Arthur as his amanuensis and effects the first instantaneous transformation by outfitting him with a new wardrobe. Exchanging his rustic garb for the fine clothes, the youth reflects that "twenty minutes ago" he had been a beggar, but now, from all appearances, he is a man of means, a solid citizen. "My senses are the sport of dreams. Some magic that disdains the cumbrousness of nature's progress, has wrought this change" (51). But it is nothing so absolute as "nature's progress" that establishes one's place in society, which is built upon appearances no more permanent than a change of clothes and is a function of an idea founded upon empirical observation. If these social appearances seem as absolute as nature, it is because our "common sense" tells us they are more substantial than they are. Men like Welbeck, who can manipulate appearances as readily as Carwin does, hold the key to the Lockean universe of Brown's Philadelphia. A foreign type (52, 57), Welbeck bears all the characteristics of the European seducer. Like Ormond, he keeps a mistress, and, like Ormond and Ludloe, he adopts a young protégé for apparently sinister purposes, swearing him to absolute candor and secrecy (62). Welbeck also promises a mysterious knowledge, the possession of which will confer social success and material opulence.

Seduced by the splendor with which Welbeck surrounds himself, Arthur pledges loyalty to his new master and begins his first task, transcribing an opus Welbeck plans to plagiarize from the manuscript left by his mistress's dead father (100). Welbeck also sees in Arthur a convenient means of giving a "new direction" to the affections of his mistress —Clemenza Lodi—who, pregnant, has grown tiresome (99). But Arthur's most important function is supposed to be as an instrument to swindle a rich lady. Mrs. Wentworth plans to bequeath her considerable fortune to one Clavering, her long-lost nephew. Welbeck plans to have Arthur convince her that Clavering is dead, so that (by means Brown imperfectly explains) Welbeck might intercept his inheritance.

The scheme itself is not overly complex, but the complications and ramifications resulting from it are typical of the tissue of Brown's narrative and of his image of society. Welbeck sends Arthur to deliver a message to Mrs. Wentworth, instructing him not to wait for the lady but merely to leave the note for her. Welbeck does plan to have Arthur convince Mrs. Wentworth that her nephew is dead, but all in good time, after he has first "artfully prepared" her mind. On his own initiative, however, Mervyn decides to deliver the letter directly into her hands. While he waits for the lady in her parlor, Arthur surveys the room. His eye lights upon a bundle of belongings he had lost during his very first hours in Philadelphia. He had sorely regretted the loss, not so much because the parcel contained all that he owned, but because among the items was a portrait of a youth who had lived with the Mervyns for some time and for whom Arthur had a brotherly affection. This unfortunate individual fell prey to a progressive insanity, which resulted in his death, witnessed by Arthur. The youth's name was Clavering.

At length, Mrs. Wentworth enters the parlor, and Arthur delivers the note; but he also explains, on his own account, that the bundle and the portrait belong to him. When he asks for their return, Mrs. Wentworth stammers: "Your picture! . . . You lost it? How? Where? Did you know that person? What has become of him?" And Arthur relates the sad end of Clavering. Though there are many such episodes in the novel, some even more involuted, this one is typical of Brown's narrative and the vision of society that his narrative technique embodies. Summary hardly does justice to its complexity, since in the novel we pick up the pieces of the narrative puzzle a few at a time from several narrators who speak at widely separated intervals. The information given in the paragraph above is drawn from six places in the text of the novel—pages 100, 63, 249, 63–5, 29–30, and 65–8, in that order. An earlier generation of readers might have summarily ascribed such fragmentary exposition to the incompetence of the storyteller. Readers bred on the likes of Faulkner, though, are more willing to accept this kind of narrative as an attempt, however imperfect, at reflecting the vicissitudes of human knowledge limited to single points of view. Less easily tolerated, especially among readers accustomed to the craft of a Faulkner, is Brown's reliance on apparently random and arbitrary coincidence.[5] Welbeck happens to seize upon Arthur Mervyn as a likely instrument with which to swindle Mrs. Wentworth. Arthur happens to know Clavering, and happens to lose a picture of him, which a servant of Mrs. Wentworth happens to find apparently abandoned in the street. And Mrs. Wentworth happens to be Clavering's doting aunt.

The most incredible coincidence, and the irony toward which Brown has worked the others, is that Welbeck's big lie just happens to be true. He wanted Mervyn to convince Mrs. Wentworth that Clavering is dead, and that is just what Arthur prematurely tries to do—since he happens to know that Clavering *is* dead. This should be a happy accident for Welbeck. What could be more effective than a swindle based upon truth? However, two additional coincidental circumstances intervene, ultimately foiling Welbeck and seriously jeopardizing Arthur's own reputation. Welbeck had intended to fabricate a plausible past for Mervyn, so that the story of his relationship to Clavering would seem authentic to Mrs. Wentworth. To this end, he pledged the youth to absolute secrecy regarding his "birth and early adventures" (62). When Arthur starts to tell Mrs. Wentworth the true story of Clavering, the pledge of silence interferes. The result is a half-concealed tale that strikes Mrs. Wentworth as evasive. A second untimely coincidence, a false report that Clavering is alive in Charleston (250), seals Welbeck's doom and nearly ruins Arthur as well, who is judged guilty through his association with Welbeck.

Brown needs the coincidences to demonstrate the limitations of perception and reason. All the empirical evidence argues that Arthur's true story about Clavering is false. If the coincidences are unlikely, they are not impossible, but our objection to them is based on a notion of literary realism that equates reality with what is usual or probable, not with what is merely possible. The extreme, even if we grant its possibility, is too readily seen as authorial fiat rather than the dramatization of an authentic vision. Brown recognized that his obsession with extreme situations violated the rules of the game of fiction. He anticipated critics' objections in the "Advertisement" to *Wieland*. "Some readers may think the conduct of the younger Wieland impossible," he admits, but he appeals to "physicians and to men conversant with the latent springs and occasional perversions of the human mind" for evidence of its basis in fact. The author does concede that cases like Theodore's are "rare," but he holds that "if history furnishes one parallel fact, it is a sufficient vindication of the Writer" (3). This doctrine may seem obstinate, even perverse; but it is no less than an aesthetic rationale for "An American Tale." Brown's imagination, like that of Poe, or the Melville of *Moby-Dick*, and so many of our most characteristic writers, was shaped by the extremity of the New World, the continuing discovery of which necessitated an imaginative departure from the usual and probable.

Drawn as it is with a heavy and uncertain hand, the coincidental plot of Brown's novel undermines commonsense applications of Lockean epistemology and the social structure Americans reared upon its assumptions. Both Welbeck and Arthur are judged on appearances because the society in which they move is structured upon the tangible and the quantifiable. A commentator schooled in the criticism of Richard Chase might note that *Arthur Mervyn* does not present the richly textured social fabric, say, of a British novel. This is less a flaw of the book, though, than it is an integral dimension of Brown's vision. The complexities of inherited familial and political ties are absent from this American tale. They are replaced by the more tangible but more mutable nexus of cash. All of Arthur's social relations result directly or indirectly from his initial association with Welbeck, whose own social connections are determined wholly by monetary transactions. For that matter, most of Arthur's own immediate social contacts are directly concerned with money, which, quantifiable and tangible, figures as the preferred medium of interpersonal relations in a society founded upon commonsense philosophy. *Arthur Mervyn* details the intellectual consequences of America's monolithic reliance on money, which represents a grotesquely incomplete attempt to transplant Old World values into the New. Absent from America are the stabilizing values of European society: hereditary social status and the politics of monarchy. Inscribed upon the social and political *tabula rasa* of the New World, the monetary civilization stands alone in all its man-made vulnerability, calling to mind the words of John Locke in his *Second Treatise of Government*: "Thus in the beginning all the World was *America*, and more so than is now; for no such thing as *Money* was any where known" (2:sect. 49). As Locke had used aboriginal America as an index against which he measured Europe, so Brown drew in *Edgar Huntly* directly upon the American wilderness to define and test the limits of civilization. The extremes of plot and coincidence that expose the tenuous and arbitrary principles of American society in *Arthur Mervyn* are less directly products of the wilderness than the adventures of Edgar Huntly, but they are born just the same of an imagination amply stocked with images of New World extremity.

It is little wonder, then, that images of the wilderness intrude into Philadelphia itself. After pledging himself to secrecy at the behest of Welbeck, Arthur has second thoughts about acting "under the guidance of another," condemning himself "to wander in the dark, ignorant whither my path tended" (63). And when Mrs. Wentworth tempts him to violate the pledge of silence, Arthur feels as if he "were walking in the dark and might rush into snares or drop into pits before I was aware of my danger" (70). Later, "bewildered" by the mounting evidence of ambiguity in Welbeck's behavior, Arthur wanders unconsciously into the rural environs of Philadelphia, "ardently pursu[ing]" his meditations until he finds himself literally "bewildered among fields and fences. It was late before I extricated myself from unknown paths, and reached home" (79). For all his complex social entanglements, it is the wilderness that claims and reclaims Arthur Mervyn in images that mock the simple philosophy Brockden Brown could not accept in the civilization of his American contemporaries.

Benjamin Franklin, according to D. H. Lawrence, tried to keep the wilderness from encroaching into the quotidian conduct of life: "He tries to take away my wholeness and my dark forest, my freedom." For the "soul of man is a dark forest, with wild life in it. Think of Benjamin fencing it off."[6] Nor could the values Franklin embodies fence off Brown's Philadelphia, whose very streets, ruler-straight in actuality, seem in this novel to merge with twisting paths in some dark forest of the mind. Yet in defining—consciously or not—his novel against Franklin, Brown adopted many of the public formulas one finds in the *Autobiography*. This is not so surprising, in view of Brown's ambivalence toward his elder colleague. The young writer's first published work was to have been a eulogistic poem on Benjamin Franklin but became one for George Washington when a "blundering printer, from his zeal or ignorance . . . or perhaps from both, substituted" one name for the other in *The State Gazette of North Carolina* on February 26, 1789.[7] The youthful Brown had been a guest in Franklin's home frequently, and the Belles Lettres Society, of which Brown had been a founder, met there occasionally as well.[8] Some seventeen years after the mislabeled tombstone inscription appeared, Brown, in 1806, published the "Character of Dr. Franklin" in his *Literary Magazine*.[9] Both of the modern commentators who take notice of the article attribute its authorship to Brown himself, ignoring Brown's own editorial comment that the "portrait" of Franklin was "taken from a foreign publication" (367). Actually the work of the Scots critic Francis Jeffrey, the article was copied with some abridgment from the *Edinburgh Review*.[10] While it is true that Brown was perpetually desperate for material to print in his magazines,[11] something more than a shortage of copy likely drew him to the figure of Franklin, particularly as Jeffrey had pictured him.

To begin with, Jeffrey's criticism of the failure of an American publisher to issue an edition of Franklin was heartily in accord with Brown's own pleas for the formation and appreciation of an American literary culture (367). More than this, Jeffrey presented Franklin as an exemplary specimen of what American life could produce:

> This self-taught American is the most rational, perhaps, of all philosophers. . . .
> Dr. Franklin received no regular education; and he spent the greater part of his life in a society where there was no relish and no encouragement for literature. On an ordinary mind, these circumstances would have produced their usual effects, of repressing all sort of intellectual ambition or activity, and perpetuating a generation of incurious mechanics; but to an understanding like Franklin's, they were peculiarly propitious, and we can trace back to them, distinctly, almost all the peculiarities of his intellectual character. (368)

One wants to take care not to push the analogy too far, but Jeffrey's remarks about the intellectual "wilderness" in which Franklin's mind developed suggest comparison with Edgar Huntly's transformation in the physical wilderness of Pennsylvania. On the one hand, America's lack of a well-developed intellectual culture (in Jeffrey's view) poses a threat to the growth of a mind bred in the New World; on the other, the intellectual wilderness provides the freedom in which an original mind may flourish:

> Regular education is unfavorable to vigour or originality of understanding. Like civilization, it makes society more intelligent and agreeable; but it levels the distinctions of nature. It strengthens and assists the feeble; but it deprives the strong of his triumph, and casts down the hopes of the aspiring. (368)

As Huntly's wilderness sojourn allowed him to realize full prowess, so Franklin's lack of a "regular"—or European—education allowed him to realize the full prowess of "understanding." Had Franklin "been bred in a college, he would have contented himself with expounding the metres of Pindar, and mixing argument with his port in the common room" (369). Or, had Boston "abounded with men of letters, he would never have ventured to come forth from his printing house; or been driven back to it, at any rate, by the sneers of the critics, after the first publication of his Essays in the Busy Body" (369).

What, in short, Brown must have seen in the article he copied from the *Edinburgh Review* is a portrait of the hero as American renaissance man.

> There are not many among the thorough bred scholars and philosophers of Europe who can lay claim to distinction in more than one or two departments of science or literature. The uneducated tradesman of America has left writings that call for our attention, in natural philosophy, in politics, in political economy, and in general literature and morality. (370)

In publishing such remarks when he did, Brown was not just adding another voice to a universal accolade. Indeed, Brown felt obliged to introduce Jeffrey's piece with the observation that "among [Franklin's] countrymen, prejudice and passion, which used to be enlisted wholly on his side, has, in some respects, become hostile to him, and an impartial estimate of his merits can perhaps only be looked for among foreigners" (367). Similarly, the 1789 tombstone eulogy seems to have been motivated by a desire to defend the character of Franklin. A. Owen Aldridge has shown that Brown's eulogistic verses were "closely modeled after a widely known attack upon Franklin which circulated in Philadelphia and elsewhere during the American revolution," so that "Brown's model . . . was not a panegyric of Franklin at all, but a malicious assault upon him and his political career." Young Brown, then, having drawn his inspiration from these verses, simply stood their satiric intention on its head in order to vindicate Franklin.[12]

Doubtless there was more than one reason for Brown's defense of

Franklin, among them his personal acquaintance with the good doctor, and a simple appreciation of his accomplishments. More than this, Brown may have recognized something of himself—his ideal self—in Franklin, especially as Jeffrey portrayed him. Perhaps Brown liked to think that an intellectual wilderness had helped to make him, like Franklin, an American renaissance man, who

> engaged in every interesting inquiry that suggested itself to him, rather as the necessary exercise of a powerful and active mind, than as a task which he had bound himself to perform. He cast a quick and penetrating glance over the facts and the *data* that were presented to him; and drew his conclusions with a rapidity and precision that have not often been equalled. (369)

Such an identification would not be entirely vainglorious. The range of Brown's interests, if not of his accomplishments, is comparable to Franklin's. One need only note the wealth of subjects touched upon in the novels, or read Brown's intellectually freewheeling journalism—the *American Register*, for example, which embraced economics, history, science, politics, agriculture, commerce, and industry. The culmination of such intellectual energy was to have been the *System of General Geography*, projected as a treatment of America, the world, and the place of our planet in the solar system and universe.

The speed of Franklin's process of thought and the idea that inquiry was for him a "necessary exercise" recall the account Brown gave to John Bernard of his own habits of composition. But Jeffrey does entertain some reservation about Franklin's intellectual traits: "He did not stop to examine the completeness of the *data* upon which he proceeded, nor to consider the ultimate effect or application of the principles to which he had been conducted" (369). Whether or not Brown saw in this a warning to himself, Paul Allen, his first biographer, did criticize a similar weakness in the young writer, a habit of letting "speculation loose without discretion" so that he was "compelled to plunge headlong into the very difficulty he would have wished most sedulously to avoid" (Allen, 107). But the single sour note in Jeffrey's article is not sufficient to account for the ambiguities in Brown's treatment of Franklin—especially in *Arthur Mervyn*—that betray the novelist's ambivalence toward him.

The first ambiguity is Brown's publication of the Jeffrey article itself. Seeing that Brown knew Franklin personally, and that his first published piece was supposed to have eulogized him, we might ask why, in 1806, he chose to copy the work of another instead of writing his own "character" of Franklin. Was it simply that, as his editorial note to the article suggests, a foreign voice had more authority with Americans where the reputation and achievement of Franklin were concerned? We have already seen how Brown not only failed to develop the utopian great plans he had cherished early in his career, but, more specifically, had failed to develop them as

American plans. The closest he ever came to articulating an American utopia was in his 1803 *Address to the Government of the United States on the Cession of Louisiana to the French*. He set his fictitious French councilor of state to explaining that space, the most abundant of New World commodities, could accomplish the utopian dream of achieving *"equality without detriment to order."* In this approach to an American version of utopia, Brown speaks through a fictitious foreigner. When he recognized in Benjamin Franklin a hero fit for an American utopia, it was an actual foreigner, Francis Jeffrey, who he let do the talking. For when Brown spoke in his own American voice, it was an Edgar Huntly he produced. Like Jeffrey's Franklin, Brown's Huntly realized in America a potential that would have lain dormant in Europe. In contrast to Franklin's American triumph, however, Huntly's was but semiconscious and, at that, did not go unpunished. Huntly was tortured with terror, physical pain, starvation, and an abiding sense of the forlorn in a life lost between two worlds. In making Edgar Huntly a man of the frontier, Brown had also to become the author of his distress. But because he did not create Jeffrey's Franklin, Brown did not have to freight his American journey with a cargo of ambivalent guilt. Franklin escaped "distress" precisely because Brown had not been his "author."

In the figure of Arthur Mervyn, Brown *does* create a version of Franklin; but Arthur does not suffer for it as badly as do the Franklinian values his progress through Philadelphia embodies. While suggesting here that the *Autobiography*, as well as Brown's more general familiarity with Benjamin Franklin, influenced the creation of *Arthur Mervyn*, it must be noted that the *Autobiography* was not issued in a reasonably complete and authentic form until William Temple Franklin's 1818 edition in Volume 1 of the "complete" *Works*. But a French translation of what is now known as the first part of the *Autobiography*, the portion ending at 1731, was issued in 1791. It was only the first of many unauthorized editions that were to appear before Brown wrote *Arthur Mervyn*. German and Swedish translations of the French edition appeared in 1792, and a poor retranslation from French into English was issued at London the next year. Also in 1793 a British edition of Franklin's *Works* was edited by Benjamin Vaughan, who made a much better retranslation of the French version of the *Autobiography*, appending to it a continuation of the narrative after 1731 by Philadelphia physician Henry Stuber. A series of American reprintings of Vaughan's edition appeared in Philadelphia and New York (1794; the New York edition was published by T. and J. Swords, who were to issue some of Brown's own works), Danbury (1795), Salem (1796), Albany (1797), and Wilmington (1799). This version of the *Autobiography* was also included in at least four American editions of the *Works* published between 1794 and 1799.[13]

In addition, then, to whatever popular myths were already circulating about Franklin, Brown had ample access to Franklin's own account of the early part of his life. Though the process of translation and retranslation had dulled Ben's prose, it did at least transmit intact his most important cultural icons, chief among which is the image of his entrance into Philadelphia. The text is drawn from the Vaughan retranslation as it was issued from Philadelphia by Benjamin Johnson in 1794:

> On my arrival at Philadelphia I was in my working dress, my best clothes being to come by sea. I was covered with dirt; my pockets were filled with shirts and stockings; I was unacquainted with a single soul in the place, and knew not where to seek for a lodging. . . . and all my money consisted of a Dutch dollar, and about a shilling's worth of coppers. (42)

Brown's image of Arthur Mervyn during his first hours in Philadelphia is similar in detail and serves the same rags-to-riches thematic purpose:

> My best clothes were of the homeliest texture and shape. My whole stock of linen consisted of three check shirts. Part of my winter evening's employment, since the death of my mother, consisted in knitting my own stockings. Of these I had three pair, one of which I put on, the rest I formed, together with two shirts, into a bundle. Three quarter-dollar pieces composed my whole fortune in money. (24)

Young Ben gives his shilling's worth of coppers to the boatman with whom he rowed to a landing on the outskirts of the city. Because Ben had helped with the rowing, the boatman is at first unwilling to accept payment, but, partly out of generosity and partly from a shrewd instinct for developing an advantageous public image, Franklin urges the coppers on him. "A man is sometimes more generous when he has little than when he has much money; probably because, in the first case, he is desirous of concealing his poverty" (Franklin, 42). The diminishment of Arthur Mervyn's fortune is due neither to generosity nor to shrewdness, but to his own inexperience and to the dishonesty of two tavern keepers: "I could not image to myself a more perfect example of indigence than I now exhibited. There was no being in the city on whose kindness I had any claim. Money I had none, and what I then wore comprised my whole stock of moveables" (*Mervyn*, 46).

For all their similarity of situation, the experiences of Franklin and Mervyn issue from diametrically opposed visions of Philadelphia and the society it both embodies and represents. Little as he has, Ben can afford to pay the boatman generously. Cheated by tavernkeepers, Arthur cannot even afford to pay the toll across the Schuylkill bridge. Two miserable meals cost Arthur all he has, while a mere three cents brings Ben the unexpected bounty of three huge (if puffy) rolls, a feast so generous that he can afford to give two surplus rolls to a mother and child he meets along the river. Arthur crosses that bridge over the Schuylkill in such a hurry that he "forgets" about paying the toll: "neither had I money wherewith to pay it."

> A demand of payment would have suddenly arrested my progress; and so slight an incident would have precluded that wonderful destiny to which I was reserved. The obstacle that would have hindered my advance, now prevented my return. Scrupulous honesty did not require me to turn back and awaken the vigilance of the toll-gatherer. I had nothing to pay, and by returning I should only double my debt. Let it stand, said I, where it does. All that honour enjoins is to pay when I am able. (27)

Even Ben is not above this kind of easy rationalization; but while it is mildly comic and certainly self-satirical in Franklin's *Autobiography*, it is necessitous in the case of Mervyn. Having sworn himself to a vegetarian life, Ben is tempted by the savor of sizzling cod. Although he had abjured the eating of flesh as a kind of "unprovoked murder," the rationalization that when fish are cut open one sees myriad smaller fish in their bellies annihilates the vestiges of his resistance. "How convenient does it prove to be a *rational animal*, that knows how to find or invent a plausible pretext for whatever it has an inclination to do!" (59–60).[14]

Like Franklin, Arthur Mervyn habitually draws lessons from his experiences. While such instances in the *Autobiography* are often amusingly facile, sometimes wry, their moral inferences drawn tongue-in-cheek (as in the fish-eating episode), they are never absurd. In *Arthur Mervyn*, however, Brown takes the moralizing tendency to grotesque lengths, demonstrating the impotence of reason in the face of essentially meaningless experience. When Arthur ventures into Mrs. Villars's brothel to rescue Clemenza Lodi from a life of easy virtue, he so pesters one of the house's inmates that she is provoked to shoot him. He is wounded—though slightly. "For a moment I was bewildered and alarmed, but presently perceived that this was an incident more productive of good than of evil. It would teach me caution in contending with the passions of another, and shewed me that there is a limit which the impetuosities of anger will sometimes overstep." Meanwhile, the woman who fired the shot becomes hysterical. "Be not frighted," Arthur tenderly if ludicrously admonishes her: "You have done me no injury, and I hope will derive instruction from this event. . . . Learn, from hence, to curb your passions, and especially to keep at a distance from every murderous weapon, on occasions when rage is likely to take place of reason" (330). One would hardly blame her if she shot again, taking more careful aim.

It is unlikely that Brown *intended* to criticize Benjamin Franklin. If anything, the character of Arthur Mervyn may have been intended as a modest version of Ben, an incarnation of the American utopian hero drawn to an accessible scale. After all, in his tombstone inscription for Franklin, Brown had hailed the good doctor as Newton's equal in philosophy, and

"America's favorite," worthy of the wreath of liberty as a crown. This was published in 1789. The odd thing is that Ben Franklin did not die until 1790. Doubtless, the "Inscription for Benjamin Franklin's Tombstone" was *intended* as a compliment, and the editor of *The State Gazette of North Carolina* thought it an even better compliment for George Washington, who had a full decade of life left to him at the time. Setting aside the question of wheher or not it is really in good taste to eulogize the living, we must observe that, in order to praise Franklin, Brockden Brown had first to bury him.

And in writing *Arthur Mervyn*, with each Franklinian gesture issuing in near disaster, Brown digs the grave a little deeper. Whereas Franklin demonstrated an uncanny ability for "doing good," managing to turn even the least promising situation to account not only for others, but for himself as well, Arthur repeatedly forces his good deeds upon the unsuspecting, with results ranging from unpleasant to disastrous. Trying to redeem the city slicker Welbeck, this bumpkin hounds him to ruin and death. Having, at his own pain and expense, journeyed to Baltimore in order to bring Mrs. Amos Watson tidings of her husband, whom Welbeck has killed in a duel, Arthur delivers his message so clumsily that his gesture of condolence nearly kills the poor woman (375). In Baltimore he also wishes to deliver into the proper hands some money Amos Watson had been carrying. It is a small fortune, but due to a number of complex circumstances and the cupidity of the woman to whom Arthur finally gives the money, Watson's legacy seems destined only to bring wealth to the undeserving and misery to the innocent (381–7).

The diabolically complex universe of Brockden Brown's Philadelphia calls to mind the portrait of New York Franz Kafka paints in his *Amerika*. As Mervyn leaves his father's Chester County farm partly because of the sexual ignominy he suffered there, so Kafka's Karl Rossmann is forced to abandon Europe because "a servant girl had seduced him and got a child by him." And, like Arthur Mervyn, Karl enters an American metropolis "hopelessly unprepared" for the bewildering maze of social relationships the city offers and represents.[15] Nothing goes as planned and no action produces simply or directly its intended result. If so simple an act of charity as young Ben's sharing his surplus rolls with a woman and child would be unthinkable in Kafka's New York and Brown's Philadelphia, how much less possible the larger-scale beneficial schemes Ben conceives for influencing and changing society as a whole? Yet Kafka, the sophisticated delineator of moral absurdity, counted "Franklin's biography" as "one of his favourite books."[16] We can guess that Franklin appealed to Kafka in the same way that he appealed to Brown: as a man of moral action, reveling in the blessed energy of a wryly willed naïveté. But *Amerika*, like Kafka's other novels, is unfinished, suggesting that the writing of fiction did not lead Kafka, anymore than it led Brown, to direct and simple ends. On the contrary, both novelists drove themselves to explore the most extreme, the most "bewildering" ramifications of even the simplest actions.

Much as they may have envied it, neither novelist could finally accept the easy universe of Benjamin Franklin's America.

For Brown, who in fact lived in the America of Franklin, the problem of acceptance was the more acute. Franklin, who was among so many other things a utopianist and writer, had succeeded where Brown, try as he might, could not. In *Arthur Mervyn* the novelist seems bent on negating Franklin's vision at every turn. Yet, behind Franklin's public spirit is a paradoxically antisocial or, at least, asocial impulse resembling Arthur Mervyn's own rhapsodic egocentrism. There is a tension between Franklin's image of himself as a self-made man and his role as a citizen in a democratic society. He is careful, for example, to inventory the individuals upon whom he had tried to depend, but who had ended by failing him. The envy of printer Samuel Keimer, who employed the ambitious Ben as a journeyman in his shop, the besotted unreliability of an early friend in John Collins, and the treachery of Governor Keith, young Franklin's would-be patron, are cataloged as parts of a cautionary tale on the dangers of relinquishing self-dependence. But, of course, these are only a few of the many personages in Franklin's memoir.

The Philadelphia of *Arthur Mervyn*, in contrast, is populated almost exclusively by Keimers, Collinses, and Keiths, men in whom confidence can be placed only with disastrous results. If, in the figure of Mervyn, Brown caricatured the Franklinian ethic to the point of comic absurdity, in Thomas Welbeck he developed a character that calls to mind a more mysterious, even sinister, side of Benjamin Franklin himself. In the versions of the *Autobiography* available to Brown, the novelist would have read a bit about Franklin's "Club for Mutual Improvement," the celebrated "Junto." For all its harmless genial good fellowship, the Junto was, after all, a secret society. The novelist might also have read Franklin's account of his disputations about religion, which were so "indiscreet" that some "pious souls" regarded him with "horror, either as an apostate or as an atheist" (1794, p. 36; cf. Labaree et al., eds., p. 71). But it was not until the "complete" *Autobiography* of 1818 that the public could read Franklin's full account of the Junto. "We had from the Beginning made it a Rule to keep our Institution a Secret," Franklin writes, explaining how satellite Juntos were organized by individual members of the original club, who kept secret from their own membership the satellite's connection with the main Junto.[17] If Brown did know anything about this, surely he would have recognized its exact resemblance to the organizational structure of the Illuminist cells known as "orients."

Though he immortalized his youth in the first portion of the *Autobiography*, it is not as a remarkable boy that Benjamin Franklin is celebrated. He was a philosopher, inventor, and statesman—in short, a practical utopianist, whose talent and power it was to manipulate individuals and governments alike. Of Brown's characters, Ormond and Ludloe—less so the more rhapsodic Adini—come closest to this; and in *Arthur Mervyn*, it is not the young hero who resembles Franklin most in his mature "utopian" aspect, but Thomas Welbeck. None of this is to suggest that Brockden Brown laid deliberate siege against the reputation of Franklin. But Brown, uncertain of his social role as an American writer, did have doubts (almost too deep for him to articulate) about his imposingly paternal fellow Philadelphian. Here was an American writer, a successful utopianist, who not only knew his place in the civilization of his country but who had actually carved out that place as he helped to create the nation itself. To the degree that the novelist reacted against Franklin, he was not alone. John Adams was meticulously vehement in his scorn for him, and William Cobbett called him a "fornicator, a hypocrite, and an infidel" in *The Life and Adventures of Peter Porcupine* (Philadelphia: William Cobbett, 1796). The most conservative faction of Federalism, the party toward which Brown himself moved in his maturity, judged Franklin to be "shrewd, dissembling as well as discerning; his charm and his humor were clever, but purposeful, even ensnaring; and he was certainly the grand master of self-promotion."[18] In addition to these public reservations about Franklin, Brown, whose fiction (we have seen) bristles with dubious fathers and father figures, may well have harbored a more personal reverence-resentment toward the spiritual, political, and intellectual patriarch discernible in Ben. As the public formulas of *Arthur Mervyn* indicate, the novelist consciously honored Franklin and his social values; but, drawing upon Brown's entire being, not just the sociable desires of his conscious will, the writing of *Arthur Mervyn* would not permit the quintessentially American values of Benjamin Franklin to stand free from ambiguity and above challenge.

In a heartlessly industrial age of laissez faire Thomas Carlyle argued that society, deny it as we might, is an organism. No member of that organism is independent of another. A poor Irish widow, Carlyle reported in *Past and Present*, "her husband having died in one of the Lanes of Edinburgh, went forth with her three children, bare of all resource, to solicit help from the Charitable Establishments of that City." All refused her, sending her from one to another, until "her strength and heart failed her: she sank down in typhus-fever; died, and infected her Lane with fever, so that 'seventeen other persons' died of fever there in consequence."

The forlorn Irish Widow applies to her fellow-creatures, as if saying, "Behold I am sinking, bare of help: ye must help me!" They answer, "No; impossible: thou art no sister of ours." But she proves her sisterhood; her typhus-fever kills *them*: they actually were her brothers, though denying it! Had man ever to go lower for a proof?[19]

It is not that Brown saw the yellow fever as a warning to his own age of Franklinian laissez faire, but that, like Carlyle after him, he found in contagious disease a dramatically apposite metaphor for the complexly inter-related patterns of civilized society. If Carlyle used the notion of epidemic disease to promote a beneficial recognition of society's organic nature, Brown seems to have conceived the necessity of social relationships as, by their nature, a kind of infection. The narrator-protagonist of "The Man at Home" is "infected" by another's bad debts; Arthur Mervyn is con-taminated by the bad reputation of the man with whom he associates; and Arthur himself, even with the best intentions, infects a host of strangers with his good deeds. Thus, in *Arthur Mervyn*, when the yellow fever ac-tually strikes Philadelphia, it comes as the objectification of a social vision operating from the beginning of the novel.

In Brown's day, opinions about the origin of the yellow fever were so divided that C. F. Volney, in his *Tableau du climat et du sol des Etats-Unis*, called the question a medical "schism": "Some maintain that it is always imported from abroad, especially from the West Indies. . . . The other party affirm, on the contrary, that this disease is capable of being generated within the country by a concurrence of certain incidents of time and place."[20] Volney gathered the evidence on both sides of the question, concluding that the theory of indigenous origin was the more sound. Brown, who took exception in the notes he appended to his translation of the *Tableau* to many of Volney's opinions, did not refute his stance on the origin of yellow fever. He did, however, expand Volney's original "Ap-pendix" to include a kind of medical handbook containing treatments for yellow fever and various other diseases, thereby somewhat mitigating the hopelessness of Volney's grisly description of the New World disease.

Brown himself published "Letters on the Yellow Fever," which argued for the native origin of the disease, in the August 1799 number of his *Monthly Magazine and American Review*. Although the "Letters" favor a theory of the domestic origin of yellow fever, the description of the 1798 Philadelphia epidemic included in them calls to mind the great plagues of Europe:

> Imagine to yourself a flourishing city, where buildings extend a league in length, and nearly a mile in breadth, a proud port, whose capacious harbour, once bearing on its bosom a forest of masts, now a wasteful expanse! A population of 70,000 souls sud-denly reduced, by flight and pestilence, to less than 6000! Imag-ine the miserable remanent shut up from the eye, and nothing to be seen but carriages bearing the infected to the hospital, or hearses carrying the dead to the grave, and each, too, deserted by every relative and friend![21]

Likewise, the fever scenes in *Ormond* and *Arthur Mervyn* invite com-parison with accounts of medieval plagues and, more recently, with Daniel Defoe's *Journal of the Plague Year*. Insofar as the idea of an epidemic figured for Brown as a metaphorical description of civilized society, and insofar as it links American civilization with European, the yellow fever expresses the novelist's most extreme fears about the direction society was taking in the New World. Which is to say that the yellow fever expresses Brockden Brown's most radically antisocial self and, therefore, his identification with the egocentric values of the wilderness. The civilization of the Old World comes to Philadelphia as a plague.

Yet, to repeat, Brown never asserted the literal importation of yellow fever. However reluctantly, he subscribed to the theory of its indigenous origin. What is more, even as he linked this New World phenomenon to the plagues of the Old, Brown suggested that the American yellow fever was also something entirely new. Constantia Dudley's reading about the great plagues of Egypt and Greece does not prepare her for the extremity of the epidemic in her native city, and Arthur Mervyn points out that, in Philadelphia, the "numbers of the sick multiplied beyond all example; even in the pest affected cities of the Levant" (129). Appropriately, then, the epidemic not only recalls European plague but also evokes images from the New World wilderness of *Edgar Huntly*. In the first throes of the disease, wandering the streets of Philadelphia, Arthur beholds a city transformed: "Never, in the depths of cavern or forest, was I equally conscious of loneliness" (141). The epidemic drives its victims to the very frontier between life and death. Arthur watches three undertakers go about their grisly work. Loading a coffin into a hearse, one of them mutters, "I'll be damned if I think the poor dog was quite dead. . . . damn it, it wasn't right to put him in his coffin before the breath was fairly gone. I thought the last look he gave me, told me to stay a few minutes" (140).

Arthur himself, searching a deserted house for Susan Hadwin's fiancé, very nearly falls victim to living burial. A looter, stumbling upon Mervyn in the house, knocks him unconscious.

> A blow upon my temple was succeeded by an utter oblivion of thought and of feeling. I sunk upon the floor prostrate and senseless.
>
> My insensibility might be mistaken by observers for death, yet some part of this interval was haunted by a fearful dream.

The dream, which is as much a perception of waking reality, is of a piece with the wilderness dreams of Clara Wieland and Edgar Huntly:

> I conceived myself lying on the brink of a pit whose bottom the eye could not reach. My hands and legs were fettered, so as to disable me from resisting two grim and gigantic figures, who stooped to lift me from the earth. Their purpose methought was to cast me into this abyss. My terrors were unspeakable, and I struggled with such force, that my bonds snapt and I found myself at liberty. At this moment my senses returned and I opened my eyes.

Only to behold "three figures," the very undertakers who had already buried one man prematurely, preparing a coffin for himself. Fortunately for Arthur, he struggles to consciousness before the undertakers actually seize him. But: "I saw into what error, appearances had misled these men, and shuddered to reflect, by what hair-breadth means I had escaped being buried alive" (148–9). Like the cave scene of *Edgar Huntly*, this episode is worthy of the obsessions of Edgar Allan Poe.

Serving Brown as the territory of fantastic indulgence—of taboos that include oedipal dreams, rhapsodism, even Ormond's "European" Illuminism—the wilderness was also a territory of horror, of living death, the excesses of passion, and the annihilation of self-identity. Insofar as Brown conceived the Old World legacy of civilization as a plague, its terror, paradoxically, demanded expression in terms of the wilderness, the very metaphor in which Arthur realizes the European-bound "happy ending" of his American tale. The novel ends with the prospect of Arthur's marriage to Achsa Fielding, his Old World "mamma." Marriage to a European, as the fulfillment of a forbidden oedipal fantasy, is symbolically a wilderness act. *Arthur Mervyn* resolves—or evades—Brown's customary crisis of identity by joining in the marriage of Arthur and Achsa America and Europe. This union of wilderness and Old World civilization entails the abandonment of that middle ground, the United States; the newlyweds plan to leave Philadelphia for Europe.

While the prospect of the marriage is the least overtly melancholy ending in Brown's fiction, it is perhaps the most subversive of conventional American—that is, United States—society. Within the rational framework of the Franklinian success story Brown found it impossible to reconcile the fullest identity of the individual (which must include values represented by the wilderness) with the idea of social structure represented at its most extreme by the Philadelphia epidemic. *Arthur Mervyn*, therefore, is a vision of the dis-ease of civilization in the New World. Brown, who had begun his literary career idly dreaming utopias, created in his most detailed portrait of an American city a plague-smitten, apocalyptic vision of an antiutopia, in which the only real sources of social relationship lie in a monetary system liable to counterfeiting and imposture or in sexual alliances smuggled into town as the counterfeiting fantasies of the asocial wilderness mind.

VII

From Oedipus to Faust:
An American Tale

Between Part 1 of *Arthur Mervyn*, which appeared in 1799, and Part 2, 1800, Brown published *Edgar Huntly*. Into Brown's "respectable" novel of Philadelphia, motifs and images of the dangerous wilderness crept with the stealth of infection. In *Edgar Huntly*, however, Brown made these his explicit subjects, as if to thrust the wilderness into the gap between the first and second parts of what, on the surface, seems his most civil novel. The source of unconscious motifs and images in *Wieland*, *Ormond*, and *Arthur Mervyn*, the wilderness emerged in *Edgar Huntly* as a fully acknowledged subject and setting. Even more, in prefatory remarks to the novel, Brown announced it as a duty of the American novelist to depict "incidents of Indian hostility, and the perils of the Western wilderness," declaring that "for a native of America to overlook these would admit of no apology" (4). He even seemed to acknowledge in these remarks the crucial link between the wilderness and the unconscious mind; for he proposed to "exhibit a series of adventures, growing out of the condition of our country, and connected with [somnambulism,] one of the most common and most wonderful diseases or affections of the human frame" (3).

The prefatory remarks to *Edgar Huntly* comprise the most explicit statements the novelist ever made about his work. But even in this novel there is a final and telling evasiveness, perhaps a genuine failure of self-understanding. The ambiguities of *Edgar Huntly* begin with the title character's motives for leaving the safety and comfort of his peaceful manor house for the pain and peril of the wilderness. Waldegrave, Huntly's dear friend and the brother of his fiancée, has been mysteriously murdered. Huntly conceives it his "duty to . . . God and to mankind" to detect the criminal and see that he is justly "punished" (8). To this end he ventures into the countryside, to the elm beneath which Waldegrave's corpse had been found. Thus, ostensibly, his initial motive for probing the "groves and precipices," the "brooks . . . pits and hollows" of the Pennsylvania frontier is an eminently civilized one: he seeks to introduce justice into the wilderness.

We have seen, though, that "duty" in Brown's fiction often masks some private, self-indulgent, even perverse motive. This is not precisely the case with Huntly. For him, duty is not so much a false motive as it is a very short-lived one. At the fatal elm, in the moonlight, he beholds a human "apparition," which he instantly connects "with the fate of Waldegrave." Half naked, the "robust and strange" figure is busy digging—a grave?—by the elm. Before Huntly can decide what to do, the man drops his spade, sits down by the pit he has dug, and weeps with "heart-bursting grief." Huntly's stern sense of justice immediately yields to sympathy, even as tears—just like those of the wretched figure before him—"find their way spontaneously to" his eyes. "My caution had forsaken me," Huntly reports, "and, instead of one whom it was duty to persecute, I beheld, in this man, nothing but an object of compassion" (11).

So Huntly advances toward him, who, in the meantime, stops weeping and again takes up his spade. He begins to "cover up the pit with the utmost diligence," as if aware of Huntly's presence and wishing to hide something from him. When Huntly calls out, the man merely looks up, gazes at him, but somehow seems not to see the caller, falling once more to oblivious tears. Huntly determines to seek an "interview," but the mysterious figure rises, seizes the spade, and, walking impassively in a profound slumber, brushes past Huntly, as the latter reports, without "appearing to notice my existence" (11). From this point Edgar Huntly's fascination with Clithero Edny mounts to an obsession. He resolves to search the wilderness for Clithero, though he cannot explain why. "For what purpose shall I prosecute this search? What benefit am I to reap from this discovery?" At last Huntly concludes that his most urgent motive is mere curiosity, which, he realizes, "is vicious, if undisciplined by reason, and inconducive to benefit"; but then he glibly concludes that "curiosity, like virtue, is its own reward" (16).

Here, as in the prefatory remarks, Brown seems to acknowledge a character motive only implicit in his earlier novels. Here is an admission of the ascendancy of an essentially irrational impulse over the reasonable motives of civilized duty. Yet, precisely in this admission, Brown causes Edgar Huntly to be most evasive. If his motive for pursuing Clithero is irrational, it is not without reason. Keeping pace with his obsessive attraction to Clithero is the growing conviction that he, Edgar Huntly, has the power to grant the mysterious man absolution for the sin of killing Waldegrave. After twice more pursuing Clithero through a mazelike wilderness landscape, Brown's obsessed hero at last confronts his quarry on the farm of Clithero's employer, Inglefield. Face to face with his pursuer there, Clithero blandly asks Huntly if he wishes to discuss "anything in particular." Three times so far Clithero has led him into the wilderness, and now, reversing roles with his prey, it is Edgar Huntly who insists that Clithero follow *him* down the path back to the portentous elm tree. There he tries to extract a confession, not by threats, but through increasingly sympathetic cajolery. "I can feel for you," Huntly insists. "I act not thus in compliance with a temper that delights in the misery of others." This sympathy rapidly intensifies into empathy, as Huntly pleads that "the explanation I have solicited is no less necessary for your sake than for mine'' (29–31).

Richard Slotkin, in *Regeneration through Violence*, suggests one reason why the actions of Clithero are so important to Huntly. "You expect," Huntly tells Clithero, "that, having detected the offender, I will hunt him to infamy and death. You are mistaken." But *hunt* Clithero is precisely what Huntly does, going so far, later in the story, as to set out a bait of food for him during a sixth foray into the wilderness (103). Slotkin, pointing out the "kinship with the frontier hunters" suggested by Huntly's very name, associates him with Indian hunters, who ritualistically identify themselves with their prey. Already "strangely drawn to Clithero," Huntly embarks upon a "hunt [that] carries his sense of kinship to its ultimate point: the hunter identifies himself with the beast he is hunting, becomes one with the thing he wishes to kill." In Clithero, then, Huntly recognizes a "double," who "represents that dark quality of Huntly's own nature which is moved by irresistible passions and impulses and which prefers nighttime and solitude to the genial day and healthy companionship."[1] By getting Clithero to confess in order that he can absolve him, Edgar Huntly is really justifying a dark part of his own being and exonerating himself.

While Slotkin's observation accounts for the mythological resonance of Huntly's identification with Clithero, the novel in and of itself sufficiently delineates psychological motives. "I am no stranger to your cares," Huntly attempts to convince Clithero, "to the deep and incurable despair that haunts you, to which your waking thoughts are a prey and from which sleep cannot secure you" (31). When he utters these words, Huntly is as yet unaware that, in diagnosing Clithero's guilt-ridden somnambulism, he is also describing his own. There are many more points at which the identities of hunter and hunted converge. Huntly first sees Clithero digging by moonlight under the elm; in the middle of the novel, we see an identical picture of Huntly, who busies himself beneath the moon digging for what Clithero had buried. It turns out to be a box, identical to one Huntly had discovered earlier in Clithero's room. That first one had been exquisitely crafted, like a puzzle, its seamless lid apparently impossible to open. "Some spring . . . secretly existed, which might forever elude the senses," a piece of handiwork perfectly suited to the enigmatic Clithero. As soon as Huntly runs his hand over the surface of the box, however, it opens. "A hundred hands might have sought in vain for this spring," but it seems as if it had been made expressly for his own hand to open. Disappointingly, there is nothing of interest to Huntly inside, so he decides to exhume whatever he had seen Clithero bury. The second box unearthed, Huntly does not bother with the niceties of secret springs. Impatiently smashing the box under his heel, he finds a manuscript inside written by one Euphemia Lorimer, who had been Clithero's adoptive mother in Ireland, and who (through a complicated but crucial chain of events we shall presently examine) had almost been murdered by Clithero.

Like Clithero, Edgar Huntly is a bit of a carpenter. In a cabinet of his "own contrivance and workmanship . . . of singular structure," containing a secret drawer opened only "by the motion of a spring, of whose existence none but the maker was conscious," Edgar Huntly has hidden his own precious manuscript, the letters of his friend and would-be brother-in-law Waldegrave. Opening the secret drawer one day to fetch the letters, he is shocked to discover them missing. Who could have taken them—for who but himself knew of the drawer, let alone how to open it? The answer, Huntly finds to his dismay, is that no one but himself had taken the letters. He had opened the drawer in his sleep, sleepwalked into the attic of his uncle's house, and secreted the documents in the angle of the two roof beams (128, 249). Clithero Edny is shocked in exactly the same manner when he opens his own box to discover that Euphemia Lorimer's papers are missing. Recall that Huntly had smashed the box containing Euphemia Lorimer's manuscript. The empty box Clithero opens is the one Huntly had found in Clithero's room, had opened as if by magic, and had himself found empty. It is empty because Clithero, sleepwalking, had removed the letters and buried them in the other box beneath the elm. Edgar Huntly is forced to acknowledge the somnambulism he shares with Clithero Edny, who "had buried his treasure with his own hands, as mine had been secreted by myself; but both acts had been performed during sleep" (267). As in *Arthur Mervyn*, where secret—antisocial—knowledge is associated with the dark seclusion of a closet, so in *Edgar Huntly* the revelation of an unconscious self is associated with the secret boxes of Clithero and Edgar. These in turn are symbolically parallel with the remote cave in the wilderness and the profound transformation that takes place in it. Huntly's first glimpse of Clithero was as an apparition, "half naked," like a savage (10). After the initiation ordeal of the cave scene, an adventure into which Clithero Edny had, emotionally, led him, Edgar Huntly emerges from the cavern "half naked," like a savage (243).

Huntly is anxious to purge Clithero of guilt and grief because he represents the nocturnal, solitary passions of his own nature. These are the very values Brown saw in himself when he explained his identity as a writer to John Bernard. And, as Clithero leads his double, Edgar Huntly, into the wilderness, so Huntly leads Brown, *his* double, after him. Brown follows Huntly not only into a fictional evocation of the Pennsylvania wilds but into that "metaphysic wilderness" defined in "Devotion: An Epistle," a territory of dark and uncontrolled intellectual speculation that leads to "nothing." As we have seen, that "nothing" comes to be identified with a nihilistic vision of the absurd limits of perception and truth; it is to this vision, after a harrowing physical and emotional chase, that Huntly's human prey finally takes him.

Richard Slotkin argues that Huntly unconsciously identifies with Clithero as the murderer of Waldegrave. Calling Waldegrave "saintly and paternal," Slotkin associates him with the authority of a father, so that Clithero comes to represent for Huntly the fulfillment of a wish to over-

come parental control, to exchange civilized restraint for the freedom of
savage life. Huntly's natural parents had been killed in an Indian raid
when Edgar was a boy. Therefore, in merging his identity with the half-
savage Clithero's, becoming something of an Indian himself, Edgar Huntly also identifies quite directly with the murderers of his *natural* parents.
Worse, he comes to blame himself for what he thinks has been the Indian
slaughter of his *adoptive* parents—an aunt and uncle—and his two sisters,
during a raid that took place while Huntly, as a result of his sleepwalking,
wandered lost in the forest. (Actually—and significantly—only the uncle,
the father-figure, has been slain; Brown spares the aunt/mother and
Huntly's sisters.) Huntly is nearly overcome with guilt at the realization
that his single-minded pursuit of Clithero has kept him away from the
family and home he should have defended (see *Regeneration*, 385–8).
Although we shall see that the ''saintly and paternal'' view of Waldegrave
is a serious oversimplification, Slotkin is right to open Brown's text to yet
another oedipal reading; but he does not tell the whole complicated story.

Clithero Edny's real crime is not the murder of Waldegrave (slain, it
turns out, by those ubiquitous Indians), but the attempted murder of
Euphemia Lorimer. Clithero tells the sad tale in a long wilderness ''interview'' with Edgar (34–85). He was born and raised in Ireland (the wild
country that gave us Carwin's mentor, Ludloe), the son of a poor tenant
farmer. The landlord, living with his wife in Dublin, was a profligate who
met a well-deserved end when he challenged a rival for his mistress's favors
to a duel. Shortly after the death of her philandering husband, the
landlady—Euphemia Lorimer—visited Edny's cottage and was so impressed with young Clithero that she took the boy back to Dublin with her.
Ostensibly, he was a servant in the great household, but he soon became
more a companion for the lady's son and, finally, was adopted by Mrs.
Lorimer as her own boy (38–9). Like Huntly, then, Clithero lived with
adoptive parents. Idolizing his foster mother as Arthur Mervyn had adored
his natural mother and her surrogate in Achsa Fielding, Clithero could not
imagine a happier situation than his.

Then he fell in love with Clarice, the illegitimate daughter of Mrs.
Lorimer's wicked twin brother, Arthur Wiatte. Like Clithero, Clarice had
been adopted by Euphemia, whom she resembles virtually as a twin—a
double (47, 78). As Arthur Mervyn found in Achsa a ''mamma'' who
could gratify his oedipal desires, so Clithero discovered Clarice. Like
Arthur, too, Clithero at first believed that his situation was too good to be
true. Judging himself socially far below Clarice, he thought that marriage
to her was an impossibility. Heartbroken at this realization, he was on the
verge of leaving Mrs. Lorimer's household when, as if to put the finishing
touch on this oedipal fantasy, the lady herself gave a prospectve marriage
between her adopted children an enthusiastic blessing.

But Clithero Edny was hardly destined for the bright fantasy future of
an Arthur Mervyn. Clarice had to postpone the wedding to journey to the
bedside of a dying friend. In the meantime, Arthur Wiatte, Euphemia's

twin brother and perhaps the only one-dimensionally evil character Brockden Brown ever created, arrived in Dublin. His appearance there was the more incredible since everyone had supposed him killed some nine years earlier in a mutiny on board the prison ship transporting him to a place of banishment for his crimes. Despite the abuses he had heaped upon her, including coercion into the unhappy marriage with the faithless Lorimer, Euphemia was passionately, pathologically devoted to her evil double. Believing her fate inextricably bound with Wiatte's, she was convinced that her life must end with his. (Neither Clithero nor Brown explains, however, why Euphemia did not die nine years earlier when she supposed her brother had been killed in the mutiny.) Although she had made many sacrifices for Wiatte, attempting desperately to repair the ruin he habitually left in his wake, she did nothing to prevent his transportation, reasoning that, given his depravity, "banishment was the mildest destiny that would befall him." With Wiatte's unexpected return, Clithero and Euphemia's new suitor, Sarsefield (who bears no relation to the Sarsefield mentioned in *Ormond*) feared that he contemplated some horrible revenge upon the sister who, he felt, had conspired to banish him.

Clithero was turning the corner of a Dublin alley when he heard a "hoarse voice" shout, "Damn ye, villain, ye're a dead man!" A pistol shot grazed his cheek, stunning and staggering him, but failing even to knock him down. Seeing that his shot had missed, Clithero's assailant muttered, "This shall do your business!" and drew a knife. Like Huntly confronted by the panther, Clithero responded spontaneously, drawing and firing a pistol he had hidden in his pocket. The dead man was Arthur Wiatte.

It mattered little to Clithero that he had acted in self-defense, and, for that matter, without knowing his assailant's identity. All he could think of was how he had signed his "mother's" death warrant by his deed, ending as well any hope of marrying Clarice. Unbalanced by the act that cut short his oedipal romance, Clithero determined to shorten Euphemia's suffering by hastening what he believed to be her inevitable end. In the darkened house, he entered the bedroom he thought was Euphemia's, gazed at a peacefully slumbering figure, raised a dagger, and was about to thrust it home—when his arm was caught by Euphemia Lorimer herself. Having mistaken Clarice's room for Euphemia's, he was about to kill his betrothed. Euphemia, overcome by shock, collapsed into a swoon Clithero mistook for death (a misapprehension under which he labors even as he tells his story to Huntly). He ran, and kept running, onto a ship, across the ocean, and into the woods of Pennsylvania.

Then, his story ended, Clithero runs away from Huntly, too, disappearing "amidst the thickets of the wood" (86). Reasoning that a person capable of attempting to murder his benefactress is also capable of killing Waldegrave, Huntly redoubles his pursuit. But now that Clithero has revealed a specifically oedipal "crime," Huntly is also the more eager to convince him of his innocence. Clithero has led Huntly, and Huntly,

Brown, through a wilderness to an oedipal revelation. But if Clithero's dark narrative is properly told in the American wilds, its action had originated in Europe. A more complete incest story than that in *Arthur Mervyn*, involving punishment as well as gratification, it is also a much more cryptic one. Whereas the "Oedipus complex" is blatant in *Arthur Mervyn*, it takes some work to uncover it in *Edgar Huntly*, to recognize that Clithero's betrothed is his adoptive mother's double, and to untangle the role Wiatte plays both in completing the fulfillment of the fantasy and in punishing it. Strictly speaking, Wiatte is Euphemia's brother and Clarice's father, and by virtue of adoption, Clithero and Clarice are brother and sister. However, in the system of symbolic equivalents of Clithero's tale, Wiatte figures as Euphemia's husband (such is her fanatical devotion to him) and Clarice figures for Clithero as the equivalent of Euphemia. Euphemia's quasi-incestuous attachment to Wiatte makes him her "husband," and therefore Clithero's "father," and Clithero's adoptive sibling relationship to Clarice compounds his identification as Wiatte's "son." In killing Arthur Wiatte, then, Clithero consummates an oedipal fantasy with the death of the wicked and oppressive father.

But there is a crucial string attached to this: the very act that consummates the fantasy ends and punishes it. Euphemia had told Clithero that she cannot live without Wiatte, so he proposes to oblige his "mother" by murdering her, thereby adding matricide to patricide. Worse, Clithero had mistaken Clarice's sleeping body for Euphemia's, and is stopped just before he dispatches his sister-mother-bride. Not only, then, does the killing of Wiatte touch off a chain of events that terminates the oedipal fantasy, but, as punishment, Clithero must carry the guilty burden of matricide and sororicide heaped upon patricide. Brown had flirted with brother-sister incest in *Wieland*, and even suggested a combination of brother-sister-mother-son incest in *Arthur Mervyn*. But not even Oedipus the King suffered through the baroque family romance of Clithero Edny, who laments, Oedipus-like, that his "misery has been greater than has fallen to the lot of mortals" (35).[2]

As with the more straightforward oedipal fantasy of *Arthur Mervyn*, the yarn Brown has Clithero spin for Huntly likely betrays an unresolved conflict within the mind of the novelist himself. But speculations about Brown's role in his personal family romance bring us, for the purposes of literary criticism, to a dead end if we do not carry the analysis beyond the merely personal. Like Ormond's seduction and threatened rape of Constantia, and Mervyn's oedipal romances, the story of Clithero is an objectification of a secret knowledge proscribed by the laws and mores of conventional society. Brown thought the revelation so offensive that he could only hint at it in intimations of primal sin and depravity. As bodied forth in Clithero's oedipal patri-matri-sororicide, Brockden Brown banishes these intimations to a wild domain in Pennsylvania. Yet, though one half of the novelist's "double mental existence" casts out this knowledge, it is not forgotten, and the other half is sent across the frontier to hunt it down. We must not overlook in this formulation the crucial fact that Europe, not wilderness America, is the scene of Clithero's drama. This presents a problem of interpretation like the one we encountered in *Ormond*, where the impulses of irrationality are embodied in a European seducer. However, as Ormond approached from the west before he attempted to rape Constantia, so Clithero absconds to the Pennsylvania wilds after his crime. Here he suffers the consequence of European guilt, becoming half savage, thereby enacting the symbolic equivalent of the passions that had driven him from the household of Mrs. Lorimer. Clithero tells his story beneath the elm where he had buried Euphemia's manuscript: the wilderness is a place in which passions are both buried and exhumed, both hidden and revealed.

In *Wieland*, the novelist reversed Joel Barlow's commonplace utopian image of America as a land of bright revelation. Edgar Huntly, too, sleepwalking out of his lightsome chamber and into a pit hidden within a wilderness cavern, wakes to a New World of utter darkness. At first he believes himself blind.

Writing about the massacre of Theodore Wieland's family, John Greenleaf Whittier judged that the "masters of the old Greek tragedy have scarcely exceeded the sublime horror of this scene from the American novelist."[3] Whittier may actually have identified in this remark one source of influence upon Brown, who once remarked that the "tragic spectacle has charms congenial to my soul, and I dwell with mingled sadness and delight on the scenes of Sophocles, Racine, and Rome" (Clark, 73). Had Whittier gone beyond the emotional impact of the ritual atrocity in *Wieland* to discuss the novel's leading intellectual motifs, his observation would have been even more acute. For, in the *Oedipus* of Sophocles, we find the epistemological theme that also obsessed Brown through his four major novels. Like Oedipus, Brown's heroes confront the limit of human capacity to discover and act upon truth. Edgar Huntly, like Oedipus, prides himself on his ability to unravel riddles. He pursues Clithero, confident not only that he is tracking the murderer of Waldegrave but also that he, Huntly, has the power to absolve Clithero of guilt. "You are unacquainted with the man before you," Clithero warns him. "You, like others, are blind to the most momentous consequences of your own actions" (34). And so Huntly is blind. Pursuing Clithero, he really hunts himself. Pitying Clithero for the unconscious, fate-driven nature of his "crime," Huntly discovers that, like him, he is also a sleepwalker, unable to give full account of his actions.

Though we can rather safely assume that Brown read *Oedipus*, determining in just what form he encountered the play requires more risky speculation. To "Henrietta G." Brown wrote that he had "received some knowledge of Greek and Latin at [Robert Proud's] Grammar School, but this knowledge will by no means qualify me to instruct others. It scarcely enables me to read these ancient authors" (Clark, 72). Even if Brown had

not—or could not have—read *Oedipus* in the original, he would have had
ample access to at least two English versions of the play. The Library Company of Philadelphia owned a copy of "The Tragedies of Sophocles.
Translated from the Greek by Thomas Fran[c]klin, London, 1757,"[4] which
contains *Oedipus*. Hocquet Caritat, New York bookstore owner and
publisher of some of Brown's own fiction, offered John Dryden and
Nathaniel Lee's version of *Oedipus* in his 1799 catalog, *The Feast of
Reason*.[5] There are no obvious verbal echoes in *Edgar Huntly* from either
of these sources, although there are some intriguing similarities. Compare
this outburst from the chorus in Francklin's translation—"O hapless state
of the human race!"—with Huntly's "Disastrous and humiliating is the
state of man!" (267). More remarkable is this passage from Dryden and
Lee. "Remember *Lajus* [Laius]," Tiresias enjoins Oedipus; to which the
King responds in soliloquy:

> Remember *Lajus!* that's the burden still:
> Murther, and Incest! but to hear 'em nam'd
> My Soul starts in me: the good Sentinel
> Stands to her Weapons; takes the first Alarm
> To guard me from such Crimes.—Did I kill *Lajus?*
> Then I walk'd sleeping, in some frightful dream,
> My Soul then stole my Body out by night;
> And brought me back to Bed e're Morning-wake.

And in these lines of Tiresias to Oedipus one may read a prophecy pro-
nounced upon Edgar Huntly:

> Thou art thy self a Riddle; a perplext
> Obscure *Aenigma*, which when thou unty'st,
> Thou shalt be found and lost.[6]

It matters less, of course, to determine just what version of *Oedipus* (if
any) Brown read than it does to recognize that the American novelist
shared with Sophocles an insight into the limits of knowledge and judgment. This is demonstrated most succinctly in Huntly's final, humiliating
gesture. Clithero, recovering from serious wounds received at the hands of
Indians, retires to the solitude of a wilderness hut. Although Clithero's
"fatal and gloomy thoughts seemed to have somewhat yielded to tranquility," Huntly is not content to let him "mope away his life in this un-
social and savage state." He reasons that Clithero is burdened by a mistaken belief that he had caused the death of Euphemia Lorimer. Huntly resolves, therefore, to tell him the truth: that Sarsefield, Edgar's friend and
former teacher, recently married Euphemia and has brought her, very
much alive, back with him to America. When Clithero refuses to believe
that this can be so, Huntly gives him as proof the couple's street address in
New York. "'Tis well!" Clithero shouts:

Rash and infatuated youth, thou hast ratified, beyond appeal or forgiveness, thy own doom. Thou hast once more let loose my steps, and sent me on a fearful journey. Thou has furnished the means of detecting thy imposture. I will fly to the spot which thou describest. I will ascertain thy falsehood with my own eyes. If she be alive, then am I reserved for the performance of a new crime. My evil destiny will have it so. If she be dead, I shall make *thee* expiate.

As he had repeatedly eluded Edgar Huntly in the woods, so Clithero disappears through the door, bound for New York (272–7).

But Edgar thinks fast. He dispatches a brief message to Sarsefield, warning him that Clithero is on the loose, and follows this note with a longer letter explaining the matter in detail. Sarsefield, in return, writes to Huntly about the consequences of his having set Clithero on Euphemia's trail, and about the additional consequence of his note and letter. Edgar's first brief note Sarsefield had narrowly prevented Euphemia from reading. She was on the verge of opening it when he entered the room and stopped her. "See how imminent a chance it was that saved my wife from a knowledge of its contents!" Sarsefeld writes. For Euphemia was pregnant, and there could be no telling what terrible effect news about Clithero would have had on her in that delicate condition. This notwithstanding, Edgar's first note was at least timely. Sarsefield alerted the authorities, who apprehended Clithero Edny in New York. Sailing back to Pennsylvania for confinement in the lunatic asylum, Clithero jumped overboard—an escape attempt or suicide?—and drowned.

But it was Euphemia Lorimer-Sarsefield who received the second letter when her husband was out of the house. After nearly dying from the shock of the news about Clithero, Euphemia suffered a miscarriage. Not only is this event the novel's epistemological coup de grâce, reiterating once and for all the myopic range of human foresight, it also sets the seal on Huntly's identification with Clithero and his oedipal romance. Richard Slotkin rightly observes that it is Huntly who fulfills Clithero's destiny, striking "down the woman and the child in her womb by a rash, unthinking deed" (*Regeneration*, 389). Actually, Huntly is implicated in Clithero's oedipal romance even more deeply than Slotkin acknowledges. Sarsefield, husband of the novel's central mother-wife, serves Huntly as a surrogate father. Huntly identifies himself as Sarsefield's "pupil" and "child," while the mentor in turn confesses "parental affection" for Edgar (231 and 248). Moreover, apparently unaware of Edgar's attachment to Mary Waldegrave, Sarsefield hints at a prospective marriage between his "son" Edgar and his adopted daughter—Clarice. Sarsefield declares to Huntly that Euphemia "longs to embrace you as a son. To become truly her son will depend upon your own choice, and that of one [Clarice] who was the companion of our voyage [from Europe to America]" (251).

Searching out the incestuous murderer, Edgar Huntly, like Oedipus, reveals the guilt in himself.

When he formulated the theory of the Oedipus complex, Sigmund Freud recognized the epistemological "moral" implicit in the legend of the Theban king. Freud quotes the chorus that closes Sophocles' play: "Fix on Oedipus your eyes, / Who resolved the dark enigma, noblest champion and most wise," but who, Freud cautions, lives like the rest of us, in ignorance of our deepest desires.[7] Edgar Huntly concludes, after he has discovered himself a sleepwalker: "Disastrous and humiliating is the state of man! By his own hands is constructed the mass of misery and error in which his steps are forever involved" (267). It is the blinding revelation for which he has hunted through the wilderness, and having caught it, it is destined to hunt and haunt him, just as it had Clithero Edny.

Renaissance Europeans were capable of asking: "Has the discovery of America been useful or harmful to mankind?"[8] We have seen that the discovery of an American New World posed challenges and threats to the Old World's conception of itself, like those Edgar Huntly confronts in the fictional wilderness of Charles Brockden Brown. Like the early European explorers, Huntly enters the New World on what he believes to be a civilized mission. He ventures into the wilderness expecting to emerge unchanged, indeed expecting to change a half-naked and half-savage apparition he finds there. But like the Europeans of the Renaissance, both Edgar Huntly and Brockden Brown return from contact with the New World profoundly changed, transformed.

There is an intriguing excursus in the novel which makes the "saintly" Waldegrave resemble the devious Ormond. Among the letters of Waldegrave, which Huntly treasures in his secret box, are youthful pronouncements upon the nature of reality. Virtually identical with Ormond's dangerous creed, Waldegrave's early belief was in a godless and wholly material universe in which necessity replaces providence, and physical matter the soul. Waldegrave suffered a conversion by and by, becoming a kind of wilderness missionary. Unlike the senior Wieland, however, he sets up as a rational teacher of poor blacks rather than as a fanatical preacher to the Indians. Despite this overwhelming testimony of mature piety, Huntly considers his friend's early doctrines harmful enough to withhold them from his fiancée, Mary, Waldegrave's sister. When she does request the letters, Huntly feels duty-bound to sort through and censor them before sending them on (125–6). But when he goes to get them in the secret drawer of his specially constructed box, he discovers that they are missing. Knowing that only he could have opened the drawer, Huntly is forced to recognize that he is a somnambulist when he finds the letters hidden in the attic (128, 249).

None of this is essential to Brown's plot. Edgar Huntly could have discovered his sleepwalking affliction more dramatically as a direct result of his experience in the cave scene. Nor does the plot demand our knowing about Waldegrave's early beliefs. If the novel itself, then, does not call for the Waldegrave detour, something in Brown must have. We know from the novelist's identification with Ormond, and from his description of writing as an unconscious and unwilled act, that he was himself drawn to the atheistic, even nihilistic, ideas of the young Waldegrave. This warrants further speculation about Huntly's treatment of his friend's letters, and also about the fate for which Brockden Brown reserves Waldegrave. Edgar's somnambulistic removal of the "dangerous" letters invites two contrary interpretations. Either the unconscious act suggests Brown's own desire to rid himself of seductive Ormondesque ideas, or it hints at a desire to preserve them, to hide them from the world and even from the censorship of his own conscious self. As to the significance of Waldegrave's having met his death in the woods at the hands of "savages," if Brown associated Waldegrave's early radicalism with the anarchistic values of the wilderness, perhaps Waldegrave's murder is the execution of poetic justice, the wild consequence of wild ideas. Or perhaps the poetic justice is the revenge the wilderness exacts upon one who has abandoned its values; Waldegrave suffers for having turned from radicalism to the bright Christianity of conventional society.

The name "Waldegrave," as a combination of the German *Wald* ("woods") and the English word *grave*, serves to link Waldegrave's letters, which Huntly hides in the attic, with Euphemia Lorimer's journal, which Clithero buries in a woodland "grave." The name also underscores the ambiguity of both Huntly's and Clithero's acts of concealment, since we are uncertain whether committing the documents to a wilderness grave signifies a desire to destroy or to preserve them. We may risk conjuring with the curious name even further. A *waldgrave*—from the German *waldgraf*—was, in "mediaeval Germany, an officer having jurisdiction over a royal forest" (*OED*). So, in perpetrating the fictional murder of a character named Waldegrave (a man whose youthful ideas savored of the "wild"), Brown possibly destroys a guardian of the forest, a kind of wilderness genius loci. Or perhaps it is Waldegrave in his saintly aspect who is destroyed—not the writer of atheist doctrine, but the pious master of a school for indigent blacks. The first interpretation would suggest Brown's repudiation of the antisocial territory of the wilderness; the second suggests that he wished to overcome the "waldgrave" who guards the forest *against* him, who prevents his entry into that unconscious territory. Waldegrave, then, emerges as an emblem of Brown's enduring ambivalence. A "sinner" turned "saint," he is associated both with the anarchistic spirit of the forest and with the repressive force that prevents access to it.

Suggestive as the ambiguities of Waldegrave are, it is important to realize that he is but a ghost in *Edgar Huntly*, dead before the narrative begins. Richard Slotkin's insights notwithstanding, Waldegrave is not a surrogate father for Huntly. Brotherly, not fatherly, and a prospective

brother-in-law at that, Waldegrave yields to Sarsefield as the principal
father-figure. In the letter to Edgar Huntly that ends the novel, Sarsefield
reproves his "son" for having so rashly sent Clithero Edny and the two
fatal messages to him and his wife: "I assure you, Edgar, my philosophy
has not found itself lightsome and active under this burden. I find it hard
to forbear commenting on your rashness in no very mild terms. You acted
in direct opposition to my counsel and to the plainest dictates of propriety." Considering that he refers to something which cost him an unborn
child and very nearly its mother as well, this is a laughably mild reproof. In
fact, it is downright fatherly: "Be more circumspect and more obsequious
for the future," he cautions (279). For its tone of paternal counsel, the
reproof is the more humiliating. In *Edgar Huntly* the oedipal drama is
played out to the end, through gratification as well as punishment, with
the father triumphant at the last. We are left only to imagine the burden
of Clithero-like guilt Huntly will have to bear for the grief he has brought
upon Euphemia and her new husband. Insofar as the oedipal adventure is
associated with the seductive and dangerous freedom of the wilderness, the
conclusion to *Edgar Huntly* signals Brown's retreat from the frontier his
hero had crossed.

In the respectable guise of an urban American success story, Brown
consummated, quite without attendant punishment and guilt, a simpler
oedipal fantasy. The second part of *Arthur Mervyn*, in which the young
hero meets and is about to marry his "new mamma," appeared a year after
Edgar Huntly. The novelist has Arthur close his story this way:

> What more can be added?
> What more? Can Achsa ask what more? She who has not been
> *only* a wife—
> But why am I indulging this pen-prattle? The hour she fixed for
> my return to her is come, and now take thyself away, quill. Lie
> there, snug in thy leathern case, till I call for thee, and that will
> not be very soon. I believe I will abjure thy company till all is
> settled with my love. Yes: I *will* abjure thee, so let *this* be thy last
> office, till Mervyn has been made the happiest of men. (446)

Unlike Arthur, Brockden Brown did not literally put away his pen when he
finished the second part of *Mervyn*; he continued to ply it for another
decade, until his death in 1810. But he did emerge from the completion of
Arthur Mervyn a remarkably transformed writer.

What more could be added, what more—after the novelist had pursued himself across the frontier of consciousness, and into a wilderness of
both dream and nightmare? Having glimpsed perhaps too much already,
the respectable citizen of Philadelphia did not put out his eyes for shame,
but shut them for the remainder of his life and career to the world of
Wieland, *Ormond*, *Edgar Huntly*, and even *Arthur Mervyn*. His last two
novels, both published in 1801, are wholehearted affirmations of bour-

geois American morality. We will barely glance at them in order to trace
the arc of Brown's late career.

Clara Howard; In a Series of Letters was resubtitled "Or, The Enthusiasm of Love" in American editions of Brown's collected works. But
the only enthusiasm exhibited is for the punctilios of conventional morality, and "love" is defined as passion in the service of a financially secure
marriage. Philip Stanley, the story's male protagonist (British editions of
the novel were named after him), begins by addressing an unidentified
correspondent:

> You once knew me as a simple lad, plying the file and tweezers at
> the bench of a watchmaker, with no prospect before me but of
> labouring, for a few years at least, as a petty and obscure journey-
> man, at the same bench where I worked five years ago! Now I am
> rich, happy, crowned with every terrestrial felicity, in possession of
> that most exquisite of all blessings,—a wife, endowed with
> youth, grace, dignity, discretion. (287)

And, we might add, endowed with wealth. *Clara Howard* (or *Philip
Stanley*) is *Arthur Mervyn* writ small.

Quite small. With nothing of *Arthur Mervyn's* subversive irony, intentional or unconscious, the courtship of Philip and Clara is related
through an epistolary series of arguments over a single moral dilemma.
Philip has been friendly, in a strictly fraternal fashion, with one Mary
Wilmot, who, although she longs to marry him, altruistically yields her
claim to Clara Howard. Clara, in her turn, loves and is loved by Philip
Stanley, but conceives it *her* duty to enjoin Philip to do *his* duty by marrying Mary—whom he does not love with (as Mervyn would put it) a
"marriage-wishing love." Thus the mercifully brief novel tugs and pulls
until Philip threatens to banish himself into the interior of the North
American continent. The timely resolution of the fastidious Clara-Philip-
Mary triangle forestalls this desperate scheme, but the point, so far as the
novelist's mature attitude is concerned, has been made. The wilderness
that, in his major fiction, held both the danger and the allure of discovering a new self, had become simply a punitive realm of social exile.
Anxiously anticipating the arrival of Philip Stanley from Wilmington,
Clara writes him from the security of her New York home: "Would to
Heaven thou hadst not this boisterous river to cross! It is said to be somewhat dangerous in a high wind. This is a land of evils,—the transitions of
the seasons are so quick, and into such extremes. How different from the
pictures which our fancy drew in [England,] our native land!" (408).

Failing to win the hand of Jane Talbot in the novel Brown named after
her, Henry Colden embarks upon the journey Philip Stanley had, in *Clara
Howard*, only contemplated. It is not into the American interior he ventures, however, but out to the farthest reaches of Europe and Asia, eventually landing upon "the desert shore of Japan; on the borders of a new

world" (229). That Colden does not travel to a specifically American "new world" matters less than our recognition that, like Philip Stanley, he entertains the pioneer's impulse to seek *a* new world. Both Stanley and Colden derive this impulse from frustration and desperation, deliberately exiling themselves from a society that—temporarily—cannot satisfy their desires. Far from directing this as criticism against the social values portrayed in *Clara Howard* and *Jane Talbot*, however, Brown is at pains to demonstrate the superiority of civilized accoutrements, notwithstanding the inhibitions and restrictions they impose, over the antisocial values of adventure. If a trip between Wilmington and New York is hazardous, how much worse a trip across the continent to the Pacific? Henry Colden, after a punishing voyage round the world, is at last welcomed into the arms of Jane Talbot, who beholds in him a weatherbeaten figure, exhausted, perhaps half savage in appearance, but whose broken health is surely destined to mend before the domestic hearth. To adopt the language of William Spengemann's *The Adventurous Muse*, Brown's muse of adventure has given way in these last novels to one of domesticity.[9]

The victim of a jealous woman's imposture, Jane Talbot is accused of infidelity to her first (now deceased) husband in an adulterous liaison she supposedly had carried on with Henry Colden. Colden, a disciple of Godwinian agnosticism, is said to have seduced Jane with views on marriage that might have been drawn from Brown's own *Alcuin*. Henry "denied (shocking!) that any thing but mere habit and positive law, stood in the way of marriage; nay, of intercourse without marriage, between brother and sister, parent and child!" (70). In *Alcuin*, his first book-length publication, Brown had deliberately courted radical notions of marriage; in the character of Ormond, a diabolical version of Henry Colden, he had found a degree of kinship; and in each of his four major novels, he had created fantasies of "intercourse . . . between brother and sister, parent and child." In *Jane Talbot*, however, the title character, far from falling prey to Colden's godless views, converts him to a proper Christianity. He returns from his adventures chastened not only in the flesh, but also in spirit. So, too, after a harrowing journey into a new world of radical ideas, having courted Godwinianism and Illuminism alike, Brockden Brown came to *Clara Howard* and *Jane Talbot* as a bourgeois Christian of Philadelphia.

In addition to his journalistic projects, ongoing since 1799, Brown wrote three or four[10] pseudonymous political pamphlets after *Clara Howard* and *Jane Talbot*. The first two, issued in 1803, treat Spain's cession of Louisiana to the French. Urging America's manifest claim to dominion over the Louisiana territory as well as the whole of the continent, *An Address to the Government* and *Monroe's Embassy* betray a Federalist's dissatisfaction with the peaceful policies of Jefferson. On a personal level, the pamphlets suggest Brown's anxious zeal to extend civilized regulation into the vast anarchy of the continental wilderness. To this end, he was willing to stir his nation to war. Brown's "historical" sketches of "Carsol" and the "Carrils and Ormes," most likely, as we have seen, composed after his six novels, may also have been the products of anti-Jeffersonian conservatism. Politically antiutopian, the feudal governments of Brown's "Sketches" are a private "utopia"—that is, a utopia only in that they represent an escape from the anxieties of the young Republic's political experiment. In this sense, the pieces foreshadow the nostalgia for things medieval that would possess the diverse likes of Mark Twain and Henry Adams.

Another document of Brown's dissatisfaction appeared the year before his death. He published early in 1809 *An Address to the Congress of the United States, on the Utility and Justice of Restrictions upon Foreign Commerce*, a measured and eloquent attack upon the embargo. As a piece occasioned by and aimed squarely at the least popular act of Jefferson's presidency, the pamphlet's broader intellectual and emotional significance should be interpreted cautiously. But Brown does not restrict himself to economic and political argument, seizing, rather, on the embargo act as an occasion for general moral reflection. Throughout its history, he argues, Europe has proven itself corrupt, even depraved:

> And alas! those who fancied that the spirit of Europe was regenerated or improved by crossing the Atlantic, are woefully mistaken. It was indeed quite ridiculous to think that *this* branch of the European body was exempted from any of the vices of *those*. How should it happen? What is there in our intellectual constitution that should make us wiser or better than our kinsmen beyond the sea? If any proof were wanting that our system of *political* justice is as narrow, selfish, depraved, unfeeling as that of European states, we have only to consider . . . the embargo.[11]

Even granting Brown the hyperbolic license of a political orator, we are justified in detecting here evidence of a final disappointment with the American experiment. Something of the same subversive spirit that had animated *Arthur Mervyn* is at work behind the 1809 *Address*. Though bourgeois American society was undercut in the novel primarily by the intrusion of wilderness values, the majority of Philadelphians Brown exhibited were as corrupt as any number of perfidious Europeans; and with Europe, Philadelphia shared its own, apparently home-grown, version of the plague.

Perhaps, though, the passage from the *Address* betrays Brown's consciousness of his own failure to transform himself into an American, to come to terms with, and to feel at home in, the New World. He had come closest to acknowledging the intimacy of his bond with America in *Edgar Huntly*. But the hero of that novel never really awakened from his sleepwalking, and the final result of his wilderness sojourn is bewilderment. In *Wieland*, Theodore is indeed transformed into a New World figure, becoming, like James Yates, the brutal caricature of an Indian in order to massacre his family. But even this "savage" act is only the culmination of his European father's religious convictions. And in three of Brown's four major novels (*Wieland, Ormond,* and *Arthur Mervyn*), a principal character—the survivor—leaves America for Europe. Edgar Huntly, who had actually penetrated the literal frontier, is reserved for a crueler fate. Deprived even of the last word in his own story, the "rash youth" is left "forlorn" in a limbo of guilt we can only imagine.

So Brockden Brown turned from the pursuit of dark knowledge in his personal wilderness to a project of outlining a neutral and impersonal universal knowledge. In the *American Register, or General Repository of History, Politics, and Science,* which he edited until his death, he attempted to chronicle the contemporary history of America and Europe, including (as the title suggests) political and scientific developments. Then, probably in 1809, Brown issued a prospectus for *A System of General Geography: Containing a Topographical, Statistical, and Descriptive Survey of the Earth as a Planetary Body, of the Solar System in General and of the Universe. In Two Volumes: The First Containing the Geography of America, the Second Containing the Geography of the Eastern Hemisphere. With Maps.*

The Faustian impulse, that desire to encompass all knowledge, was not a development entirely of Brown's late years. The European and American chronicles of the *American Register* and the *System of General Geography* recall the Belles Lettres Society, which Brown organized with some friends about the year 1789. A principal task of the society was to determine "the relation, dependence, and connection of the several parts of knowledge" (Allen, 14). Occupied as a youth with utopian great plans, Brown was a child of the century of great plans—ambitious and comprehensive projects for understanding and improving the human condition. Even Benjamin Franklin, whose good works were often conceived on a humbler scale, was capable of the grandiose "Proposal for Promoting Useful Knowledge among the British Plantations in America."[12] The chronicles and the *Geography,* as they hark back to the sorting and classifying projects of Brown's youth, recall Franklin's eighteenth-century passion for encompassing, sorting, and classifying the myriad departments of life. D. H. Lawrence complained that Ben was trying to fence in the dark forest of his soul. The wilderness of Brown's fiction possessed the novelist, holding him helpless as a blindman within its dark embrace. But Brown craved sight of the forest, sight of it whole, and, like Lawrence's Franklin, craved mastery of it. Where literary imagination had failed him in this, maps, charts, and calculations might succeed.

To dominate the wilderness and what it represented in himself, Brown had finally to repudiate the hero of his major novels, a figure who probed blindly though boldly for an urgent yet uncertain knowledge. Reflecting upon the thirty-nine years of Brown's life, we see that the three-year space in which he wrote *Wieland, Ormond, Arthur Mervyn,* and *Edgar Huntly* was little more than an incursion of the wilderness into the text of his total career. By abandoning Oedipus to bring to birth in himself a Faust,

Brown, in a sense, returned to the ambitions of his youth. But the Faustian schemes of earlier years, allied to the dangerous utopianism of a Ludloe and Ormond, courted the custom of the devil. The projects of his later life were instead the plodding and measured occupations of one who professed a conservative Philadelphia Christianity. In his *Geography*, Brown proposed to fence the entire wilderness within the continent and place the Americas in their proper geographical relation to the Eastern Hemisphere, putting both East and West together into a world, and setting that in the solar system, and the solar system safely in the universe. The scale of this final work was worthy of Faust all right, but Brown was no longer willing to risk the damnation of a radical enthusiasm. It is impossible to say how far along the writer was on this final project when he succumbed to consumption in 1810.[13]

Still, a Faust needs some devil to buy his soul. But Brown's soul, his darkest literary self, had already proven diabolic, and the only "devil" to whom he could sell it now was respectability itself. Not that the Faustian gesture of Brown's closing years was devoid of a certain desperate nobility. It was, after all, a manner of Faustian myth, a thirst for original but universal knowledge, that informed the work of the United States' own Renaissance. At their best, though, Poe, Hawthorne, and Melville, as well as Emerson, Thoreau, and Whitman realized both the light and the dark sides of the Faustian project. In their finest and most characteristic work, they reconciled, or were at least artistically conscious of, the ineluctable claims self, society, and the universe made upon them. Possibly if, instead of cautious misunderstanding, Charles Brockden Brown had found in his contemporaries the catalytic sympathy Melville discovered in Hawthorne, and Thoreau and Whitman in Emerson, his kinship with what we call our greatest romantics would be more obvious. But Elihu Hubbard Smith and William Dunlap, admirable, learned, industrious, were finally conventional men, quite unlike the extraordinary spiritual colleagues who collaborated, with unusual good fortune, upon an American Renaissance. These writers, half a century after Brown, found in themselves and in each other the strength to bear the blindness of Oedipus while struggling, like Faust, toward the light of knowledge.

Notes

Introduction

1. [John Neal,] in "American Writers," *Blackwood's Edinburgh Magazine* 16 (1824), p. 425. Page references hereafter will be cited in the text. The comment on "unnecessary precision" appears in *Blackwood's* 16, p. 415. The best account of Neal's life and career is Benjamin Lease, *That Wild Fellow John Neal* (Chicago: University of Chicago Press, 1972).

2. The Sharples portrait is reproduced in the Kent State *Wieland*, the Dunlap portrait in the Hafner reprint of *Ormond*. Dunlap may have thought that Sharples had gotten the better likeness (see Dunlap, *Diary*, p. 815).

3. John Bernard, *Retrospections of America, 1797–1811* (1887; rptd., New York: Benjamin Blom, 1969), p. 252.

4. George Lippard, "The Heart-Broken," *Nineteenth Century: A Quarterly Miscellany* 1, no. 1 (January, 1848), pp. 19–27. Page references hereafter will be cited in the text.

5. Charles E. Bennett, in his Introduction to his facsimile of Allen, shows how the first volume of what was to be issued as Dunlap's *Life of Charles Brockden Brown* is far more the work of Allen. Wherever possible, reference is made in this study to Bennett's facsimile since it is both fuller than Dunlap's first volume (Dunlap excised portions that were apparently distasteful to Brown's family) and more readily available. Reference to Dunlap will be confined to material not included in Allen. The Dunlap *Life* appeared in 1815; the abridgment, *Memoirs of Charles Brockden Brown, the American Novelist*, was published in London by Henry Colburn in 1822.

6. See "The Squatter," *New England Magazine* 8 (February, 1835), pp. 97–104, and *Logan: A Family History* (Philadelphia: H. C. Carey and I. Lea, 1822), Vol. 1, p. 9.

7. *American* appears as *Amenean* in the *Blackwood's* article. A ransacking of dictionaries of Americanisms, Britishisms, and nonstandard English reveals no word approaching *Amenean*; since Neal discusses Brown as an American author, it seems safe to read the word as a typographical error for *American*.

8. Leslie A. Fiedler, *Love and Death in the American Novel* (New York: Dell, 1966), p. 132.

9. In order to enhance the mythic-mysterious image of Brown, Fiedler declares it impossible "to discover . . . what Brown looked like. According to one standard biography his hair was straight and 'black as death,' his complexion pale, sallow, and strange, accented by the 'melancholy, broken-hearted look of his

eyes.' '' Fiedler continues (without footnotes): ''Another account describes him as 'short and dumpy, with light eyes and hair inclining to be sandy''' (133–4). The first quotation is of course from Neal—hardly a ''standard biography''—and the second is from Bernard. Neal never saw Brown; Bernard had seen him; Fiedler mystifies himself unduly.

10. Nathaniel Hawthorne, *Mosses from an Old Manse* (1846; rptd., Columbus: Ohio State University Press, 1974), vol. 10, pp. 173–4.

11. *Mosses*, p. 378; the next quotation is from p. 380.

12. See Sydney J. Krause and Jane Nieset, ''A Census of the Works of Charles Brockden Brown,'' *Serif* 3 (December, 1966), pp. 27–55.

13. James Fenimore Cooper, *Notions of the Americans: Picked up by a Travelling Bachelor* (London: Henry Colburn, 1828), vol. 2, pp. 145–6; and ''Preface'' to *The Spy: A Tale of the Neutral Ground* (New York: Wiley and Halstead, 1821), pp. vi–vii.

14. Washington Irving, *Works* (New York: Putnam, 1888), vol. 4, p. 507.

15. Lulu Rumsey Wiley, in *Sources and Influences of the Novels of Charles Brockden Brown* (New York: Vantage, 1950), produces even more doubtful instances of Brown's ''influence'' on Irving. But Wiley's book is thoroughly undependable.

16. Stanley T. Williams, *The Life of Washington Irving* (New York: Oxford Book Co., 1935), vol. 1, pp. 41, 122, 247; and vol. 2, p. 263; see also Pierre Irving, *Life and Letters of Washington Irving* (New York: Putnam, 1864), vol. 2, p. 47.

17. A search through Merton M. Sealts, *Melville's Reading: A Check-List of Books Owned and Borrowed by Herman Melville* (Madison: University of Wisconsin Press, 1966) failed to turn up any of Brown's volumes; nor is the name C. B. Brown to be found in the indexes of Jay Leyda, *The Melville Log* (New York: Harcourt, Brace, 1951), nor in the *Letters* (New Haven: Yale University Press, 1960). Lulu Rumsey Wiley's speculations about Brown's influence upon Melville are as unreliable as her remarks about Brown and Irving. Her most plausible assertion, that Melville borrowed a scene of spontaneous human combustion in *Redburn* from *Wieland*, is convincingly contested by Elizabeth Wiley, ''Four Strange Cases,'' *Dickensian* 58, no. 337 (May, 1962), pp. 120–5, and by George Perkins, ''Death by Spontaneous Combustion,'' *Dickensian* 60, no. 342 (Winter, 1964), pp. 57–63.

18. See, for example, [E. T. Channing,] Review of Dunlap's *Life* of Brown, *North American Review* 9 (June, 1819), pp. 58–77, and [W. H. Gardiner,] review of Cooper's *The Spy*, *North American Review* 15 (July, 1882), pp. 250–82. Patricia Parker, *Charles Brockden Brown: A Reference Guide* (Boston: G. K. Hall, 1980) presents a comprehensive list of early reviews with brief summaries.

19. The Prescott piece (1834) was reprinted from Jared Spark's *Library of American Biography* as ''Charles Brockden Brown, the American Novelist'' in W. H. Prescott, *Biographical and Critical Miscellanies* (New York: Harper, 1845). See also George Barnett Smith, ''Brockden Brown,'' *Fortnightly Review* 30 (September, 1878), pp. 399–421; see p. 399.

20. Brown's ''anticipation of Fenimore Cooper, in fictional exploitation of the redskins, is a . . . stroke of pioneering ingenuity'' (Harry Levin, *The Power of Blackness: Hawthorne, Poe, Melville* [New York: Knopf, 1958], pp. 21–2).

1. Irreconcilable Oppositions

1. There are many articles on American literature: see for example, the review of ''Poems, Chiefly Occasional, by the late Mr. Clifton,'' *Monthly Magazine* 3

(December, 1800), pp. 426–33; item eight under "Notices of American Writers and Publications," *Literary Magazine* 2 (August, 1804), p. 345; and "Why the Arts Are Discouraged in America," *Literary Magazine* 6 (July, 1806), pp. 76–7; also see the *American Register* 1 (1807), p. 174. For comments on commercial and industrial independence from Europe see the following in the *Literary Magazine*: 7 (June, 1807), p. 460, and 8 (October, 1807), pp. 150–1.

A Note on Authorship: As the articles in these journals are mostly anonymous, save for an occasional initial, one can often do little more than conjecture as to precisely which Brown himself wrote. It may be assumed, certainly, that Brown exercised editorial control over all of the articles. Bennett, in "The Charles Brockden Brown Canon," has identified with a high degree of certainty a small number of articles as products of Brown's pen. But in the absence of positive evidence, subject and style have served as a guide in attribution throughout this study. It should be further noted that Clark, pp. 134–5, reports that contributions from "The Friendly Club"—the New York literary circle from which Brown had expected a good deal of material—were disappointingly small. Clark observes that Brown was responsible, if not always as writer, at least as "editor and rewriter," for all the literary reviews in the *Monthly Magazine*. Warfel, p. 221, quotes a letter from Brown to John Blair Linn (July, 1804) in which Brown complains that in the June number of the *Literary Magazine* all of the original prose, save one article, "I have been obliged to supply myself."

2. See Warfel, pp. 207 and 211-4, for an account of the furor created by the pamphlet.

3. [Charles Brockden Brown,] *An Address to the Government of the United States on the Cession of Louisiana to the French, and on the Late Breach of Treaty by the Spaniards; Including the Translation of a Memorial of the War of St. Domingo, and Cession of the Missisippi [sic] to France, Drawn up by a French Counsellor [sic] of State* (Philadelphia: John Conrad, 1803), pp. 62–6. Page references hereafter will be cited in the text.

4. Charles Brockden Brown, trans., *A View of the Soil and Climate of the United States* (Philadelphia: John Conrad, 1804), note on pp. 338–9. Brown's translation is free, but the only substantive change he makes is the rendering of *Anglo-Américains* (*Tableau*, p. 367) as simply *Americans*. Elsewhere, it should be noted, Volney himself sometimes writes *Américains*.

5. This and the next two quotations are from "On the Scheme of an American Language," *Monthly Magazine* 3 (July, 1800), pp. 2–3. Bennett, p. 129, demonstrates Brown's authorship.

6. [Charles Brockden Brown?], review of Webster's *Brief History of Epidemic and Pestilential Diseases*, *Monthly Magazine* 2 (April, 1800), p. 296. See comment on authorship, note 1, above.

7. The phrase is Richard Slotkin's, from *Regeneraton through Violence: The Mythology of the American Frontier, 1600–1860* (Middletown, Conn.: Wesleyan University Press, 1973), p. 382; like Slotkin, Cecelia Tichi, in "Charles Brockden Brown, Translator," *American Literature* 44, no. 1 (March, 1972), pp. 1–12, ignores evidence of Brown's ambivalence on several points throughout the translation of the *Tableau* as well as Brown's praise for Volney in the preface to the translation.

8. D. H. Lawrence, *Studies in Classic American Literature* (1923; rptd., New York: Viking, 1972), p. 47.

9. All nineteenth-century editions number two consecutive chapters 14; 15 here is actually 16.

10. See Boyd Carter, "Poe's Debt to Charles Brockden Brown," *Prairie Schooner* 27 (Summer, 1953), pp. 190–6; David Lee Clark, "Sources of Poe's 'The Pit and the Pendulum,'" *Modern Language Notes* 44 (June, 1929), pp. 349–56; Carmen Ford, "Poe's Debt to Charles Brockden Brown," M.A. thesis, University of Iowa, 1940; David H. Hirsch, "Another Source for 'The Pit and the Pendulum,'" *Mississippi Quarterly* 23, no. 1 (Winter, 1969–70), pp. 35–43, and "The Pit and the Apocalypse," *Sewanee Review* 76 (Autumn, 1968), pp. 632–52; R. T. Kerlin, "*Wieland* and 'The Raven,'" *Modern Language Notes* 31 (December, 1916), pp. 503–5; Burton R. Pollin, "Poe and Godwin," *Nineteenth-Century Fiction* 20 (December, 1965), pp. 237–53; and G. R. Thompson, *Poe's Fiction: Romantic Irony in the Gothic Tales* (Madison: University of Wisconsin Press, 1973), pp. 151–2.

11. John Filson, *The Discovery, Settlement and Present State of Kentucke* (1784; rptd., New York: Corinth, 1962), p. 31.

12. Harold Bloom, *The Anxiety of Influence: A Theory of Poetry* (New York: Oxford University Press, 1973), pp. 15–6.

13. Washington Irving, *A Tour on the Prairies* (1835; rptd., Norman: University of Oklahoma Press, 1956), p. 55.

14. William Carlos Williams, *Selected Essays* (New York: New Directions, 1969), p. 134.

15. Ralph Ellison, *Shadow and Act* (London: Secker and Warburg, 1967), p. xv.

16. Warner Berthoff, "The Literary Career of Charles Brockden Brown," Ph.D. dissertation, Harvard, 1954, p. 27. For an example of the confusion between Brown's actual and fictional lives, see Eleanor M. Tilton, "'The Sorrows' of Charles Brockden Brown," *PMLA* 69 (December, 1954), pp. 1304–8, and Bennett, pp. 144–53.

17. Leslie A. Fiedler, *Love and Death in the American Novel* (New York: Dell, 1966), p. 145.

18. John Bernard, *Retrospections of America, 1797-1811* (1887; rptd., New York: Benjamin Blom, 1969), p. 252. Next quotation, pp. 253–4.

19. Brown uses the phrase "favourite pursuit" in an unpublished letter (Princeton University Library: AM2534) of March 16, 1803, to Rev. Samuel Miller, who had solicited Brown's comments on his *Retrospect of the Eighteenth Century* (1803). See also Allen, p. 10. Brown's last project was to have been *A System of General Geography*.

20. The Hakluyt volume in which the Hore narrative is found is listed on p. 87 (item 244) of the 1789 *Catalogue of Books Belonging to the Library Company of Philadelphia* (Philadelphia: Zachariah Poulson, Jr., 1789). Although Brown left almost no record of his reading, we can narrow the range of speculation about Brown's sources by ascertaining what books, germane to the themes of his fiction, were available to him. Warfel, p. 25, reports the Brown family's membership in the Library Company at least as early as Charles's childhood, although Library Company librarian Edwin Wolf, 2nd, reports in a letter to A. A. (October 21, 1978) that C. B. B. did not acquire a share in his own name until August 10, 1809 ("Record Book B, p. 275"). He did present the Library with copies of *Wieland, Ormond, Edgar Huntly*, and *Clara Howard* "when they were first published" (Austin Gray, *Benjamin Franklin's Library: A Short Account of the Library Company of Philadelphia, 1731-1931* [New York: Macmillan, 1937], p. 46). This suggests an association of some kind between Brown and the Library dating at least from 1798. In any event, one did not have to be a shareholder to use the Library.

21. Richard Hakluyt, *Principal Navigations* . . . (London: J. M. Dent, 1907), vol. 5, p. 340.

22. Brown, trans., *A View*, p. 138n.

23. Although throughout the earlier portions of the *Tableau* Volney places great emphasis on the effects of climate, later in his book he seems to modify this view, observing that "climate and constitution . . . are causes subordinate to laws and government" in shaping the character of nations (Brown, *A View*, pp. 350–1).

24. Benjamin Rush, "An Oration Delivered before the American Philosophical Society, Held in Philadelphia on the 27th of February, 1786; Containing an Enquiry into the Influence of Physical Causes upon the Moral Faculty" (Philadelphia: Charles Cist, 1787), p. 17.

25. Rush, "An Oration," p. 19. The doctor makes further remarks on the relation hunger and extremity bear to the moral and intellectual faculties in one of his *Six Introductory Lectures to Courses of Lectures upon the Institutes and Practices of Medicine, Delivered in the University of Pennsylvania* (Philadelphia: John Conrad; Baltimore: M. and J. Conrad; Washington City: Rapin, Conrad and Co., 1801), "On the Influence of Physical Causes in Promoting an Increase of the Strength and Activity of the Intellectual Faculties of Man."

26. John Gilmary Shea, ed. and trans., *Perils of the Ocean and Wilderness; or, Narratives of Shipwreck and Indian Captivity* (Boston: Patrick Donahoe, 1857), p. 29.

27. Michel Guillaume Jean de Crèvecoeur, *Letters from an American Farmer* (1782; rptd., New York: Dutton, 1957), pp. 43 and 48; owned by the Library Company (*Catalogue*, p. 99, item 1261); see note 20, above.

2. Metaphysic Wilderness

1. John Davis, *Travels of Four Years and a Half in the United States of America during 1798, 1799, 1800, 1801, and 1802* (1803; rptd., New York: Holt, 1909), pp. 163–4 and 164n.

2. [Charles Brockden Brown?], "Notices of American Writers and Publications," item 8, *Literary Magazine* 2 (August, 1804), p. 345. See note on authorship, Chapter 1, note 1, above.

3. This and the subsequent quotations from a journal kept by Brown are preserved in Dunlap, *Life*, vol. 2, pp. 51–2.

4. "Devotion: An Epistle" (1794), *American Register* 3 (1808), pp. 567–78; rptd., Clark, pp. 319–29. All quotations—including this one—are from Clark, pp. 322–5.

5. William Carlos Williams, *In the American Grain* (1925; rptd., New York: New Directions, 1956), p. 225. Page references hereafter will be cited in the text.

6. Van Wyck Brooks, "America's Coming of Age" in *Three Essays on America* (1934; rptd., New York: Dutton, 1970), pp. 52, 55, and 48.

7. Edwin Fussell, *Frontier: American Literature and the American West* (Princeton: Princeton University Press, 1965), p. 173.

8. For Poe on Brown, see review of Cooper's *Wyandotté* (1843), Poe, vol. 11, p. 206; *Marginalia* (1844), Poe, vol. 16, p. 41; review of a translation of *Ettore Fieramosca* by Mussimo D'Azeglio (1845), Poe, vol. 12, p. 224; review of *The Wigwam and the Cabin* by W. G. Simms (1845), Poe, vol. 12, p. 249. Poe promised an essay on Brown (which he never produced) in *The Literary Examiner and Western Monthly* 1 (August, 1839), pp. 316–20. See John Ward Ostrom, *The Letters of Edgar Allan Poe* (New York: Gordian Press, 1966), vol. 1, p. 117.

9. See Chapter 1, note 10.

10. David Lee Clark, "Sources of Poe's 'The Pit and the Pendulum,'" *Modern Language Notes* 44 (June, 1929), pp. 349–56. The Clark article also cites additional sources for Poe's story. Also see David Hirsch, "Another Source for 'The Pit and the Pendulum,'" *Mississippi Quarterly* 23, no. 1 (Winter, 1969–70), pp. 35–43; and Maragaret Atherton, "An Additional Source for Poe's 'The Pit and the Pendulum,'" *Modern Language Notes* 48 (June, 1933), pp. 349–56.

11. Boyd Carter, "Poe's Debt to Charles Brockden Brown," *Prairie Schooner* 27 (Summer, 1953), pp. 190–6.

12. G. R. Thompson, *Poe's Fiction: Romantic Irony in the Gothic Tales* (Madison: University of Wisconsin Press, 1973), p. 152.

13. George Six, *Dictionnaire Biographique de Généraux & Amiraux Francais de la Révolution et de l'Empire (1792-1814)* (Paris: Libraire Historique et Nobilaire, 1934), vol. 2, pp. 64–5. Atherton (note 10, above) demonstates that Poe was likely familiar with Antonio Llorente's *History of the Spanish Inquisition*, a possible source of Poe's knowledge of Lasalle.

14. Cf. David H. Hirsch, "The Pit and the Apocalypse," *Sewanee Review* 76 (Autumn, 1968), pp. 632–52.

15. See H. D. Thoreau, *Walden* (1854; rptd., Boston: Houghton Mifflin, 1957), p. 62; and *A Week on the Concord and Merrimack Rivers* (1849; rptd., Boston: Houghton Mifflin, 1893), p. 401: "The frontiers are not east or west, north or south, but wherever a man *fronts* a fact."

16. Ralph Waldo Emerson, "Experience," in *Essays: Second Series* (1844; rptd., Columbus: Merrill, 1969), p. 54.

17. Ernest Hemingway, *A Farewell to Arms* (New York: Scribner's, 1929), p. 185; "Nature," in *Selections from Ralph Waldo Emerson* (Boston: Houghton Mifflin, 1957), pp. 33–4.

18. Fussell, *Frontier*, p. 218.

19. Thoreau, *Walden*, p. 109.

20. Richard Slotkin, *Regeneration through Violence: The Mythology of the American Frontier, 1600-1860* (Middletown, Conn.: Wesleyan University Press, 1973), p. 68.

21. William Spengemann, *The Adventurous Muse* (New Haven: Yale University Press, 1977), passim; see the Introduction for an outline of Spengemann's approach.

22. See Chapter 1 of Richard Chase, *The American Novel and Its Tradition* (Garden City, N.Y.: Doubleday, 1957), especially pp. 1–13. Page references hereafter will be cited in the text.

23. "The Difference between History and Romance," *Monthly Magazine* 2 (April, 1800), pp. 250–3 and 251–2.

24. F. O. Matthiessen, *American Renaissance* (New York: Oxford University Press, 1941), p. 263.

25. See Samuel G. Goodrich, *Recollections of a Lifetime* (New York and Auburn: Miller, Orton, and Mulligan, 1857), vol. 2, pp. 203–4, for Scott on Brown. See also Tremaine McDowell, "Scott on Cooper and Brockden Brown," *Modern Language Notes* 45 (January, 1930), pp. 18–20. William B. Cairns, in *British Criticisms of American Writings, 1783-1815* (University of Wisconsin Studies in Language and Literature, no. 1, 1918), p. 13, reports that in 1824 or 1825 Scott called Brown "America's greatest novelist up to that time." Cairn gives no source for the quotation, which likely is a garbled version of John G. Lockhart's opinion mistakenly attributed to Scott (see Goodrich).

3. New World Genesis, or the Old Transformed

1. "An Account of a Murder Committed by Mr. J—— Y——, upon His Family, in December, A.D. 1781," in *New York Weekly Magazine* 2, nos. 55 and 56 (July 20 and 27, 1796), pp. 20 and 28; rptd., *Philadelphia Minerva* 2, nos. 81 and 82 (August 20 and 27, 1796), n. pag. An anonymous reviewer of *Wieland* recognized the Tomhannock murder as a source for the novel in the *American Review and Literary Journal* 1 (January, 1801), pp. 333–9. J. C. Hendrickson, in "A Note on *Wieland*," *American Literature* 8 (November, 1936), pp. 305–6, identifies J—— Y—— as James Yates.

2. Carl Van Doren, "Early American Realism," *Nation* 99 (November 12, 1914), pp. 577–8.

3. A facsimile of the outline is reproduced together with a transcription in the Kent State *Wieland*. Page references hereafter will be cited in the text.

4. Michel Guillaume Jean de Crèvecoeur, *Letters from an American Farmer* (1782; rptd., New York: Dutton, 1957), p. 35.

5. In *Posthumous Works of Ann Eliza Bleecker* (New York: T. and J. Swords, 1793). *The History of Maria Kittle* was also published in a separate edition in 1797 by Elisha Babcock, Hartford. All references are to the 1793 edition and will be cited in the text.

6. Edwin Fussell, *Frontier: American Literature and the American West* (Princeton: Princeton University Press, 1965), p. 10.

7. See Kendall B. Taft, ed., *Minor Knickerbockers* (New York: American Book, 1947), p. 378, n. 3.

8. "Though it has been virtually ignored by literary historians, the amazing influence that [C. M. Wieland's] *Oberon* evidently exerted would seem to make this pioneer metrical romance easily the most influential foreign literary work of the time. . . . In a steady stream [Wieland's] writings . . . appeared in countless editions and *well over 375 translations into no less than 14 other languages!*" (Werner W. Beyer, *The Enchanted Forest* [New York: Barnes and Noble, 1963], pp. ix and 2). See also Harry R. Warfel, "Charles Brockden Brown's German Sources," *Modern Language Quarterly* 1, no. 2 (September, 1940), pp. 357–65.

9. John McCarthy, *Fantasy and Reality: An Epistemological Approach to Wieland* (Bern and Frankfurt: Lang, 1974), pp. 9 and 12.

10. See the Warfel article cited in note 8. For more on Brown's use of C. M. Wieland, see John G. Frank, "The Wieland Family in Charles Brockden Brown's *Wieland*," *Monatshefte* 42, no. 7 (November, 1950), pp. 347–53.

11. Christoph Martin Wieland, *The Trial of Abraham. In Four Cantos. Translated from the German* (Norwich, Conn.: John Trumbull, 1778), p. 28. Page references hereafter will be cited in the text.

12. See the entries under "Albigenses" and "Waldenses" in Ephraim Chambers, *Cyclopaedia; or, An Universal Dictionary of the Arts and Sciences*, 5th ed. (London: D. Midwinter, 1741–3), and in the second volume of the 1753 *Supplement* (London: Printed for W. Innys, 1753). Accounts by later authorities are found in Samuel Macaulay Jackson et al., eds., *The New Schaff-Herzog Encyclopedia of Religious Knowledge* (New York: Funk and Wagnalls, 1910); James Hastings et al., eds., *Encyclopaedia of Religion and Ethics* (New York: Scribner's, 1958); and Edwin H. Palmer et al., eds., *The Encyclopedia of Christianity* (Wilmington: National Foundation for Christian Education, 1964), vol. 1.

13. Larzer Ziff, "A Reading of *Wieland*," *PMLA* 77 (March, 1962), pp. 51–7; see pp. 51 and 54.

14. Charles Chauncy, "Enthusiasm Described and Cautioned Against: A Sermon Preach'd at the Old Brick Meeting House in Boston, the Lord's Day after the Commencement, 1742" (Boston: J. Draper and S. Eliot, 1742), p. 3. Page references hereafter will be cited in the text.

15. Erasmus Darwin, Zoönomia; or, The Laws of Organic Life (Philadelphia: T. Dobson, 1797), pt. 2, vol. 1, p. 444.

16. William L. Hedges, "Charles Brockden Brown and the Culture of Contradictions," Early American Literature 9 (Fall, 1974), pp. 107–42 (see pp. 110 and 112).

17. [Charles Brockden Brown,] An Address to the Congress of the United States, on the Utility and Justice of Restrictions upon Foreign Commerce (Philadelphia: C. and A. Conrad, 1809), p. vi.

18. William Smith, History of New-York, from the First Discovery to the Year 1732 (1757; rptd., Albany: Ryer Schermerhorn, 1814), pp. 201–3 and 202n. A second edition was issued by Mathew Carey in Philadelphia, 1792.

19. Except where noted otherwise, the information that follows is drawn from Charles West Thomson, "Notices of the Life and Character of Robert Proud, Author of 'The History of Pennsylvania,'" in Memoirs of the Historical Society of Pennsylvania (Philadelphia: McCarty and Davis, 1826; rptd., Philadelphia: Lippincott, 1864), vol. 1, pp. 417–35.

20. Robert Spiller et al., The Literary History of the United States, 4th ed. (New York: Macmillan, 1974), p. 137.

21. Although Proud affixed the date of the "Plaintive Essay" in good Quaker fashion, substituting the simple "6 mo." for the pagan June, he dated the "Vox Naturae" from "Philadelphia, Christmas Day, 1782." Quaker practice, as set out in Rules of Discipline, and Christian Advices of the Yearly Meeting of Friends for Pennsylvania and New Jersey (Philadelphia: Samuel Sansom, Jr., 1797), enjoins against distinguishing days and months by pagan names and condemns "Fasts and Feast Days and Times, and other human Injunctions and Institutions relative to the Worship of God." From all appearances temperamentally unsuited to the spirit of Woolman and Penn, Proud, in the privacy of manuscript, was also capable of heterodoxy in a significant detail of Quaker practice.

22. "Letters of Robert Proud," Pennsylvania Magazine of History and Biography 34 (January, 1910), p. 62–73; see p. 63.

23. [Charles Brockden Brown], review of Proud's History of Pennsylvania, Monthly Magazine 1 (June, 1799), pp. 216–7. For authorship see Bennett, p. 129.

24. Robert Proud, History of Pennsylvania (Philadelphia: Zachariah Poulson, Jr., 1797), vol. 1, pp. 7–8. Page references hereafter will be cited in the text.

25. See Herman Melville, Redburn: His First Voyage (1849; rptd., New York: Doubleday, 1957), pp. 236–7. For a discussion of Melville's possible borrowing from the spontaneous combustion scene in Wieland, see note 17, Introduction.

26. So the Reverend Charles Chauncy questioned the metaphor of illumination employed by proponents of The Great Awakening. He doubted the validity of any "joy" or "assurance" vouchsafed by "a direct Light shining in" the mind of an enthusiast rather than by "Evidence . . . from the Word of GOD." Chauncy warned that "the Joy of these Times [the decade of the Awakening] is too generally the Effect of this sudden Light, and not of a strict and thorow Examination." It is "infinitely dangerous for Men to trust to this light, and depend upon the Joy arising from it, without the concurring Testimony of their own Consciences, upon clear and full evidence." (Charles Chauncy, Seasonable Thoughts on the State of Religion [Boston: Printed by Rogers and Fowle for Samuel Eliot, 1743], p. 123.)

27. Joel Barlow, *The Vision of Columbus: A Poem in Nine Books* (Hartford: Hudson and Goodwin, 1787), bk. 7, p. 204

28. See Kenneth Silverman, *A Cultural History of the American Revolution* (New York: Crowell, 1976), passim and p. 232, for a discussion of the "rising glory" motif. Brown wrote his own "Rising Glory of America" (1787), a poem transcribed in his father Elijah's manuscript journal (Historical Society of Pennsylvania: AM03399, item 4).

29. Hugh Blair, *Lectures on Rhetoric and Belles Lettres*, 2d ed., corrected (London: W. Straham, T. Cadell, and W. Creech, 1785), vol. 2, pp. 204–13. Page references hereafter will be cited in the text. On the great popularity of Blair in America, see William Charvat, *The Origins of American Critical Thought, 1810-1835* (Philadelphia: University of Pennsylvania Press, 1936), pp. 29–31.

30. [Charles Brockden Brown,] "The Difference between History and Romance," *Monthly Magazine* 2 (April, 1800), pp. 250–3.

31. "Read Brown's 'Carwin,' as far as he has written it" (Smith, August 8, 1798, p. 460).

32. Two articles summarize the controversy: Robert Hobson, "Voices of Carwin and Other Mysteries in Charles Brockden Brown's *Wieland*," *Early American Literature* 10 (Winter, 1975–76), pp. 307–9; and David Lyttle, "The Case against Carwin," *Nineteenth-Century Fiction* 26 (December, 1971), pp. 257–69.

33. Howard Mumford Jones, *O Strange New World* (New York: Viking, 1967), pp. 227–72.

34. Plato, "Apology," in Benjamin Jowett, trans., *The Dialogues of Plato* (Boston: Houghton Mifflin, 1962), pp. 66–7.

35. Jean Brun, *Socrates*, trans. Douglas Scott (New York: Walker and Co., 1962), pp. 66–7

36. Darwin, *Zoönomia*, pt. 2, vol. 1, p. 444.

37. Anthelme Chaignet quoted in Brun (see note 35, above).

38. J. H. Eliott, *The Old World and the New* (Cambridge: At the University Press, 1972), p. 8.

39. Jones, *New World*, p. 14; cf. Anne Bradstreet's "sweet-tongu'd Philomel" in stanza 26 of the *Contemplations*.

40. Washington Irving, *A Tour on the Prairies* (1835; rptd., Norman: University of Oklahoma Press, 1956), p. 108.

41. Jeremy Belknap, *A Discourse Intended to Commemorate the Discovery of America by Christopher Columbus* . . . (Boston: Apollo Press, 1792), p. 34.

42. Thomas Morton, *Columbus; or, The Discovery of America. An Historical Play. As Performed at the Theatre-Royal, Covent-Garden, London* (Boston: William Spotswood, 1794). The play had its American premiere in New York, September 16, 1797. William Dunlap praised the production. See George C. D. Odell, *Annals of the New York Stage* (New York: Columbia University Press, 1927), vol. 1, p. 463; and William Dunlap *History of the American Theatre and Anecdotes of the Principal Actors* (1832; rptd., New York: Burt Franklin, 1963), vol. 1, p. 372.

43. [Charles Brockden Brown?], review of Jeremy Belknap, *American Biography* . . . (Boston: Isiah Thomas and Ebenezer T. Andrews, 1794), *Monthly Magazine* 1 (July, 1799), pp. 282–7. See note on authorship, Chapter 1, note 1.

44. Alexander Martin wrote an addendum to Morton's *Columbus* entitled "A New Scene Interesting to the Citizens of the United States of America, Additional to the Historical Play of Columbus, by a Senator of the United States." Published in 1798 by Benjamin Franklin Bache at Philadelphia, the fragment sounds a

utopian theme closely resembling Barlow's; Martin even borrows Barlow's Hesper —albeit adorned in "Roman cap"—to guide Columbus through a vision of the United States. See Richard Walser, "Alexander Martin, Poet," *Early American Literature* 6 (Spring, 1971), pp. 55–61.

45. Wayne Franklin, in "Desperate Imagination: Tragedy and Comedy in Brown's *Wieland*," *Novel* 9 (Winter, 1975), pp. 147–63, shows how Brown was influenced by Shakespeare in the mixture of tragic and comic modes in *Wieland*.

4. Great Plans: A Foreword to *Ormond* and *Arthur Mervyn*

1. *American Register* 1 (1807), pp. 215 and 220. Clark, p. 257, credits the review to Brown; the note Brown appended to the review, however, says that it is the work of a "friend." Even if Brown was not the author of the review, his note, stressing the "importance" of the *Columbiad*, shows that he was enthusiastic about the poem. Brown, as editor of the *American Register*, must have written the announcement in the next issue of the magazine: "In the department of fine arts, we meet with a work which, in extent and value, cannot be expected to present itself very often" (2 [1808], p. 159).

2. Joel Barlow, *The Vision of Columbus: A Poem in Nine Books* (Hartford: Hudson and Goodwin, 1787), bk. 4, p. 131.

3. John Bernard, *Retrospections of America, 1797-1811* (1887; rptd., New York: Benjamin Blom, 1969), p. 252.

4. Smith, p. 256. The review Smith cites is in the *Monthly Review*, 2d series, 20 (August, 1796), pp. 524–32.

5. Bennett, p. 179. One manuscript is at the Historical Society of Pennsylvania, Dreer Collection, AM03399; another is at the Humanities Research Center, University of Texas at Austin.

6. The "extracts" from the unpublished portions of *Alcuin* included in Allen were "written in the fall and winter of the year 1797" (Allen, 71).

7. Warfel, pp. 70–2. The "Sketches" were included in Allen, pp. 170–222, and appear in an altered version in Dunlap, *Life*, vol. 1, pp. 170–258.

8. Warner Berthoff, "Charles Brockden Brown's Historical 'Sketches': A Consideration," *American Literature* 28, no. 2 (May, 1956), pp. 147–54.

9. Berthoff (see note 8, above) suggests that the "Sketches" were composed in 1803 or later; Bennett, pp. 233–43, dates them from 1803.

10. For Brown's involvement with the Belles Lettres Society and his speech on education, see Allen, pp. 17–21 and 23. Emilius is identified in Charles E. Bennett's Introduction to Allen, p. xiv.

11. Desmond Guinness and Julius Trousdale Sadler, Jr., *Palladio: A Western Progress* (New York: Viking, 1976), p. 9. See also their chapter on Palladian influence in North America.

12. Howard Mumford Jones, *O Strange New World* (New York: Viking, 1967); see especially pp. 269–72.

13. [Charles Brockden Brown,] *An Address to the Government . . .* (Philadelphia: John Conrad, 1803), p. 44.

14. Allen, pp. 359–87. Bennett, pp. 167–75, fixes the date of "Adini" at 1797. The fragment is the most finished of the "Ellendale" materials.

15. Brown or his editors, Allen and Dunlap, have confused matters. Instead of "Mr. Ellen," the text reads "my father." Raff, the narrator, is an orphan, and while it is possible that he might refer to his guardian, Mr. Malcombe, as "father," it is clear that Adini is speaking here not with Malcombe but with Mr. Ellen.

16. Quoted in William Charvat, *The Origins of American Critical Thought, 1810-1835* (Philadelphia: University of Pennsylvania, 1936), p. 36.

17. Two letters from Brown to Miller regarding the *Brief Retrospect* are preserved in the Princeton University Library. AM2534 is dated March 16, 1803, and AM2536, June 20, 1803.

18. Harry R. Warfel, ed., *The Rhapsodist and Other Uncollected Writings by Charles Brockden Brown* (New York: Scholars' Facsimiles and Reprints, 1943), p. 6. Page references hereafter will be cited in the text.

19. Charles Brockden Brown, "The Man at Home," in Warfel, ed., *Rhapsodist*, pp. 27-30.

20. William Marsden, *The History of Sumatra, Containing an Account of the Government, Laws, Customs, and Manners of the Native Inhabitants* (2d ed., London: Printed for the author, 1784), facing p. 166. We can safely assume Brown's knowledge of Marsden not only because Brown's Rejang characters are identical to Marsden's, but also because Abraham Rees's *Cyclopaedia; or Universal Dictionary of Arts, Sciences, and Literature* (Philadelphia: Samuel F. Bradford, n.d.) cites Marsden in its article on Sumatra. "An Inventory of the Property of Charles Brockden Brown" reproduced in Clark, p. 331, lists the *Cyclopaedia* among the novelist's possessions. The first edition of the *History* (1783) was available in the Library Company *Catalogue* (1789, p. 27, item 385).

21. The letter, February 15, 1799, is in Dunlap, *Life*, vol. 2, p. 97.

5. Utopian Romance

1. For Dunlap's reading of *The Algerine Captive*, see the *Diary*, p. 174. Smith requested a copy of the novel from Joseph Dennie, Jr., on September 5, 1797, and read at least part of it by December 22 (Smith, pp. 357 and 409). The review of *The Foresters* appeared in the *Monthly Magazine* 1 (September through December [combined issue], 1799), pp. 434-8.

2. See "Novel Reading," *Literary Magazine* 1 (March, 1804), pp. 401-5, and "On the Cause of the Popularity of Novels," 7 (June, 1807), pp. 410-5.

3. For praise of Richardson, see Clark, p. 64. The influence of Godwin on Brown has been noted by virtually every commentator on the novelist. See Brown's own statement in Allen, p. 106. On November 5, 1796, Brown and Smith heard fellow member of the Friendly Club William Johnson read from *Hermsprong; or Man as He Is Not* and "were pleased." Brown—February 13, 1797—"began to dramatise 'Hermsprong'" (Smith, pp. 243 and 290).

4. Both record reading "James the Fatalist and His Master," Smith on May 19, 1798 (*Diary*, p. 445), and Dunlap three days later (*Diary*, pp. 259-60).

5. Leslie A. Fiedler, *Love and Death in the American Novel* (New York: Dell, 1966), pp. 78-89.

6. "A Census of the Works of Charles Brockden Brown," *Serif* 3 (December, 1966), pp. 34-5. The figure on *Charlotte* is from Clara M. and Rudolf Kirk's Introduction to their edition of the novel (New Haven, Conn.: College and University Press, 1964), p. 30.

7. All that survives of the novel are an "Advertisement" in the *Weekly Magazine* 1, no. 7 (March 17, 1798), p. 202, and "An Extract from 'Sky-Walk,'" also in the *Weekly Magazine* 1, no. 8 (March 24, 1798), pp. 228-31.

8. It is difficult to determine how much firsthand knowledge of the 1793 epidemic Brown had; he was touring Connecticut with E. H. Smith during the height of the disease in Philadelphia. See Warfel, p. 44. Clark, pp. 160-2, reports

that Brown had "witnessed the early scenes of the plague of 1793" and that he may also have known Mathew Carey's *Short Account of the Malignant Fever* (1794). Brown was in Philadelphia during the 1797 epidemic there.

9. Warfel, p. 118; Warner Berthoff, "The Literary Career of Charles Brockden Brown," Ph.D. dissertation, Harvard, 1954, p. 33.

10. Exiled revolutionists, Martinette and her father apparently chose to live under the assumed name of Monrose—though this is never explicitly explained by Brown (p. 208).

11. Most of what follows is drawn from Vernon Stauffer, *New England and the Bavarian Illuminati*, Columbia University Studies in History and Economics (New York: Columbia University Press, 1919), vol. 82.

12. Jedidiah Morse, *A Sermon Delivered at the New North Church in Boston* . . . (Boston: Samuel Hall, 1798). Also Stauffer, *New England*, pp. 9-12.

13. See Stauffer, *New England*, pp. 106–21, for the Democratic Societies; p. 136, for the threat against Philadelphia; p. 292, for Morse's "discovery" of Illuminati in Virginia and New York. Morse's "official, authenticated lists" were highly dubious (pp. 294–300).

14. Morse was known to Brown as the author of *The American Universal Geography* (Elizabethtown: Shepard Kollock, 1789, with many later revisions and editions) and *The Elements of Geography* (Boston: I. Thomas and E. T. Andrews, 1795, with other 1795 editions and many later editions). Brown cites Morse in his prospectus for *A System of General Geography* (p. 3).

15. The Library of Congress *Catalog* lists two British editions in 1797. A third and fourth British edition appeared in 1798, with a second printing of the fourth edition that same year. A reprinting of the third edition was issued from Philadelphia and a reprinting of the fourth from New York in 1798.

16. John Robison, *Proofs of a Conspiracy* . . . (4th ed., New York: George Forman, 1798; rptd., Boston and Los Angeles: Western Islands, 1967), pp. 66 and 71, and "Carwin," pp. 281-2; *Proofs*, p. 68, and "Carwin," pp. 283ff.; and *Proofs*, p. 61.

17. [Charles Brockden Brown,] "The Editor's Address to the Public," *Literary Magazine* 1 (October, 1803), pp. 4–5. Although this passage is a blanket retraction that must include his novels, the particular "something" for which he takes "much blame" may well be the outrageous *Address* on the Louisiana cession, published in January of 1803.

18. The historical "Sketches," probably composed in 1803 or later, are fictions, but their dryly precise and wholly impersonal chronicle style partakes more of "history" than "romance." Though fiction, the "Sketches" are not novels.

19. Both Donald Ringe, in *Charles Brockden Brown* (New York: Twayne, 1966), p. 58, and Warfel. p. 131, point this out.

20. Benjamin Franklin, "Information for Those Who Would Remove to America," in Russel B. Nye, ed., *Autobiography and Other Writings* (Boston: Houghton Mifflin, 1958), p. 188.

6. The Rise of Arthur Mervyn

1. Charles Brockden Brown, "The Rhapsodist" (1789), in Harry R. Warfel, ed., *The Rhapsodist and Other Uncollected Writings by Charles Brockden Brown* (New York: Scholars' Facsimiles and Reprints, 1943), pp. 13–5.

2. David Lyttle, "The Case against Carwin," *Nineteenth-Century Fiction* 26 (December, 1971), pp. 257–69.

3. See Elizabeth S. Kite, "The 'Pineys' " *Survey: A Journal of Constructive Philanthropy* 31 (October 4, 1913), pp. 7–13 and 38–40.

4. . . . from the arched roof
   Pendant by subtle Magic many a row
   Of Starry Lamps and blazing Cressets fed
   With *Naptha* and *Asphaltus* yielded light
   As from a sky. . . .   (*Paradise Lost*, bk. 1, ll. 726–30)

5. For Norman S. Grabo, in *The Coincidental Art of Charles Brockden Brown* (Chapel Hill: University of North Carolina Press, 1981), such coincidental structures are the very essence of Brown's craft.

6. D. H. Lawrence, *Studies in Classic American Literature* (1923; rptd., New York: Viking, 1972), pp. 18–19, and pp. 10 and 11.

7. Allen, p. 17; the poem is reproduced in Clark, p. 46.

8. Allen, p. 18; Clark, pp. 45 and 113.

9. *Literary Magazine* 6 (November, 1806), pp. 367–74. Page references hereafter will be cited in the text.

10. See Clark, p. 242 and p. 242, n. 53; and A. Owen Aldridge, "Charles Brockden Brown's Poem on Benjamin Franklin," *American Literature* 38, no. 5 (May, 1966), p. 243, n. 11. Jeffrey's article, a review of "The Complete Works" of Franklin (London: J. Johnson, 1806), appeared anonymously in the *Edinburgh Review* 8 (July, 1806), pp. 327–44. It is reprinted in *Contributions to the Edinburgh Review by Francis Jeffrey* (London: Longman, Brown, Green, and Longmans, 1844), vol. 1, pp. 136–57.

11. See Chapter 1, n. 1, above.

12. Aldridge, "Charles Brockden Brown's Poem on Benjamin Franklin," pp. 230–5.

13. For information on early editions of the *Autobiography*, see the Introduction to Leonard W. Labaree et al., eds., *The Autobiography of Benjamin Franklin* (New Haven: Yale University Press, 1964), pp. 26–37; Paul Leicester Ford, *Franklin Bibliography* (New York: Privately published, 1889), pp. 179–213; and entries in Charles Evans's *American Bibliography* (New York: Peter Smith, 1941).

14. Here the consequences of translation and retranslation are painfully evident. Franklin had actually written: "So convenient a thing is it to be a *reasonable Creature*, since it enables one to find or make a Reason for every thing one has a mind to do" (Labaree et al., eds., *Autobiography*, p. 88).

15. Edwin Muir, trans., *Amerika* (New York: New Directions, 1946) pp. 3 and 21.

16. Max Brod, Afterword, *Amerika*, p. 298.

17. Labaree et al., eds., *Autobiography*, pp. 170–1.

18. Richard D. Miles, "The American Image of Benjamin Franklin," *American Quarterly* 9 (Summer, 1957), pp. 120–1 and 118.

19. Thomas Carlyle, *Past and Present* (1842; rptd., Boston: Houghton Mifflin, 1965), pp. 150–1.

20. Charles Brockden Brown, trans., *A View of the Soil and Climate of the United States of America* (Philadelphia: John Conrad, 1804), p. 246.

21. [Charles Brockden Brown?], "Letters on the Yellow Fever," *Monthly Magazine* 1 (August, 1799), pp. 324–30; see especially p. 325; the quotation is from p. 326.

7. From Oedipus to Faust: An American Tale

1. Richard Slotkin, *Regeneration through Violence: The Mythology of the American Frontier, 1600-1860* (Middletown, Conn.: Wesleyan University Press, 1973), pp. 384-6. Page references hereafter will be cited in the text.

2. David Brion Davis also explores the oedipal theme in *Edgar Huntly*. See *Homicide in American Fiction, 1798-1860: A Study in Social Values* (Ithaca: Cornell University Press, 1957), pp. 94-100.

3. John Greenleaf Whittier, "Fanaticism," in *Writings* (Boston: Houghton Mifflin, 1895), vol. 7, p. 393.

4. See the Library Company *Catalogue*, p. 298, item 47. See Chapter 1, note 20, above.

5. Hocquet Caritat, *The Feast of Reason and the Flow of Soul, A New Explanatory Catalogue of H. Caritat's General and Increasing Circulating Library* (New York: M. L. & W. A. Davis, 1799), p. 118.

6. For the quotations from the Francklin *Oedipus*, see Bernadotte Perrin, ed., *Greek Dramas* (New York: Appleton, 1900), p. 184; for Dryden and Lee, see John Dryden, *Dramatic Works* (London: Nonesuch, 1932), pp. 394 and 393.

7. James Strachey, trans., *The Interpretation of Dreams* (New York: Avon, 1965), pp. 296-7.

8. J. H. Elliott, *The Old World and the New, 1492-1650* (Cambridge: At the University Press, 1972), p. 1.

9. William Spengemann, *The Adventurous Muse* (New Haven: Yale University Press, 1977), passim. In *The Coincidental Art of Charles Brockden Brown* (Chapel Hill: University of North Carolina Press, 1981), pp. 131 and 142, Norman S. Grabo speculates—and he is careful to present the idea as a speculation—that *Clara Howard* and, possibly, *Jane Talbot* were written before Brown's four major novels, though published after them. Professor Grabo bases his speculation on his view of the novelist's career as a progress toward an increasing mastery of craft and theme. Since *Clara Howard* and *Jane Talbot* are so obviously inferior to the major novels, Grabo suggests that they were apprentice works belatedly published. But, as with so much else concerning the novelist, there is no hard evidence to corroborate this. The present discussion, which identifies these two novels as the first stage in Brown's retreat from the territory explored in the major works, assumes that *Clara Howard* and *Jane Talbot* were indeed the last novels Brown wrote.

10. There is no dispute over Brown's authorship of the 1803 *Address . . . on the Cession of Louisiana*, the 1803 *Monroe's Embassy* (a follow-up to the cession *Address*), or the 1809 *Address* on the embargo. Clark, p. 261, argues that a pamphlet entitled *The British Treaty of Commerce and Navigation* (1807?) is not Brown's. Dunlap, *Life*, vol. 2, pp. 69-74, does attribute it to Brown; so does Bennett, pp. 11-13.

11. [Charles Brockden Brown,] *An Address to the Congress of the United States, on the Utility and Justice of Restrictions upon Foreign Commerce* (Philadelphia: C. and A. Conrad, 1809), p. 37.

12. The "Proposal" was issued as a broadside on May 14, 1743. See Leonard W. Labaree et al., eds., *The Papers of Benjamin Franklin* (New Haven: Yale University Press, 1959), vol. 2, pp. 378-83.

13. The prospectus was published in Philadelphia and is undated. The Shaw-Shoemaker *American Bibliography* assigns it to 1809. See Charles E. Bennett's Introduction to Allen, pp. vi-vii, for a discussion of the fate of the project.

Index